Beyond the Impasse:
The Promise of a Process Hermeneutic

Cover. A nineteenth-century woodcut of an illustration by an anonymous artist. "[The disciples said to Jesus when they reached Emmaus], 'Stay with us, for it is toward evening and the day is now far spent.' . . . '[And] he opened to us the scriptures.'" —Luke 24:29, 32 RSV

1. *Reimagining America. A Theological Critique of the American Mythos and Biblical Hermeneutics*
   by Charles Mabee
2. *Norman Perrin's Interpretation of the New Testament. From "Exegetical Method" to "Hermeneutical Process"*
   by Calvin R. Mercer
3. *The Community of Interpreters. On the Hermeneutics of Nature and the Bible in the American Philosophical Tradition*
   by Robert S. Corrington
4. *The Poetics of Revelation. Recognition and the Narrative Tradition*
   by Diana Culbertson
5. *Faith and the Play of the Imagination. On the Role of Imagination in Religion*
   by David J. Bryant
6. *The Second Naiveté. Barth, Ricoeur, and the New Yale Theology*
   by Mark I. Wallace
7. *Reading Sacred Texts through American Eyes. Biblical Interpretation as Cultural Critique*
   by Charles Mabee
8. *Hermeneutics as Theological Prolegomena. A Canonical Approach*
   by Charles J. Scalise
9. *A Common Sense Theology. The Bible, Faith, and American Society*
   by Mark Ellingsen
10. *The Politics of Biblical Theology. A Postmodern Reading*
    by David Penchansky
11. *Making Sense of New Testament Theology. "Modern" Problems and Prospects*
    by A. K. M. Adam
12. *Theology as Cultural Critique. The Achievement of Julian Hartt*
    by Jonathan R. Wilson
13. *Beyond the Impasse. The Promise of a Process Hermeneutic*
    by Ronald L. Farmer

Beyond the Impasse

The Promise
of a Process Hermeneutic

by
Ronald L. Farmer

MERCER UNIVERSITY PRESS

ISBN 0-86554-558-8   MUP/P126

BS
476
.F37
1997

Beyond the Impasse.
The Promise of a Process Hermeneutic.
Copyright ©1997
Mercer University Press, Macon, Georgia 31210-3960 USA

Library of Congress Cataloging-in-Publication Data

Farmer, Ronald L., 1952–   .
Beyond the impasse : the promise of a process hermeneutic /
by Ronald L. Farmer.
xvi+270pp. 6x9" (15x23cm.) —
(Studies in American biblical hermeneutics ; 13)
Includes bibliographical references and indexes.
ISBN 0-86554-558-8 (pbk. : alk. paper).
1. Bible—Hermeneutics.   2. Process Theology.
I. Title.   II. Series.
BS476.F37   1997
220.6'01—dc21   97-18448

CIP

Contents

Foreword by William A. Beardslee ix
Editor's Preface by Charles Mabee xi
Preface xv

Part One
The Impasse
Chapter 1
The Quest for a Satisfying Hermeneutic 3
    The Historical-Critical Method 4
    Classical Liberalism's Progressive Revelation 5
    The Biblical Theology Movement 7
    Existentialist Interpretation 11
    The New Hermeneutic 17
    Literary Criticism 26
    Deconstruction 32
    The Impasse 45
    A Process Hermeneutic 46

Chapter 2
Language, Worldview, and the Hermeneutical Enterprise 51
    The Four Phases of Language 52
    The Emerging Worldview:
        From Substance Thinking to Event Thinking 58

Part Two
Beyond the Impasse
Chapter 3
The Process Worldview 71

Chapter 4
Process Hermeneutic: The Nature of Language 83
    Whitehead's Theory of Perception 84
    Whitehead's Theory of Language 93

Chapter 5
Process Hermeneutic: The Nature of Texts 103

Chapter 6
Process Hermeneutic: Validity in Interpretation
and Theological Norms 109
   Historic Routes of Living Occasions 110
   Creative Transformation 114
   The Community of Interpretation 118

Chapter 7
Process Hermeneutic: An Assessment 121
   Author Intent or Indeterminate Meaning? 121
   The Value of Religious Language 122
   The Excision of Problematic Elements 123
   The Essentialist vs the Evolutionary Approach 125
   The Nature of Authority 126
   History, Freedom, and Divine Activity 128
   Symbolism 128
   Narrative and Myth 129
   Confessionalism or Public Discussion? 130
   The Role of the Interpreter's Community 130
   New Categories for Interpretation 131
   A Descriptive or Hermeneutical Task? 131
   Inspiration and Revelation 131

Part Three
Process Hermeneutic Applied

Chapter 8
The Lamb and the Beast: The Apocalypse of Power.
Revelation 4–5 in Process Hermeneutic 135
   Two Conceptions of Power 135
   Recent Study in Early Christian Apocalypticism
   and the Apocalypse to John 141
      Genre Analysis 142
      Sociohistorical Analysis 142
      Literary Analysis 144
   Analysis of Revelation 4–5 149
   Hermeneutical Reflections on John's "Undercurrent" 158

Chapter 9
Transforming a Paradox: Universal/Limited Salvation
in the Apocalypse to John 163
    Limited Salvation in the Apocalypse 164
    Universal Salvation in the Apocalypse 170
    Statement of the Paradox 180
    Transforming the Paradox 184
    Conclusion 193

Excursus
Reimaging the Apocalyptic "End" 195

Appendix
An Overview of Whitehead's Cosmology 199
    Actual Entities/Occasions 200
    Creativity 206
    Eternal Objects 207
    God 213
    The Phases of Concrescence 221
        Phase One. Conformal Feelings 223
        Phase Two. Conceptual Feelings 224
        Phase Three. Physical Purposes 228
        Phase Four. Propositional Feelings
           and Intellectual Feelings 229
        The Final Phase. Satisfaction 236
    Enduring Objects and the Macrocosmic World 236

Bibliography 255

Indexes 265
    Author Index 265
    Subject Index 268

*For Patricia,
my partner in the adventure of life*

Foreword

Ronald L. Farmer brings together a broad and discerning competence in the field of hermeneutics and a thorough grasp of the "constructive postmodern" perspective of process philosophy. This combination enables him to open a path of interpretation which leads beyond the impasse of a cafeteria-style mixture of methods on the one hand and the limitation of shared meaning to self-enclosed communities on the other, which so often seems to be the outcome of recent developments in interpretation theory. Farmer fully recognizes the linguistic and situational aspects of all interpretation, but he insists that these are not the whole story. Public discourse is possible (though always in process and never a final expression) because the relational character of reality means that we are constituted by one another and by all that happens, and thus have data accessible to us for communication about the realities from which language arises.

The priority of relations and of events is widely if somewhat intuitively recognized today. Farmer's exposition of process thought provides a matrix within which the relational and event character of reality can be seen to cohere, and to provide a framework for understanding language which does justice both to its inexact, provisional, and imaginative character, and to its ability to express, if always provisionally, the shape of the far wider nonlinguistic reality from which language arises. A strong feature of the book is that the reader can linger over the very fine presentations of Whiteheadian/process categories and absorb the reorientation of our imagination which they carry with them, or bypass most of these for the time being to grasp the overall picture of a relational reality.

Farmer turns to the Book of Revelation to show how a process hermeneutic can work in practice. A number of recent interpreters have noted features of this book that run counter to the thrust of its most vivid images of overruling power and limited salvation—notably images of God's power as persuasive and depending on a human response, and images of a wider or total salvation. Farmer's careful study of the literary structure (note, for instance, his insight into the "bracketing" of coercive power by persuasive power, and his perception of the dialectic between what John hears and what he sees), and of the interplay of images shows both how what seems to be a mere "undercurrent" can be constitutive for the wider meaning, and how a seeming paradox can be transformed to offer a more comprehensive vision of justice. This is a rich book which provides a thorough and perceptive introduction to hermeneutics from a process perspective.

William A. Beardslee

Editor's Preface

Whereas American biblical hermeneutics shares in the twentieth century European philosophical quest to overcome traditional Western metaphysics, it seems to me the foundation for this quest is grounded in its own distinctive rationale. Much of the European discussion has centered on language and linguistic analysis. Structuralism, deconstruction, and postmodernism are recent intellectual children of that discussion. The spirit of the Continental discussion in particular seems to have been preoccupied with tearing down the legacy of impositional, hierarchical, patriarchal (ecclesiastical) thought. In short, the way of thinking associated with traditional philosophy and Christian theology is viewed as an obstacle to the liberation and growth of the human spirit. Not surprisingly, all too frequently the fabric of intellectual argument tends toward the agonistic and the adversarial. While the ultimate goal may be to rebuild, ideological deadwood needs clearing from the land of our intellectual labor before the constructive impulse can come to the fore.

From its inception the American trajectory of "antimetaphysics" is characterized as a constructive element rather than a destructive one. The American impulse tends to build intellectually upon the recognition of the primacy of experience. Impositional resistance is far more easily cast aside, and the task takes less of our creative juices. Perhaps it is simply because substantially less meaningful tradition in the culture exists to tear down. Or perhaps it is because there is an inbred intellectual confidence in experience as such. While acknowledging the fragility of experiential interpretation, the American impulse is to favor it over dogmatic thought. This perception holds generally in the culture; it holds in theological thinking as well. The obstacles to growth bequeathed by past ideas tend to be viewed more as inconveniences than full-fledged obstacles, because after all they come to us in mere words, and words can never adequately replace experience. Experience, especially as mediated to us through immediate experience, seems generally to be perceived as both prior to and deeper than linguistic formulation. And, it exists independently of it.

In the book you have before you, Ron Farmer has outlined a constructive proposal for biblical hermeneutics that is congruent with the American spirit of experiential primacy. He has made the first contribution to the Studies in American Biblical Hermeneutics series from the standpoint of process thought—a position foundationally mapped out by the British philosopher Alfred North Whitehead. Process hermeneutics offers a substantial alternative to more mainstream historical-critical approaches to the Bible that, when used exclusively, tend to make the Bible more a museum piece than a revelation from God.

A provocative way of conceptualizing the approach of Alfred North Whitehead might be to ask, "Suppose God were a verb, rather than a noun . . . ?" This question might serve as a centerpiece for the recognition of the way Whitehead joins the twentieth century project to overcome "substance thinking" (his words) in Western thought. Borrowing the language of Northrop Frye, we might say that Whitehead believed we need to move from modern mechanistic, descriptive modes of thought to a way of thinking that both recaptured and moved beyond some of the traditional components of metaphorical and transcendental ways of thinking. He believed the answer lay in uncovering the *process* undergirding all of reality, an approach he called "event thinking" rather than "substance thinking." This is a promising way of understanding the primacy of experience over dogmatic thinking. It is a constructive way to build a provocative and universal approach to understanding the Bible.

While the reader will emerge with a good introductory understanding of Whitehead's philosophy and its relevance for biblical studies, the book delivers far greater rewards. Unsatisfied with a discourse that talks *about* the Bible, Farmer provocatively engages the Book of Revelation from the standpoint of process thought. His hermeneutical method helps uncover the crucial importance of this problematic book for developing key Christian themes that have particular relevance for the American democratic context: the persuasive character of God's power and the paradox of limited/universal salvation. It would be difficult to imagine a more innovative and persuasive way of exhibiting the promise of process hermeneutics. This is a well-conceived and well-written book that will richly reward the reader. I rejoice than an important gap has now been filled in our project of finding new meaning in the Bible by taking our cultural context as constitutive.

August 1997   *Charles Mabee*
Ecumenical Theological Seminary, Detroit

Preface

In the opinion of many, contemporary biblical scholarship has reached an impasse. In an effort to describe and underscore the significance of this impasse, "Part One. The Impasse" opens with a chapter briefly chronicling the author's personal quest for a satisfying hermeneutic, a quest which in many respects parallels the history of modern biblical interpretation. This survey focuses on nineteenth- and twentieth-century attempts to bridge the formidable gap between the ancient texts and their contemporary theological and ethical appropriation. Two of the more important aspects of the hermeneutical impasse—language and worldview—receive special attention in chapter 2.

In "Part Two. Beyond the Impasse" my own formulation of a process hermeneutic is set forth in five chapters. Rather than developing the hermeneutic from the side of process philosophy—that is, as a purely theoretical discussion of the hermeneutical implications of Whiteheadian thought—I develop it from the side of biblical studies—that is, as answering practical questions arising from the current impasse in biblical hermeneutics such as, What is the nature of language? What is the nature of texts? What constitutes a valid or normative reading of a text? Can an eclectic appropriation of the various exegetical methods (or "tool box raiding" as some affectionately call it) escape the charge of being ad hoc?

All too often books dealing with hermeneutics are entirely theoretical in nature. "Part Three. Process Hermeneutic Applied" attempts to overcome this shortcoming by applying the process hermeneutic to several well-known exegetical difficulties. The appendix provides interested readers a more thorough treatment of Whitehead's cosmology than is presented in part two. By placing this discussion in an appendix, readers are not required to master the more technical aspects of Whitehead's thought until/unless their own questions make a more detailed discussion relevant.

Although it would be impossible to name all of the individuals who have contributed to my thinking, a few acknowledgments are in order. Over the past several years I have presented various aspects of this manuscript to my former colleagues in the Religious Studies Department at the University of Missouri, at regional and national meetings of the Society of Biblical Literature, and at the Center for Process Studies in Claremont, California. Feedback on these occasions has been invaluable. I am especially indebted to three pioneers in the development of a process hermeneutic—William A. Beardslee, John B. Cobb, Jr., and Russell Pregeant—who read an earlier draft of the entire manuscript. Each offered constructive criticism and encouragement. Professor Beardslee also graciously wrote the forward to this volume.

I also want to thank Charles Mabee, editor of Mercer University Press's Studies in American Biblical Hermeneutics series, for his interest in my work and his guidance in seeing it through to publication.

Finally, a special word of appreciation is due to Patricia Adams Farmer, my partner in the adventure of life, who first introduced me to process thought and has been supportive of this project in countless ways.

Ronald L. Farmer

Part One

The Impasse

Chapter 1

The Quest
for a Satisfying Hermeneutic

My first exposure to the theological and ethical use of the Bible was within the context of a fundamentalist church. In such churches the Bible is viewed as a "fixed deposit." According to this perspective, "the revelation of God contained in the Bible is complete; all that is required is the *redepositing* of this tradition, completely unchanged, to successive generations." The goal of biblical interpretation, then, is to make modern life conform as closely as possible to a "golden era" in the past. "The interpreter simply takes the Bible as it is (that is, interprets it literally) and seeks parallels or correspondences between contemporary and biblical situations. Where correspondences are found, the present, analogous situation is made to conform as closely as possible to the biblical situation."[1]

This method of biblical interpretation forced me onto the horns of a dilemma. My academic pilgrimage—most notably my high school natural and social science courses—increasingly led me to view reality, especially the human situation, in a manner which was at odds with the teachings of the church of my childhood. For example, my education and family upbringing led me to view women and men as equals. Yet, my church exhorted me to adopt a patriarchal stance based upon its reading of the Bible. What was I to make of this?

---

[1]Ron Farmer, "The 'Transmission of Tradition' and the 'Academic Freedom-Ecclesiastical Control' Debate: Three Models," *Perspectives in Religious Studies* 17 (1990): 129.

Also troubling to me was the static understanding of spirituality undergirding this approach to the Bible. Is the goal of religion simply the redepositing of an unchanging tradition to succeeding generations? Viewing the Bible as a fixed deposit of God's revelation limits its significance to situations for which there is a close parallel. "This limitation results in the Bible becoming increasingly incapable of addressing contemporary concerns."[2] Should not an adequate spirituality be oriented to living in the contemporary world rather than calling for a repetition of the past? In my experience, life was thoroughly evolutionary, not static.

As is frequently the case when young people are forced to choose between intellect and religion—a crisis which inevitably arises when the only form of religion known is fundamentalist in nature—I left the church. Toward the end of my undergraduate college years, however, an existential crisis reawakened deep spiritual concerns which had lain dormant for several years. Fortunately, my former church had recently called a pastor who held more moderate theological convictions. I found his theology more compatible with my educational and life experiences, but I still did not know what to do with the Bible. My hermeneutical quest led me to enter seminary.

• The Historical-Critical Method •

Discovery of the historical-critical method of biblical studies resolved my dilemma—at least for a time. Learning that the sacred text grew out of the real experiences of real people and therefore was *historically* and *culturally conditioned* was most liberating. I also found the method's reliance upon reason rather than the imposed authority of the church to be congruent with my approach to knowledge in all other areas of life. Just like the reformers before me, I felt confident that bypassing church tradition would enable the Bible to speak for itself. I wholeheartedly adopted the historical-critical method and devoted myself to the exegetical task. Of course, I quickly found that the better I understood the historical, cultural, and social setting of a text (what it "meant"), the less I

---

[2]Farmer, "The Transmission of Tradition" 130.

knew what to make of it as canonical literature (what it "means"). Having come to appreciate the vast historical and cultural differences between the biblical and the contemporary worlds, I realized that I must construct some sort of hermeneutical bridge capable of spanning this immense chasm if there were to be any intercourse between the two worlds.

In seeking to distinguish between a text's meaning and its cultural garb, I came to view the interpretive task as being twofold: engaging in the descriptive task of historical-critical exegesis (as prolegomena[3]), followed by the normative task of discovering the "timeless truth" or "religious essence" of the text for use in theological and ethical reflection.[4] I discovered that this approach to the interpretive task had taken several different forms. I explored each in turn.

• Classical Liberalism's Progressive Revelation •

First, I explored the classical liberalism of the nineteenth and early twentieth centuries. Influenced by Hegel's theory of history, and later by Darwin's theory of evolution, these interpreters approached the Bible as a record of "the progressive revelation of God," that is, God's revelation to humanity as people were able to discover it. Having discerned a text's original meaning through historical-critical exegesis, the interpreter then considers the place it occupies in the progress of revelation. Are the ideas the text expresses primitive and therefore transcended by later, higher ideas? Or are the ideas reflective of or at least in harmony with the later, more mature stages of the progress of revelation? Problematic texts (for example, miracles and ideas or acts that seem immoral to the "enlightened" conscience of a modern interpreter) were merely the partial gropings or misconceptions of earlier stages in

---

[3]To be satisfying, contemporary meaning cannot be "inconsistent with historical-critical methods and conclusions," but contemporary meaning and significance cannot "develop simply out of the data uncovered by historical research" (Edgar V. McKnight, *Postmodern Use of the Bible: The Emergence of Reader-Oriented Criticism* [Nashville: Abingdon Press, 1988] 48).

[4]My quest eventually led me to conclude that the attempt to discover a text's "essence" is wrongheaded.

the religious education of humankind and thus are to be discarded. Modern religious life must be a development of the timeless ethical principles of the later stages of revelation.

Although I was tempted to embrace classical liberalism's hermeneutic because of its evolutionary approach to spirituality and its facile excision of problematic material, I found several of its presuppositions to be questionable at best. To begin with, this approach was in harmony with the nineteenth- and early twentieth-century belief in inevitable progress and the correlated liberal view of human nature. However, two world wars separated by a worldwide depression destroyed this overly optimistic belief in progress, and events of the last fifty years have hardly served to reinstate this naïve optimism.

Also problematic was the positivist manner in which the historical-critical method was practiced. In the hands of the liberal exegete this tool had for its goal the total elimination of the interpreter's subjectivity in dealing with historical objects. Not only was the impossibility of this goal finally admitted, but more importantly the hermeneutical relevance of the interpreter gradually came to be recognized.[5] For example, the tendency of interpreters to modernize the later stages of revelation, especially the historical Jesus, became apparent. Through the work of Albert Schweitzer,[6] even the historical Jesus became "a stranger to our time" and hence problematic for theological and ethical appropriation.

On a related note, any method which demands that modern application be developed from (and only from) the original meaning finds itself faced with serious problems. To begin with, several of the so-called "assured results" of historical criticism have come to be questioned. Frequently the results of the historical-critical method are either too tenuous to use for satisfying application or too meager for a comprehensive application (for example, the authentic sayings of Jesus). Even when these assured results are substantial, the move to application is in fact based on some philosophical system; that is, the metahistorical framework

---

[5]The significance of this insight will become clear below.
[6]Albert Schweitzer, *The Quest of the Historical Jesus* (London: A&C Black, 1910; New York: Macmillan, 1948).

supporting the application is not derived from the historically verifiable data but is supplied by the interpreter.[7] Practitioners of this methodology seldom acknowledged, or more likely were not consciously unaware of, the role their worldview played in the hermeneutical process.

• The Biblical Theology Movement •

The two decades following the Second World War witnessed a distinctly American attempt to construct a hermeneutical bridge: the biblical theology movement. Although influenced by Continental dialectical (neoorthodox) theology,[8] this movement was largely the product of a new generation of Protestant scholars in the United States living in the wake the fundamentalist-modernist controversy of the preceding generation. In their opinion, biblical scholarship "had deteriorated into an exercise in trivia, in which tragic process the profound theological dimensions were overlooked."[9] They did not reject the historical-critical method as such, but rather desired to move beyond this preliminary stage of biblical research to the heart of the Bible, its theological dimension. I certainly identified with their quest.

Although the biblical theology movement resembled the progressive revelation approach of classical liberalism, there was a crucial difference. Whereas the earlier approach emphasized the progressive revelation of truth as humans were able to receive it—that is, revelation as human discovery—the biblical theology movement focused primarily on the mighty acts of God in history as revelatory; only in a secondary and inferential manner did human interpretation of these objective, historical acts enter the picture. Thus, the biblical theology movement attacked liberalism

---

[7]See below for Bultmann's contention that adherence to some philosophical system is inescapable, and the discussion in chap. 2 of the relationship between worldview and the hermeneutical enterprise.

[8]E.g., Barth's (*Romans*) assertion that humans cannot know God as an object of their investigation. Between God and humankind exists a gulf which only God can bridge; consequently, God can only be known as a subject acting upon humans.

[9]Brevard S. Childs, *Biblical Theology in Crisis* (Philadelphia: Westminster Press, 1970) 15.

as well as fundamentalism: "The emphasis on history as a vehicle for revelation was set over against seeing the Bible as a reflection of eternal truths, or a deposit of right doctrine, or particularly a process of evolving religious discovery."[10]

This emphasis on the self-revelation of God in history appeared to solve several problems.[11] (1) This perspective enabled interpreters to approach objective, historical events as related to divine activity; this was not possible as long as the Bible was viewed as the history of human religious development. Likewise, exegetes could discuss the subjective element of human interpretation of these events without destroying the concept of the self-revelation of God. Although the mighty acts of God in history are objective, the events are not in themselves revelatory; they must be viewed from a particular perspective, the perspective of faith. Thus, redemptive history (*Heilsgeschichte*) is distinct from verifiable historical events (*Historie*). Moreover, for redemptive history to be truly redemptive it must be existentially appropriated. (2) The emphasis upon revelation as an event of divine self-disclosure shifted the content of revelation away from doctrine and propositional formulations concerning God to an encounter with God. The exact content of the encounter was considered secondary or inferential from the event. (3) The fragmentation of the Bible associated with historical criticism was overcome. Behind the various written sources, oral traditions, and redactions was one continuous line of historical, revelatory events: thus, one can discern a unity to the Bible in midst of diversity. (4) History also provides the means to bridge the gap between the past and the present. Israel's history becomes the church's history, and by means of "liturgical recital"—which allows participation in past redemptive events—it can become the modern reader's history. The God who acted redemptively in the history of Israel and the church is still at work: redemptive history (*Heilsgeschichte*) continues in the life of the institutional church in the preaching of the Word, in the sacraments, and in social ministry.

---

[10]Childs, *Biblical Theology in Crisis*, 39.
[11]Childs, *Biblical Theology in Crisis*, 40-41.

Although I was initially attracted by the promising rhetoric, closer examination revealed that the problems the biblical theology movement claimed to have solved had in fact been glossed over. For example, although it was affirmed that the Bible, a fully human book, was the vehicle for the Word of God, the exact relation of the Bible and revelation was never clarified. Did revelation reside in the text, in some event behind the text, or in a combination of text and event? Similarly, the biblical theologians agreed that revelation was mediated through history, but the attempt to define the nature of history led to serious disagreements. What was the relationship between *Historie, Heilsgeschichte,* and *Traditionsgeschichte*? These ambiguities led to various inconsistencies within the movement. For example, "whenever historical events were in historical doubt, the interpretation of the sacred history was said to carry the theological meaning. [But when] an event had historical support, the historically real quality of the biblical history was passionately affirmed." Similarly, the biblical theologians "used biblical and orthodox language to speak of divine activity in history, but at the same time continued to speak of the same events in purely naturalistic terms."[12]

I also found problematic one of the central tenants of the biblical theology movement. As part of their polemic against both liberalism and fundamentalism, these interpreters argued that there was a distinctive biblical mentality. This mentality—which underlies the New Testament as well as the Hebrew Bible—was identified as "Hebrew" as opposed to "Greek." The difference in mentality, in the approach to reality, can be seen in the difference between the two languages, they argued. The dominant part of speech in Greek is the substantive, the word which describes or designates a *thing*; in Hebrew, the dominant part of speech is the verb, the word of *action*. Greek mentality, then, is abstract, rationalistic, and static, whereas Hebrew mentality is personal, psychological, and dynamic. This emphasis on a distinctive biblical mentality led to a further proposal. In contrast to the history of religions school (*religionsgeschichtliche Schule*) which stressed the influence of the religious and cultural environment on the religion of Israel and

---

[12]Childs, *Biblical Theology in Crisis,* 64-65.

the early church, both in form and content, the biblical theologians argued that the Bible's appropriation of environmental elements was distinctive and unique. Therefore, instead of emphasizing the similarities, the biblical theologians stressed the differences. The Bible, especially the Hebrew Bible, was held to have consistently transformed environmental influences into a unique expression of faith.

Many scholars were quick to argue that the contrast between Hebrew and Greek mentality had been overdrawn.[13] At the same time, the emphasis on the distinctiveness of the Bible over against its environment began to be replaced by a renewed interest in comparative studies. Doubtless, the discoveries of the Dead Sea Scrolls and the Nag Hammadi texts played an important role in this shift in scholarly interest. Moreover, scholars such as James Barr argued that it is both wrong and dangerous for theology "to try to set up any exact correlation between degree of distinctiveness and degree of revelatory value."[14] For the biblical theologians were not merely arguing that only by adopting an ancient perspective could a modern interpreter understand the Bible (what it "meant"); they were actually advocating that only by returning to this unique biblical perspective could modern faith be genuinely Christian. "They insisted that the Biblical message must be retained in its historical form and continued to fight hard against any separating of form from content whether by means of idealistic, existential, or psychological maneuvers."[15] If liberal interpreters had been guilty of modernizing the Bible to make it acceptable to the modern age, then the biblical theologians were guilty of the opposite error, that of adopting an archaizing stance. Should one canonize the historically and culturally conditioned ancient worldview? Do ancient ways of thinking and acting represent absolute and unchanging ways of relating to God?

And finally, although the biblical theology movement had been concerned with the notion of hermeneutics to some degree—at

---

[13]E.g., James Barr, *The Semantics of Biblical Language* (London: Oxford University Press, 1961).

[14]James Barr, *Old and New in Interpretation: A Study of the Two Testaments* (New York: Harper & Row, 1966) 63.

[15]Childs, *Biblical Theology in Crisis*, 71.

least as a polemic against the restrictions of historicism—I found that it made no significant contribution to hermeneutical theory. In fact, reaction to the movement constituted a step backward: a call for a strict separation between the work of the historian and the work of the theologian.[16] Thus, the failure of the biblical theology movement actually widened the hermeneutical gap.

• Existentialist Interpretation •

One of the most important twentieth-century attempts to construct a hermeneutical bridge is the existentialist interpretation of the Bible, an approach most closely associated with Rudolf Bultmann and his students. Although Bultmann acknowledged the legitimacy of and engaged in historical criticism, he emphasized that the Bible must also be interpreted in a manner so that it speaks as the Word of God. The kerygma cannot be established by historicism's inquiry into the reliability of the tradition, for all historical knowledge is relative, and any Word thus established would also be relative. Neither can it be discovered by liberalism's elimination method which reduces the Bible to some timeless ethical residue. In place of these failed approaches Bultmann proposed a program of "demythologizing" or "existentialist interpretation." According to this approach, the interpreter seeks the understanding of human existence—that is, what constitutes authentic human existence—that is expressed *through* the mythological language of the Bible.[17] This attitude toward life is then expressed in the categories of existential philosophy to challenge the modern person to a genuine existential decision.

---

[16]E.g., *Interpreter's Dictionary of the Bible,* s.v. "Biblical Theology, Contemporary" by Krister Stendahl.

[17]Bultmann ("New Testament and Mythology," in *Kerygma and Myth I,* ed Hans Werner Bartsch [New York: Harper & Row, 1953, 1961]) defined mythology as "the use of imagery to express the otherworldly in terms of this world and the divine in terms of human life, the other side in terms of this side. For instance, divine transcendence is expressed as spatial distance" (10n.2). "The real purpose of myth is not to present an objective picture of the world as it is, but to express man's understanding of himself in the world in which he lives. Myth should be interpreted not cosmologically, but anthropologically, or better still, existentially" (10).

The purpose of demythologizing the Bible is to remove stumbling blocks to the faith of modern people such as belief in a three-storied universe, divine intervention, angels and demons, death as a punishment for sin, Christ as a preexistent divine being, substitutionary satisfaction by the death of Jesus, the resurrection and ascension of Jesus, and the imminent end of the world marked by the returning Son of Man on the clouds of heaven. According to Bultmann, to expect a modern person to accept the ancient mythical view of the world as true would be both senseless and impossible. "It would be senseless, because there is nothing specifically Christian in the mythical view of the world as such. It is simply the cosmology of a prescientific age. Again, it would be impossible, because no man can adopt a view of the world by his own volition—it is already determined for him by his place in history."[18] This demythologizing program must be distinguished from liberalism's approach to the Bible. Whereas liberalism eliminates what is incredible (such as myth) retaining only the timeless residue, demythologizing decodes or interprets myth's meaning. Myth bears a meaning that lies behind the uncongenial language; this meaning needs to be set free by restatement in more congenial language. By means of the demythologizing process, the interpreter "peels away" the husk, the mythological garb, to arrive at the kernel, the understanding of human existence it clothes.[19] In support of this approach, Bultmann noted that certain of the New Testament writings themselves—especially the Gospel of John and

---

[18]Bultmann, "New Testament and Mythology," 3. Bultmann went on to acknowledge that a person's worldview "is not absolutely unalterable, and the individual may even contribute to its change. But he can do so only when he is faced by a new set of facts so compelling as to make his previous view of the world untenable. He has then no alternative but to modify his view of the world or produce a new one" (3). See chap. 2 below for a discussion of the relationship between worldview and the hermeneutical enterprise.

[19]"As far as its content is concerned, Christian faith is nothing other than that freedom from the past and openness for the future that is the original possibility of authentic human existence. . . . In other words, Bultmann reduces the entire contents of the traditional Christian confession to one fundamental assertion: *I henceforth understand myself no longer in terms of my past, but solely in terms of the future that is here and now disclosed to me as grace in my encounter with the church's proclamation.*" Schubert M. Ogden, *Christ without Myth: A Study Based on the Theology of Rudolf Bultmann* (New York: Harper & Brothers, 1961) 113-14.

the letters of Paul—engage in the process of demythologizing earlier Christian traditions.

In response to charges that this approach subordinates the interpretation of the Bible to an alien philosophical system, Bultmann set forth three points. First, he noted that "every interpretation is actualized by the framing of specific questions." He acknowledged that these questions need not be framed consciously, "but unless they are framed the texts have nothing to say to us." Second, "the right question to frame with regard to the Bible—at any rate within the Church—is the question of human existence." In fact, the ultimate purpose of the interpretation of any text "is to realize consciously the possibilities it affords for the understanding of human existence," possibilities a person is free to accept or reject. People are driven by an urge to inquire existentially about their own existence. Moreover, the church itself proclaims that the Bible, as the Word of God, addresses the reader concerning his or her own existence. Third, he pointed out that interpreters are dependent upon terminology which has come down to them by tradition, "though it is accepted uncritically and without reflection, and every traditional terminology is in one way or another dependent upon a particular philosophy." But, he argued, "it is vital that we should proceed neither uncritically nor without reflection. . . . In fact, there is no reason why we should not admit that what we are concerned with is the 'right' philosophy." He clarified that he is not suggesting that one adopt existentialism as "a final philosophical system" or that it is necessary for exegesis "to take over the actual answers that philosophy gives to the existential question of the meaning" of human existence. "The 'right' philosophy is simply one which has worked out an appropriate terminology for the understanding of existence, an understanding involved in human existence itself." For Bultmann, the obvious choice for modern people is existentialism.[20]

---

[20]Rudolf Bultmann, "Bultmann Replies to His Critics," in *Kerygma and Myth I*, ed Hans Werner Bartsch (New York: Harper & Row, 1953, 1961) 191-93. Bultmann anticipated this charge in his original manifesto, "New Testament and Mythology": "Some critics have objected that I am borrowing Heidegger's categories and forcing them upon the New Testament. I am afraid this only shows that they are blinding their eyes to the real problem. I mean, one should rather

Bultmann's critics can be divided into three groups: right wing, left wing, and center. Critics on the right[21] fault him for demythologizing (and hence denying) the "historical facticity" of such redemptive events as the incarnation, the atonement, the resurrection, the ascension, and the second coming. They assert that the biblical concept of God's salvific activity in history (*Heilsgeschichte*) requires a real relationship between historically verifiable facts and Christian faith. Although they admit that historical research cannot uncover the saving dimension of past historical events, they insist that "revelation is . . . always more than history, not only history, *but not without history.*" Moreover, these critics argue that "the concepts and pictorial ideas of the New Testament are indissociably connected with what they express. They do not need demythologizing, but only translation into the language and conceptual world of any given time."[22]

In sharp contrast, critics on the left,[23] with whom I found myself in agreement, fault Bultmann for not applying his methodology consistently. For example, although he insisted that the kerygma is not interested in historical research, he nevertheless

---

be startled that philosophy is saying the same thing as the New Testament and saying it quite independently" (25). He went on to point out "the crucial distinction between the New Testament and existentialism, between the Christian faith and the natural understanding of Being. The New Testament speaks and faith knows of *an act of God through which man becomes capable* of self-commitment, capable of faith and love, of his authentic life" (33; emphasis added).

[21]E.g., Julius Schniewind, "A Reply to Bultmann," and Helmut Thielicke "The Restatement of New Testament Mythology," both in *Kerygma and Myth I*, ed. Hans Werner Bartsch (New York: Harper & Row, 1961); Karl Barth, "Rudolf Bultmann—An Attempt to Understand Him," *Kerygma and Myth II*, ed. Hans Werner Bartsch (London: S.P.C.K., 1962); and Walter Künneth, "Bultmann's Philosophy and the Reality of Salvation," *Kerygma and History: A Symposium of the Theology of Rudolf Bultmann*, trans. and ed. Carl E. Braaten and Roy A. Harrisville (Nashville: Abingdon Press, 1962).

[22]Künneth, "Bultmann's Philosophy and the Reality of Salvation," 107, 115 (emphasis added). Yet as Schubert Ogden (*Christ without Myth*, 134), a left-wing critic, correctly stated, the position of the right-wing critics is essentially "what is obviously mythology is to be accepted merely because it is in the New Testament . . . the only way the position of the 'right' can be maintained is by some form of special pleading."

[23]E.g., Fritz Buri, "Entmythologisierung oder Entkerygmatisierung der Theologie," *Kerygma and Myth II*, ed. Hans Werner Bartsch (London: S.P.C.K., 1962) and Schubert M. Ogden, *Christ without Myth*.

tied his existentialist interpretation to an objective fact—the "thatness" of the historical Jesus. But if the kerygma is tied to a historical event, then it cannot be uninterested in historical research; or if it is improper to attempt to "justify" faith by historical research, then it cannot be tied to a historical fact. These critics also charge that he did not go far enough in his demythologizing program. He left the act of God in Jesus as a remnant of mythology: that is, he argued that Christian faith is to be interpreted as the possibility of authentic existence open to all humankind (as in existential philosophy), yet he also argued that it is only because of the uniqueness of the Christ-event that authentic existence is possible. A consistent application of existentialist interpretation, however, would lead to the dissolution of the specific possibility of Christian existence into a general possibility of humankind as such (that is, a possibility that has always and is always being given). Such a move would overcome the problem of Christian exclusivism: the possibility of authentic existence available through the proclamation of the Christ-event is not different in kind from the possibility God makes available to humans at all times and in all places. The Christ-event is not unique but rather is a supreme example; what matters is not faith in Christ, but faith in God as illustrated in the proclamation of Jesus as the Christ.[24]

The critics "in the center"—his own students[25]—disagreed with Bultmann on two points. First, Bultmann argued that any quest of the historical Jesus is irrelevant for faith because faith rests on the kerygma, not on so-called facts of history. The cross-and-resurrection is not a past fact of salvation (*Heilsgeschichte*) but a present saving event (*Heilsereignis* or *Heilsgeschehen*). How can a past phenomenon, God's act in Christ, continue to be "eventful"? This

---

[24]"Contrary to Bultmann, . . . the New Testament does *not* affirm that in Christ our salvation 'becomes possible.' It affirms, rather, that in him what has always been possible now 'becomes manifest,' in the sense of being decisively presented in a human word of witness" (Ogden, *Christ without Myth*, 143). Ogden supports this statement by appealing to Rom 1:18-23; 3:21; 4:1-25.

[25]E.g., Ernst Käsemann, "The Problem of the Historical Jesus," *Essays on New Testament Themes* (London: SCM Press, 1964); Günther Bornkamm, *Jesus of Nazareth* (New York: Harper & Row, 1960); and James M. Robinson, *A New Quest of the Historical Jesus* (London: SCM Press, 1959).

past event is made present through proclamation.[26] Although Bultmann's students agreed with him in rejecting *Heilsgeschichte* in favor of *Heilsgeschehen* or *Heilsereignis*,[27] they argued that there must be more continuity between the historical Jesus and the kerygmatic Christ than the mere fact that Jesus existed. Thus, because they judged Bultmann's "no quest" to be dangerously close to docetism, they began a "new quest" of the historical Jesus. These "post-Bultmannians"[28] followed their mentor in recognizing the priority of the kerygma—the gospels are kerygmatic: Jesus is always the Christ of faith, never the historical Jesus. Likewise, they regarded as illegitimate any attempt to "prove" faith historically. Nevertheless, they believed that a quest back through the kerygma would reveal a Jesus behind it who, particularly in his authentic sayings, is consistent with the church's proclamation. That is, they felt that they would find that the understanding of existence in the

---

[26]Bultmann, "New Testament and Mythology," 36-42:
To believe in the cross of Christ does not mean to concern ourselves with a mythical process wrought outside of us and our world, with an objective event turned by God to our advantage, but rather to make the cross of Christ our own, to undergo crucifixion with him. . . . In its redemptive aspect the cross of Christ is no mere mythical event, but a historic (*geschichtlich*) fact originating in the historical (*historisch*) event which is the crucifixion of Jesus. . . . the resurrection is not a mythological event adduced in order to prove the saving efficacy of the cross, but an article of faith just as much as the meaning of the cross itself. Indeed, *faith in the resurrection is really the same thing as faith in the saving efficacy of the cross.* . . . How do we come to believe in the saving efficacy of the cross? . . . the way in which the cross is proclaimed. It is always proclaimed together with the resurrection. Christ meets us in the preaching as one crucified and risen. He meets us in the word of preaching and nowhere else. The faith of Easter is just this—faith in the word of preaching. . . . The word of preaching confronts us as the word of God. It is not for us to question its credentials. It is we who are questioned, we who are asked whether we will believe the word or reject it. But in answering this question . . . we are given an opportunity of understanding ourselves. . . . Through the word of preaching the cross and resurrection are made present: the eschatological "now" is here, . . .

[27]As will be indicated below, Ernst Fuchs and Gerhard Ebeling altered Bultmann's *Heilsereignis* or *Heilsgeschehen* (saving event) to *Sprachereignis* (language event) and *Wortgeschehen* (word event) respectively. This change in terminology is part of their attempt to focus the saving event in language itself.

[28]This term indicates the desire of his students to move beyond Bultmann in certain important respects.

he meant by the event-character of "the language of being," he contrasted it with "the everyday language of the subject-object dilemma." Heidegger's language does not function as a sign designating a given content by means of commonly accepted sounds. Nor does his language express the ineffable inner experience of the speaker. According to such an understanding it is the speaker himself or herself who comes to expression in language; consequently, such language is always inadequate because of its derivative, objectifying character. Such language is secondary and results from "the forgetfulness of being characteristic of the West, which has produced a 'degeneration of language'," for example, language which has degenerated into scientific terminology.[38] For Heidegger, uncorrupted language is "the house of being." Being unveils itself calling forth thought, calling forth a response. Humans then speak, making audible the silent tolling of being. Primal language—being unveiling itself—needs the thinker or poet as its loudspeaker so that less perceptive people may hear the tolling of being. Such human language, then, is an-swer, correspond-ence, re-speaking. Thus, a poet's (or thinker's) language is not an "object" for study but rather an "event" in which the subject matter that called forth the language is so revealed that it calls forth a response in the hearer or reader. The goal in reading poetry, then, is to hear the voice of being, to which the poet's words answered, with sufficient clarity so that the reader is also called upon to answer.[39]

The turn in Heidegger's thinking sketched above accounts for many of the differences between Bultmann and his students. Although it is true that in both the earlier and later Heidegger hermeneutic "has to do with interpreting being, the later Heidegger does this in terms of the path of language rather than in terms of the structures of *Dasein*."[40] Whereas Bultmann relied upon the earlier Heidegger for his understanding of the structures of human existence, his students relied upon the later Heidegger for their

---

[38]Heidegger was attempting to overcome the modern or descriptive view of language—with its tyranny of the subject—which he viewed as the final state in the decay of language. See chap. 2.

[39]Robinson, "The German Discussion of the Later Heidegger," 49-51.

[40]Robinson, "The German Discussion of the Later Heidegger," 52.

understanding of language. For Bultmann, language is the objectification of an understanding of existence, "an objectification that is itself contrary to the understanding seeking expression in it." Language is merely a "vehicle" for transmitting or conveying an understanding of existence (the "content" or "subject matter"). In keeping with this view of language it follows that the movement in Bultmann's hermeneutic is "away from language—of which mythological language serves as a model—back to the understanding prior to, and more authentic than, the language." For his students, however, language is not "an objectification behind which one must move in establishing the understanding of existence objectifying itself therein." On the contrary, language is "constitutive of self-understanding, rather than merely its secondary objectification." The author of a text is not actually the one who is expressing himself or herself in language; rather, the author is simply re-speaking or answering the call of being. The question to ask of a text, then, is not "What was the author's intent?" but "What shines forth in this text?"[41] Language, in the sense of a language event,[42] has the power to bring into being something that was not there prior to the words being spoken. This "performative"[43] aspect of language stands in sharp contrast to Bultmann's view of language as a mere vehicle conveying a subject matter which is separate from the language itself.

For the post-Bultmannians hermeneutic is basically "translation." Because people hear the call of being in terms of their socio-historical world,[44] language which served as a language event

---

[41]Robinson, "Hermeneutic Since Barth," in *The New Hermeneutic*, ed. James M. Robinson and John B. Cobb, Jr, (New York: Harper & Row, 1964) 37-38, 46, 49.

[42]As noted above, Gerhard Ebeling used the term *Wortgeschehen* (word event) whereas Ernst Fuchs preferred *Sprachereignis* (language event).

[43]Performative language does not merely say something, it does something. Examples of performative language are wedding vows, a sentence pronounced by a judge, a provision in a will, and a declaration of war. Although the "power" of language is alien to the modern worldview, it was common in the ancient world (e.g., the Bible) and in primitive cultures (see chap. 2). See Robert W. Funk, *Language, Hermeneutic, and Word of God: The Problem of Language in the New Testament and Contemporary Theology* (New York: Harper & Row, 1966) 26-28.

[44]One should also note that Fuchs and Ebeling (like Heidegger) affirmed the linguisticality of existence. The "world" in which a person lives is given to him or her in language (language understood broadly; see above). Although this

in one setting may not serve as a language event in another setting. Translation will be required for the language event to happen again. This translation is not just a matter of finding a word for each word of the text; such a process may result merely in repeating what was once said instead of enabling the language event to happen anew. Translation involves transporting the subject matter (which, with respect to the Bible, is the Word of God[45]) from then to now. Sometimes this translation (the sermon) requires stating the subject matter in a way that is radically different from or even contradictory to the way it was expressed in the text so that it can once again become a language event demanding a response from the hearer.[46] Proponents of the new hermeneutic note that this phenomenon of translation is found in the New Testament itself as the original language event expressed in the language of Palestinian Judaism was translated so that people in the Hellenistic world could experience it.

One final characteristic of the new hermeneutic must be mentioned. Whereas in other approaches it is the biblical *text* that is interpreted, in the new hermeneutic it is the *interpreter* who is interpreted.[47] A text exists for the language event that was its origin and that will be its future. Thus, because the goal of interpretation is the reoccurrence of the language event, the end result is that the interpreter is interpreted; in the language event the interpreter is addressed by the Word of God; in the language event

---

world is largely inherited as part of a particular language tradition, it can be placed in question by new experiences. These minor (or major) "crises"—which call for a readjustment of (or a break with) the traditional way of understanding the world and/or self—are the language events that so concern proponents of the new hermeneutic.

[45]The language of the Bible is not identified with God's Word but is viewed as an answer to God's Word; thus, the language of the Bible is the linguistic path to God's Word.

[46]When existentialist interpretation is understood as the interpretation of the text with regard to the language event, guidance is provided for both historical criticism and the sermon. Historical criticism is to approach the text as a proclamation that has taken place; the sermon is to proclaim in the present what the text proclaimed in the past (i.e., the sermon is to execute the aim of the text which is the uttering of the Word of God).

[47]This was also true of Bultmann's approach, but the new hermeneutic made it more explicit with its emphasis on the language event.

the interpreter is called from inauthentic existence to authentic existence. Thus, the text, by means of the sermon, is a hermeneutical aid for interpreting present experience.

To many biblical scholars outside the Bultmannian school, the new hermeneutic seemed to be an inner scholarly debate expressed in esoteric terminology and hence was ignored. Those who took the time to understand the movement, however, found it to be an important advance in hermeneutical theory. Nevertheless, the approach has its weaknesses.

One frequent criticism of the new hermeneutic, like existentialist interpretation in general, is that it is too individualistic; the focus is on the individual and the crisis of decision. Although this is an important aspect of the biblical witness, the Bible is primarily communal or social in its outlook. Moreover, the emphasis on the power of the text to create a crisis of decision by calling the reader's world into question (e.g., the parables and aphorisms of Jesus) does not do justice to the full range of biblical genres. The Bible contains other genres which do not create confrontation, such as narratives which tend to create a sense of continuing identity for readers by showing them where they have been and where they are going.[48]

A related criticism is that the new hermeneutic fails to expand adequately Bultmann's narrow anthropology and conception of faith. Humans are more and seek more than what existentialist interpretation allows. According to existentialism, humans are primarily conative and so the focus is on freedom and the desire for authenticity. Yet as Amos Wilder noted, such an anthropology is but an "existentialist skeleton of human nature, a kind of X-ray photograph." Humans are also creative artisans and symbol-users "endowed with intellect, sentiment, imagination" and they seek fulfillment in all these dimensions. Thus, faith is concerned with reason and imagination as well as with will.[49]

---

[48]See William A. Beardslee, *Literary Criticism of the New Testament* (Philadelphia: Fortress Press, 1969) 81.

[49]Amos N. Wilder, "The Word as Address and the Word as Meaning," *The New Hermeneutic*, ed. James M. Robinson and John B. Cobb, Jr. (New York: Harper & Row, 1964) 202-15. See also John B. Cobb, Jr., "Faith and Culture," *The New Hermeneutic*, ed. James M. Robinson and John B. Cobb, Jr. (New York: Harper & Row,

A third negative charge is that, in spite of its claim to the contrary, existentialist interpretation (even of the post-Bultmannian type) is a variation of classical liberalism's approach to the Bible in which the essential kernel—now understood to be the text's existential meaning rather than a timeless truth—is to be separated from its nonessential husk. Many scholars, especially those informed by literary criticism, have pointed out that a text's "content" cannot be separated from its linguistic "form"; on the contrary, its content can be discerned *only in terms of* the cultural and historical categories in which it is expressed by the author *and* in which it is perceived by the reader. There is never a state in which the content is "formless," whether it be viewed from the perspective of author or reader. Underlying all existentialist approaches is the unfounded conviction that the categories of existence are universal and thus provide the means by which the subject matter of the Bible can be translated into contemporary language. In reality, "the givenness of existence in every age is composed of distinctive factors that form human existence, so that there is no such thing as a final analysis of existence itself."[50] In light of the radically historical nature of existence, language is always more than the mere vehicle for a text's content. In many respects, the medium *is* the message. Granted, one can distinguish between content and form in theory, but this does not mean that the two can be separated in practice. There simply is no such thing as "formless content." The search for a text's essence—whether that kernel be understod as a timeless truth (as in classical liberalism), an act of God (as in the biblical theology movement), or its existential meaning (as with Bultmann and his students)—is misguided.

One of the promising aspects of the new hermeneutic lay in its concern for literary form and language. But instead of this concern leading to a dialogue with literary scholars, the new hermeneutic turned instead to the philosophy of language (Heidegger) and

---

1964).

[50]John Dillenberger, "On Broadening the New Hermeneutic," in *The New Hermeneutic*, ed. James M. Robinson and John B. Cobb, Jr. (New York: Harper & Row, 1964) 161. See also Robert W. Funk, "The Hermeneutical Problem and Historical Criticism," in *The New Hermeneutic*, esp. 189-92.

theology. For example, they examined the parables of Jesus as language events but did not also treat them as metaphors. The needed interface of the philosophy of language and literary criticism "had to wait until the discussion moved to America."[51]

• Literary Criticism •

The literary criticism of the Bible, to which my quest next led, grew out of the Anglo-American New Criticism of the early decades of the twentieth century. Prior to this time, critics of literature viewed texts as "windows to meaning which lay beyond them"; the new critics "rebelled by construing texts as mirrors within which meaning was locked up."[52] As Dan Via so aptly described it, "the historical critic looks through the text to what it refers or points to and treats the text as evidence for something else, while the literary critic looks at the text for what *it* says in itself by means of the patterning or shaping—the informing—of its content."[53] Historical criticism, especially in its historicist form, had emphasized genetic or causal explanation to such an extent that the text was reduced to its historical causes; in reaction, the new literary criticism focused on the text as a self-contained, self-regulated system. The New Critics gave attention to "poetics," how literature is "made,"[54] but the making that concerned them was not the causal activity *extrinsic* to the text but rather the linguistic and literary relationships *intrinsic* to the text.

---

[51]Norman Perrin, *Jesus and the Language of the Kingdom: Symbol and Metaphor in New Testament Interpretation* (Philadelphia: Fortress Press, 1976) 123. Perrin pointed to Robert Funk's *Language, Hermeneutic, and Word of God* as the pioneering integrative work.

[52]Norman R. Petersen, *Literary Criticism for New Testament Critics* (Philadelphia: Fortress Press, 1978) 24.

[53]Dan O. Via, Jr., "Editor's Foreword," in Norman R. Petersen, *Literary Criticism for New Testament Critics* (Philadelphia: Fortress Press, 1978) 5. Another comparison: historical criticism views the text as a "shell" which contains the real "meat" being sought (historical information); once the desired information is obtained, the shell is discarded. Literary criticism emphasizes the "delight" of literature rather than its "use" and is thus as concerned with the shell as with the meat.

[54]"Poetics" is derived from the Greek verb *poiein*, "to make."

The New Critics considered a text to be an autonomous whole to be interpreted apart from any reference beyond itself, that is, in abstraction from the author, the reader, or the "real" world. Moreover, they maintained that a literary work could not be replaced by an interpretation of it (for example, a commentary): the rich symbolism and structure of literature addresses the reader holistically and awakens intuition whereas the abstract language of interpretation offers only rational explanation; symbolism can combine a wide variety of notions into a single impression whereas abstract language can only present one idea at a time. As a result, whenever symbolism is translated (reduced they would say!) into the abstract language of rational explanation there is a loss of meaning. Therefore, in place of rational interpretation these literary critics urged an encounter with the text itself, a participation in the imaginative world created by the text.

Norman Petersen correctly noted that the parallel revolt against historicism in biblical studies

> took the form of theological hermeneutics rather than of poetics. Concerned with the principles of understanding and of interpretation, the hermeneutical revolution associated with the introduction of existential phenomenology by . . . Rudolf Bultmann became separated from poetic questions because it focused on the content rather than on the composition of biblical texts. Biblical students . . . distinguished between the study of the theological things referred to in the texts [*Sachkritik*] . . . and historical criticism, *to which matters of textual poetics were relegated.*[55]

Unencumbered by the separation of poetics from hermeneutical considerations, literary criticism's intrinsic study of the text results in meaning which is not confined to authorial intent; in this manner the "hermeneutical gap" is bridged.

In the opinion of the practitioners of literary criticism, reading the Bible as literature means retrieving it from the museum in which historical criticism had confined it. Moreover, literary criticism deals with dimensions of faith frequently omitted in other approaches to the Bible: imagination and creativity. "The moral

---

[55]Petersen 27; emphasis added.

and intellectual dimensions of faith have always been central to Christian theology, but too often the imaginative and creative side of faith has been suspect or ignored." Yet the inclusion of this dimension is essential because "creativity is a central component not merely in the 'human response' of faith, but also in the very structure which evokes faith." The inclusion of this dimension results in a transformation of the typical understanding of faith because "a theology which takes imagination and creativity seriously will not be willing to limit them to functioning only in the initial stage of faith or in some uniform expression of it. Some element of spontaneity, or new vision, will have to be a possibility in the continuing history of faith."[56]

I found the literary approach to biblical interpretation helpful in a number of ways, especially its ability to make the text immediately available for theological reflection and its attention to imagination and creativity. But as with historical criticism, I found literary criticism too reductionistic in its methodology. I could not bring myself to ignore the historical dimension of texts. Literary critics blamed my reluctance upon having invested so much time and energy in the historical-critical method. Doubtless there was some truth in their charge, but something far more important was also at stake. I could not bring myself to abandon the radical historicity of human existence.

I was happy to discover that I was not alone in my hesitation to embrace this methodology as the goal of my hermeneutical quest. There were also literary critics for whom the retreat from historical criticism to a "text-centered" literary criticism—the legacy of New Criticism to biblical studies—had not been entirely satisfying. Edgar McKnight, for example, has proposed a "radical reader-oriented literary criticism . . . which views literature in terms of readers and their values, attitudes, and responses." Such an approach is

> postmodern in that it challenges the critical assumption that a disinterested reader can approach a text objectively and obtain verifiable knowledge by applying certain scientific strategies. A

---

[56]Beardslee, *Literary Criticism of the New Testament*, 75.

radical reader-oriented approach sees the strategies, the criteria for criticism and verification, the "information" obtained by the process, and the use made of such "information" in light of the reader.[57]

Thus, radical reader-oriented criticism stresses the role of the reader—as opposed to the text or the author—in the hermeneutical process. In this approach the reader is no more autonomous than the text or author; on the contrary, reader and text and author are interdependent. Nevertheless, it is the reader who makes sense of the text. "Readers make sense of the Bible in the light of their world, which includes not only linguistic and literary tools but also worldviews that influence the sorts of meanings and the methods that are satisfying."[58]

McKnight labeled his approach "radical" reader-response criticism to distinguish it from earlier stages of reader-response criticism in which the variability of readers' responses were viewed with suspicion. In an effort to maintain the concept of validity in interpretation, earlier reader-response critics judged between proper and improper readings on the basis of the "objective" text. Only when it was recognized that literature is a conventional category dependent upon the subjective perception of the reader—that is, there is no neutral "language of literature" to serve as the foundation for judgment of a reader's response—was there a radical departure from the assumptions of New Criticism. This development in literary criticism was influenced by philosophy's abandonment of modernism's foundationalist epistemology—that is, a proposition may be advanced whose truth is demonstrable without any assumptions and from which further theories can be

---

[57]McKnight, *Postmodern Use of the Bible*, 14-15.

[58]McKnight, *Postmodern Use of the Bible*, 58. "In biblical studies, the distinction between the material work itself and what the work comes to be in the perception and actualization of readers has been taken to be the result of a lack of information and/or critical capacity. As knowledge and capacity develop, more accurate perception and actualization take place. But it seems impossible to dispute the idea that biblical texts have been perceived differently because of different worldviews and because of developments within a particular worldview. The ancient and medieval church could only perceive the Bible in the light of its Platonic worldview, and the church following the Enlightenment could not perceived the Bible apart from consideration of its historicity" (145-46). See chap. 2.

developed in a linear fashion—for postmodernism's circular episte-mology—that is, "knowledge is justified in a circular fashion through the relationship of the results obtained to the beginning point."[59]

In addition to the epistemological revolution, McKnight also cited developments in the fields of hermeneutics, structuralism and poststructuralism, and phenomenology as contributing to the rise of radical reader-response criticism. The influence of the hermeneu-tical tradition associated with Heidegger is evident in those forms of reader-response criticism that view the task of understanding a text not as discovering an inner meaning contained in the text but rather as unfolding the possibility of being indicated by the text. I found this happy marriage of the philosophy of language and literary criticism very promising.

In radical reader-response criticism, the opposition between French structuralism, which emphasized order and necessity, and poststructuralism (or deconstruction), in which order is replaced with radical disordering, has been mediated in the broader struc-tural tradition. According to structuralism in this broader sense, "literature is a system standing in correlation with other systems that help to define literature." Literature is influenced by changes in culture, and vice versa. "A dialectical relationship also exists between the individual and culture"; no longer is the individual viewed as a mere passive reactor to the environment or the possessor of innate ideas that automatically unfold. Because of the dynamic interaction of text, culture, and reader, "the reader is no longer an irrelevant individual, superimposing private associations

---

[59]McKnight, *Postmodern Use of the Bible*, 16-18. McKnight acknowledged that "the limits of knowledge and the failure to establish some final foundation for knowledge have been applied in a dramatic fashion in literature in the skeptical deconstruction associated with Jacques Derrida [see below]. Skepticism, however, is not the only possible conclusion. Skepticism results from the assumption that foundationalism is the only route to knowledge, or that the only kind of knowledge that counts is that which is based on foundationalism. A reader-oriented approach results from the assumption that knowledge (epistemology) is always related to life (ontology) and that the only sort of knowledge that really counts is knowledge grounded in life" (18-19).

onto a social meaning, but an active force who is indispensable to meaning from the beginning."[60]

The role of the reader is also emphasized in the phenomenological tradition. For example,

> the work of art itself is distinguished from the work as an aesthetic object that is constituted or actualized through the intentional act of reading. The complexity of a literary work and its apprehension are such that readers cannot give themselves equally to all of the components of the total apprehension. Only a few of the multiplicity of experienced and interwoven acts become central. The rest are only co-experienced.[61]

Because this is so, there is constant change with regard to which component acts are central to any particular reader at any particular moment. Thus, "the same literary work is apprehended . . . in various changing 'aspects.'"[62]

Although I find much of McKnight's approach convincing and hermeneutically satisfying, his radical reader-oriented literary criticism, and similar proposals, raise several important questions. Acceptance of these postmodern approaches means acknowledging two points: that the interpretation of a text involves a universe of interdependent systems, and that the factors involved in interpretation are dynamic (understandings of self, world, text, meaning, and so forth continue to change). Therefore, the question that immediately arises, and which McKnight himself posed, is, "How can interpretation take place within a dynamically expanding system, consisting of dynamic elements?" One common solution is to attempt to refute or ignore the implications of relativism involved in adopting a radical reader-oriented approach.

> The particular universe within which we make sense is so compelling that it is difficult to appreciate the relativism of methods and meanings. We "know" intuitively and emotionally that the meanings validated by our experience in our world are true in some final way. Even when we recognize intellectually the

---

[60]McKnight, *Postmodern Use of the Bible*, 20 (see also 143-62).
[61]McKnight, *Postmodern Use of the Bible*, 20.
[62]McKnight, *Postmodern Use of the Bible*, 20-21.

inevitability of some type of relativism, we attempt to ignore or refute it because relativism seems to mean that all of our facts are false or at least that no important fact can be verified.[63]

McKnight's solution, with which I find myself in agreement, is to understand the relativity involved as indicating "not that truth is unattainable but that it is attainable in all the various universes. Truth is discovered and expressed in terms that make sense within a particular universe of meaning." That such truth is not final, objective, trans-historical truth should not be disturbing, for such truth could not touch humankind (due to the radically historical nature of human existence). Relative truth which is "consistent with the various systems that cohere in a particular universe of meaning [is] true—or truthful."[64]

A second set of questions also arise from McKnight's approach. His radical reader-oriented literary criticism entails the coordination of numerous interpretative methodologies, "a universe of interdependent systems"[65] as he described it. But how can these diverse systems of meaning be combined without the combination appearing *ad hoc*? Was not Bultmann right? Is not some philosophical system required to undergird a *coherent*, methodologically interdependent and inclusive approach to biblical interpretation? In the absence of such an undergirding metaphysical system, as I engaged in radical reader-oriented criticism I found myself pushed in the direction of deconstruction.

• Deconstruction •

One of the most influential postmodern developments in the interpretation of texts is the rise of deconstructive literary criticism. Named[66] by Jacques Derrida who introduced the methodology to

---

[63]McKnight, *Postmodern Use of the Bible*, 59.

[64]McKnight, *Postmodern Use of the Bible*, 59.

[65]McKnight, *Postmodern Use of the Bible*, 58.

[66]As Robert Con Davis and Ronald Schleifer (*Contemporary Literary Criticism: Literary and Cultural Studies*, 2nd ed. [New York: Longman, 1989] 206) noted, "Derrida named his critique 'deconstruction' because of the way he showed that meanings and values, by their very nature, are so mutually interdependent in systems of thought as to be continually destabilizing to each other and even to

American scholars in 1966, "deconstruction has become the critical rage (or, depending upon point of view, outrage)."[67] American scholars who have played important roles in the dissemination of deconstructive thought—or as some would prefer say, those responsible for bringing the plague to American scholarship and teaching—include Paul de Man, Geoffrey Hartman, Harold Bloom, and J. Hillis Miller—the "Yale School." Biblical scholars and theologians significantly influenced by deconstructive criticism include John Dominic Crossan, Thomas J. J. Altizer, Carl Raschke, Charles Winquist, Joseph S. O'Leary, Mark C. Taylor, and Stephen D. Moore.[68]

In order to understand deconstructive criticism, one must begin with the modern linguistic understanding of the sign. Ferdinand de Saussure[69] asserted that no intrinsic relationship exists between the two parts of the sign, the signifier and the signified; the bond between them is purely arbitrary. A signifier is a unit of sound, an arbitrary division of the abstract sound spectrum (or in the case of a graphic sign, a sound-image, for example, the letters "c-a-t"); a signified is a concept, an arbitrary division of the conceptual field; and the relationship between a signifier and a signified is arbitrary in that no objective, natural, or inevitable link exists between the

---

themselves." See below for an expansion of this idea.

[67]G. Douglas Atkins, *Reading Deconstruction/Deconstructive Reading* (Lexington: University Press of Kentucky, 1983) 1.

[68]Representative works include John Dominic Crossan, *In Parables: The Challenge of the Historical Jesus* (New York: Harper & Row, 1973), *The Dark Interval: Towards a Theology of Story* (Niles IL: Argus Press, 1975), *Raid on the Articulate: Comic Eschatology in Jesus and Borges* (New York: Harper & Row, 1976); Thomas J. J. Altizer, *Total Presence: The Language of Jesus and the Language of Today* (New York: Seabury Press, 1980); Thomas J. J. Altizer, Max A. Meyer, Carl A. Raschke, Robert P. Scharlemann, Mark C. Taylor, and Charles E. Winquist, *Deconstruction and Theology* (New York: Crossroad, 1982); Mark C. Taylor, *Deconstructing Theology* (New York: Crossroad, 1982), *Erring: A Post Modern A/Theology* (Chicago: University of Chicago Press, 1984); and Stephen D. Moore, *Mark and Luke in Poststructuralist Perspectives: Jesus Begins to Write* (New Haven: Yale University Press, 1992).

[69]Saussure (*Course in General Linguistics*, trans. Wade Baskin (New York: McGraw-Hill, 1959 [1915]) pioneered a new direction in linguistic studies. Instead of asking etymological, diachronic questions with respect to particular linguistic formations, he asked synchronic questions with respect to how elements of language are configured so as to produce their effects.

signifier and the signified (that is, a signifier could be replaced by any other sound unit if it were accepted by the speech community). Signs, then, are made possible by *differences* between sounds. For example, the sound "cat" is intelligible to those who speak English not because of what it is, because there is no resemblance between the sound (or its appearance when written) and the animal we call a "cat." Rather, the sound is intelligible because of what it is not: "cap," "cab," "bat," "rat," and every other sound. Because the sign is a structure of difference, that which is signified by the signifier is never present in and of itself: signified and signifier never become one; the word is not the thing. The arbitrary nature of signs means that words have no real (or absolute) referential value; the thing could have been signified by any other word. "In language there are only differences, *without positive terms* [that is, without absolute referents]."[70]

Derrida's own analysis of the sign, based on Saussure's assertion that the sign marks a place of difference, led him to several important insights. He noted that the possibility of a sign substituting for the thing in a system of differences depends upon deferral, upon putting off into the future any grasp of the thing "itself." To indicate both the differing and deferring structure of the sign Derrida coined the word *differance* (the French verb *différer* has both meanings).

Whereas Saussure observed that meaning derives from the differences between one element and others in the system, Derrida pointed out that difference works within as well as between elements. The perception of one element within a system requires the perception of the differences between it and other elements; thus, each element must refer to elements other than itself in order to be. This *trace* of the other as other makes thought possible; indeed, the notion of trace—as distinct from the actual content of difference—is logically prior to the actual differences which exist between two elements in a system.[71]

---

[70]Saussure, *Course in General Linguistics*, 165.

[71]One should note, however, that the notion of trace means that a "thing" is not defined simply by its difference from "another"; because a thing differs from "itself" (see the discussion on "simple presence" below)—i.e., a trace of the "other" is always present—it cannot be simply defined.

In addition to making thought possible, the notion of trace renders the idea of "simple presence" impossible; an element is never present in and of itself but always bears within it the trace of the other. With respect to Western metaphysics' desire for simple presence, Derrida wrote: "Without the possibility of *differance*, the desire of presence as such would not find its breathing-space. That means by the same token that this desire carries in itself the destiny of its nonsatisfaction. *Differance* produces what it forbids, makes possible the very thing that it makes impossible."[72] At the same time *differance* denies simple presence, it also denies the opposite notion of total absence. Indeed, all of the central oppositions of metaphysics are denied: for example, presence/absence, truth/error, good/evil, identity/difference, being/nothingness, life/death, nature/culture, mind/matter, soul/body, man/woman, master/slave, transcendent/immanent, necessary/contingent, simple/complex, nature/culture, object/representation, history/fiction, literal/metaphorical, text/interpretation. Each element of an opposition bears the trace of the other, undermining the opposition; either/or becomes both/and.

Merely neutralizing these and other opposition is not sufficient. According to Derrida, such oppositions always involve "a violent hierarchy. One of the two terms governs the other (axiologically, logically, etc.) or has the upper hand. To deconstruct the opposition, first of all, is to overturn the hierarchy at a given moment."[73] But this is only the first step for a deconstructive critic; the next step is to overthrow the reversal. "The 'trace' creates this ceaseless undoing/preserving oscillation. The undoing is no more necessary than the preserving, for without the latter another term would be privileged in a new hierarchy, simple opposition being maintained through reversal, and the 'trace' ignored."[74]

Derrida's distinctive approach to traditional binary oppositions is also reflected in the term *supplément*. This French word, like *differance*, has two meanings: an addition and a substitute. Instead

---

[72]Jacques Derrida, *Of Grammatology*, trans. Gayatri Chakravorty Spivak (Baltimore: Johns Hopkins University Press, 1976) 143.

[73]Jacques Derrida, *Positions*, trans. Alan Bass (Chicago: University of Chicago Press, 1981) 41.

[74]Atkins, *Reading Deconstruction/Deconstructive Reading*, 21.

of opposing "A" to "B," as in traditional logic, "B" is both added to "A" and substituted for it. "A" and "B" are neither opposed nor equated because the trace of the other meaning is always there to undermine the distinction between substitute and addition.

According to Derrida, then, nothing escapes *textuality*, the system of traces. "Anything that can be known will be articulated *as a text* within a system of differences . . . *without positive terms.*"[75] There is no privileged signified outside the system of differences. And as G. Douglas Atkins remarked: "Once we rethink the metaphysical concept of 'reality' in 'textual' terms (there are no philosophical regulations of truth, the thing itself being a sign and all 'facts' being in 'fact' interpretations, as Nietzsche argued), we are left with a world of texts, all of which possess a certain 'fictive' or 'literary' quality."[76] All texts (for example, social texts or literary texts) "produce meanings, but since the production of meaning cannot be arrested through a relationship with absolute referents (positive terms) or absolutely closed contexts (centers or grounds), textuality will always be in progress and unfinished—thus, undecidable."[77]

Traditional literary critics have desired "meaning" or "truth" outside the system of differences, stable meaning that is present "behind" or "under" the textual surface. But because there is no privileged signified outside the system of differences, there is no such meaning. The deconstructive critic seeks to avoid the temptation to break the endless chains of substitutions which condemn a critic to endless interpretation and escape to a haven outside contingency and temporality. Aware of the differential quality of language, the deconstructive critic

> seeks the moment in any text when its duplicity, its dialogical nature, is exposed. . . . seeks the text's navel, the moment when any text will differ from itself, transgressing its own system of values, becoming undecidable in terms of its apparent system of

---

[75]Davis and Schleifer, *Contemporary Literary Criticism: Literary and Cultural Studies,* 208.

[76]Atkins, *Reading Deconstruction/Deconstructive Reading,* 23.

[77]Davis and Schleifer, *Contemporary Literary Criticism: Literary and Cultural Studies,* 208.

meaning. . . . This undoing, made necessary by the "trace," and so by the duplicitous quality of words and texts, must not be confused with the simple locating of a moment of ambiguity or irony that is somehow incorporated into a text's system of (monological) meaning; rather, it is the moment that threatens the collapse of that entire system.[78]

Literary texts, then, move dynamically beyond and even contrary to any purposiveness that can be attributed to their authors. Therefore, a close reading of a text may lead both to the author's purpose and to the deconstruction of that purpose by means of the text's language, for there is an unresolvable conflict between textual declaration and textual description. "The text tells the story of this conflict. But the conflict is not between two completely different positions, there being no way ever to separate one completely from the other."[79] The trace of the one is always present in the other.

Although deconstruction has been embraced by scholars in many fields, it has not gone unchallenged. As is often the case when radically new methodologies are introduced, deconstruction has suffered considerable misunderstanding, even caricature; indeed, most of the following negative criticisms appear to be based on misunderstandings of various types. For example, one charge frequently leveled against Derrida and other deconstructive critics is that they are needlessly obscure. In evaluating this charge, one must acknowledge that their writings *are* quite difficult. Doubtless, one of the reasons they are so hard to understand is that they write within the more abstract Continental tradition instead of the more familiar Anglo-American empirical tradition. But the main reason for this difficulty is that many readers expect language "to be a mirror reflecting truly the nature and contents of the 'object' being described."[80] But this is precisely the understanding of

---

[78]Atkins, *Reading Deconstruction/Deconstructive Reading*, 25. Compare Gayatri Chakravorty Spivak, "Translator's Preface" in Derrida, *Of Grammatology*, xlix: "The desire for unity and order compels the author and the reader to balance the equation that is the text's system. The deconstructive reader . . . [seeks] the moment in the text which harbors the unbalancing of the equation, the sleight of hand at the limit of a text which cannot be dismissed simply as a contradiction."

[79]Atkins, *Reading Deconstruction/Deconstructive Reading*, 11.

[80]Atkins, *Reading Deconstruction/Deconstructive Reading*, 26. See the discussion

language the deconstructive critics call into question, for language is never a simple means for the presentation of truth. Because language is a system of differences, every use of language—even the most critical philosophical or scientific text—manifests the trace. It is impossible to transcend the endless chain of signifiers and reach some privileged signified behind the text and thereby "get the meaning." Deconstructionist writings simply make this ubiquitous aspect of language more apparent than do other texts.

A second frequently voiced criticism is that deconstructive critics have abandoned the usual interpretive procedures. For example, it is frequently alleged that these critics place all readings, even the most arbitrary, on the same level; there appears to be no way to evaluate the validity of various readings. This charge, however, is not correct. The fact that a deconstructive reading does not allow one privileged meaning to escape the system of differences does not mean that all readings are equal. For an interpreter to shine light upon one aspect of a text involves casting shadows on others, or even relegating them to the darkness. Nevertheless, some readings penetrate more deeply into a text than do others. Thus, rather than proposing that all readings be valued alike, deconstructive critics actually call for the recognition of the limits of all readings.

Moreover, in disputing the allegation that they abandon the usual interpretive procedures, deconstructionists point out that they preserve as well as undo traditional or unequivocal readings of a text (failing to understand the trace, the opponents of deconstruction have focused exclusively on the undoing side of the undoing/preserving oscillation). Indeed, deconstructionists begin their interpretation in the traditional manner. They insist, however, that "any traditional or unequivocal reading is always already bifurcated, divided within, equivocal. . . . Instead of being on the outside, distinct, and separate . . . the deconstructive [reading] already lies within the traditional. Or is it the other way around?"[81] The situation is frequently described in terms of host and parasite. Whereas opponents only construe the metaphor so

---

of the descriptive phase of language in chap. 2.

[81] Atkins, *Reading Deconstruction/Deconstructive Reading*, 7-8.

that the deconstructive reading is the parasite, one could equally well claim that the traditional reading "is the parasitical virus which has for millennia been passed from generation to generation in Western culture in its language and in the privileged texts of those languages."[82] However the metaphor be construed, the important point is that each reading requires, indeed, contains the other and therefore is no longer a simple identity.

Many opponents of deconstruction label it nihilistic, "the denial of all truth, of meaning, of authorial intent, of reference, of reality, and more." If it were true that deconstructive criticism allowed a reader to construct *any* meaning at all, then it would be nihilistic. But this is not deconstruction's understanding of the interpretive process. Deconstruction does signal "an end—not the end of meaning but the end of privileged and protected notions of text, meaning, truth, reader."[83] According to deconstructive thought, the act of reading does involve an active intervention on the part of the reader. Reading is never an objective identification of the meaning present in or beneath or behind a text. On the contrary, "each reader takes possession of the work for one reason or another and imposes on it a certain pattern of meaning." This creation of meaning is an expression of a will to power, an attempt to become master (á la Nietzsche).[84] Subjectivists and some hermeneuticians (for example, the Bultmannian school) use this analysis of the act of reading to reverse the traditional hierarchy—objective meaning (truth)/subjective meaning (fiction)—in support of the autonomous consciousness. Deconstruction, however, cannot rest content with merely reversing the hierarchy (which would only perpetuate, not transform, hierarchization), as if the autonomous consciousness is a foundation. According to deconstructive critics, there is *no* foundation. Object cannot exist without subject (and vice versa) or truth without fiction (and vice versa), for the elements forming an (illusory) opposition are actually accomplices due to the system of differences and the trace. The trace keeps

---

[82]J. Hillis Miller, "The Critic as Host," in *Deconstruction and Criticism* (New York: Seabury Press, 1979) 222.

[83]The Bible and Culture Collective, *The Postmodern Bible* (New Haven: Yale University Press, 1995) 145.

[84]J. Hillis Miller, "Tradition and Difference," *Diacritics* 2 (1972): 6, 12.

differance in play. Thus, although deconstructionist criticism seeks to avoid the interpretive mastery that imports meaning into texts (and the world) under the guise of transcendent truth outside the play of difference, it does so in a way more radical than nihilism or subjectivism. In its recognition of the "fictionality of things" deconstruction acknowledges the "doubleness of what is, . . . the complicity of truth and fiction."[85]

Another common accusation is that deconstruction is deeply antithetical to the humanist tradition.[86] Based on the mythological affirmation of a "cosmic continuum," the humanist tradition posits a meaningful world characterized by primal and final unity. However, because of the system of differences—which both makes the dream possible and its fulfillment impossible—unity has always been deferred; a gap perpetually remains which the humanist tradition has failed to close. Unable to move outside the system of differences and thereby locate a transcendental referent which could bestow order and meaning, the humanist tradition has—in the opinion of many—fallen into a state of bankruptcy. That deconstruction is antithetical to the humanist tradition is obviously a true accusation. But rather than presenting nihilism as the only alternative, deconstruction offers a way out of the present bankruptcy. Indeed, rather than pining with nostalgia for the lost security of meaning never in fact possessed or placing confidence in linear progress,[87] Derrida called for "a Nietzschean *affirmation*—the joyous affirmation of the freeplay of the world and without truth, without origin, offered to an active interpretation. . . . [This affirmation] plays the game without security."[88]

Atkins, among others, has compared deconstructionist thought to the Yahwist-prophetic tradition. To appreciate this comparison

---

[85]Atkins, *Reading Deconstruction/Deconstructive Reading*, 29.

[86]For the purpose at hand, the following characteristics of the humanist tradition are of special importance: faith in reason, human nature, stable meaning, objective norms of interpretation, and the critic's subservience before a text which the critic is merely to describe objectively.

[87]See Atkins, *Reading Deconstruction/Deconstructive Reading*, 30-31.

[88]Jacques Derrida "Structure, Sign, and Play in the Discourse of the Human Sciences," in *The Structuralist Controversy: The Languages of Criticism and the Sciences of Man*, ed. Richard Macksey and Eugenio Donato (Baltimore: Johns Hopkins University Press, 1972) 264-65.

one must note the contrast between Hebraic and Hellenistic thought. In the Hellenistic-humanist tradition, the notion of sign has always implied the existence of an intelligible meaning to which it refers. What is signified is the center which precedes the sign as its ground or foundation. But if signification "is determined by the system of differences wherein each sign is inscribed, rather than by the presence of a signified inside *and outside* language, then it is clear that language has no center," no foundation. "There is no Transcendental Signified, no fullness of presence—only difference." In this discovery, deconstruction destroyed the crowning feature of Hellenism, logocentrism: "the idea of the *logos*, the transcendent principle of structure and order that conveys meaning to secondariness."[89] There is no *logos*. The world as perceived by deconstructionists, then, is dehellenized, without intrinsic order or structure or meaning.

Certain theologians[90] have called for the dehellenization of Christianity for several decades. These scholars attack Christianity's bondage to the transcendent, impassive God derived from Greek metaphysics. Rather than viewing the world as governed by this sovereign God's eternally fixed, all-encompassing purpose, they boldly assert that God has no such plan. But because humans experience themselves as purposeful creatures, they are unable to believe the world is devoid of purpose and so project purposiveness on the cosmos—usually assigning themselves a crucial place in the *telos*! "Strange as it may appear to some," Atkins correctly observes, "these theologians' rejection of the age-old mythological and Hellenic notion of a *telos* and of an order ordained by God and built into the nature of things stems from a recognition that such thinking is unbiblical."[91] In contrast to the patterned and

---

[89] Atkins, *Reading Deconstruction/Deconstructive Reading*, 39-40; emphasis added.

[90] E.g., Paul Tillich, John A. T. Robinson, Leslie Dewart, Thomas J. J. Altizer, John Dominic Crossan, and Harvey Cox.

[91] Atkins, *Reading Deconstruction/Deconstructive Reading*, 42. Atkins's statement, though correct, needs qualification. Certainly there are passages in the Bible which contain ideas compatible with much of Hellenistic thought. For example, the apocalyptic eschatology of early Judaism and early Christianity looked for the ending of *this* world. But the Hebrew prophets and the historical Jesus called for the ending of *world*; John Dominic Crossan has referred to this as permanent eschatology, "the permanent presence of God as the one who challenges world

closed Hellenistic world which allowed humans to ground their existence in the nature of things thereby giving life meaning, order, and security, the biblical or Hebraic vision is quite unsettling. According to the prophets, Yahweh is not to be identified with the idols of the human mind, with nature, with place, or with structure of any kind. Yahweh is known only in divine acts within a radically open-ended conception of history (or more correctly stated, Yahweh does not act *in* history or time; rather, the presence of God which calls for creaturely response *creates* history and time). "The Yahwist vision is stubbornly restless, probing, skeptical, constantly engaged in an effort to demystify and demythologize, attempting to reveal the constructedness and fictionality of all things."[92] The effort of the Hebrew prophets and Jesus was to expose all wishful thinking masquerading as religion in order to find a God who is not a mere projection. Therefore, all attempts to construct a coherent, closed, settled (and hence secure) worldview are condemned as idolatry; God calls for a trusting response in the face of an uncertain, open-ended future.

The dehellenization of theology and Derrida's call for freeplay have many similarities: e.g., both attack the quest for stable meaning or final words about reality, human pride, and the belief in inevitable progress culminating in the unfolding of all of life's secrets. Likewise, the results of both are similar: freedom, the freedom to create the future. Nevertheless, there is an important difference between the radical theologians and Derrida. Derrida denies that dehellenization can ever be complete. Because of the trace, it is impossible to step outside metaphysics, for "the attempt to do so will be couched in the very terms the antimetaphysician aims to dislodge."[93]

In spite of the "bad press" deconstructionist thought has received, I found that it stresses several of the key ideas that my hermeneutical quest has led me to value: (1) that the reader

---

and shatters its complacency repeatedly" (*In Parables*, 26). Many recent scholars agree with Crossan that permanent not apocalyptic eschatology forms the dominant (though not only) strand of biblical thought.

[92]Atkins, *Reading Deconstruction/Deconstructive Reading*, 46.

[93]Atkins, *Reading Deconstruction/Deconstructive Reading*, 48. The point about the inescapability/insufficiency of metaphysics resurfaces in chap. 2.

"creates meaning" in reading a text, (2) that the meaning of a text is open ended, that there is no privileged reading, (3) the stress on interconnectedness and relationality, and (4) that we have genuine freedom to create the future. Moreover, deconstruction's "fascination with the marginal, the secondary, the repressed, and the borderline"[94] clearly opens the door to ideological criticism, including those of the liberationist variety that I find so needed and helpful: feminist, so-called third world, and black criticism.

These and other attractive features of deconstructionism notwithstanding, I nevertheless have not been able to embrace it as the end of my quest. The major difficulty I have with deconstructionist thought is the claim that we are locked in a linguistic universe: words only refer to other words; language has no real referential value beyond itself. In some respects, deconstructionist philosophy is similar to, but more radical than, Kant's distinction between the noumenal and the phenomenal.[95] Anything that transcends language—for example, the "real" world, God—is in principle, then, inaccessible to us. But I am not convinced of this thorough-going epistemological solipsism. Sometimes I am dimly aware of prelinguistic experience. As Gerald Janzen described it, "we experience more than we know, and we know more than we can think; and we think more than we can say; and language therefore lags behind the intuitions of immediate experience."[96] If there is, indeed, human experience underlying linguistic experience, then there must be some genuine connection to that which is beyond the linguistic universe. And if I am somehow interconnected with that which is beyond me, then so is my language, at least to some degree.[97]

---

[94]*The Bible and Culture Collective*, 121.

[95]See chap. 2.

[96]J. Gerald Janzen, "The Old Testament in 'Process' Perspective: Proposal for a Way Forward in Biblical Theology," *MAGNALIA DEI: The Mighty Acts of God. Essays on the Bible and Archaeology in Memory of G. Ernest Wright*, ed. Frank Moore Cross, Werner E. Lemke, and Patrick D. Miller, Jr. (Garden City NY: Doubleday, 1976) 492.

[97]See chaps. 3 and 4. Cf. Marjorie Hewitt Suchocki, "Deconstructing Deconstruction: Language, Process, and a Theology of Nature," *American Journal of Theology and Philosophy* 11 (1990): 133-42, and her "Constructing Theology in a Deconstructive Age," in *Religion and the Postmodern Vision*, ed. Ron Farmer

I am also unconvinced by deconstruction's skepticism on another plane. In contrast to structuralism whose aim, "typical of most Western thought, is to find ways of 'understanding' phenomena through models of explanation that offer *coherent* pictures of the order of things," deconstruction "aims at describing the limits of understanding." The Western mind has been trained to accept authority only by positing its center or foundation as that beyond which one cannot go. But as the deconstructive critic examines the assumptions, tests the so-called self-evident truths, and uncovers the unexamined axioms at the center or foundation of various claims to knowledge and understanding, the investigation reveals an underlying authority (or center or foundation) beneath the prior authority, and so on. This regress of certainty, this decentering, destroys all notions of self-evident and absolute foundations in knowledge. As a result, modern Western culture is in the ironic state of *knowing* that knowledge is ultimately problematic.[98]

But is skepticism the only possible conclusion? As McKnight correctly noted, "skepticism results from the assumption that foundationalism is the only route to knowledge, or that the only kind of knowledge that counts is that which is based on foundationalism." In place of the foundationalist theory of knowledge, McKnight advocated a circular theory "whereby knowledge is justified in nonlinear, or circular, fashion through the relationship of the results obtained to the beginning point." In literature, for example, the meaning of a word is bound up with the meaning of the sentence in which it occurs, and the meaning of the sentence is dependent on the meaning of the words composing it; a mutual causality exists. The illustration can be extended. The sentence is embedded in a larger literary unit which in turn is related to nonliterary systems such as culture. Thus, meaning is dependent upon circles and circles of circles.[99] Knowledge gained in this manner can never be absolute, but it can be true relative to certain

---

(Columbia: University of Missouri Press, 1992).

[98]Davis and Schleifer, *Contemporary Literary Criticism: Literary and Cultural Studies*, 205-207.

[99]McKnight, *Postmodern Use of the Bible*, 18. Instead of McKnight's "circle" imagery (which may carry negative connotations for many) I prefer the image of a non-linear web of relationships.

circles. And relative truth is a far cry from either absolutist claims or skepticism.

Likewise, the metaphysical agnosticism espoused by deconstructionists seems overstated. The argument that one cannot construct a metaphysical system with any sense of finality is convincing; but as Derrida himself noted, it is impossible to step outside metaphysics altogether because of the trace. If both extremes are impossible, then the effort to construct a "provisional" worldview (one open to and expecting modification) would seem to be not only justified but wise. Everyone lives out of basic presuppositions which form a type of implicit, though frequently unacknowledged, metaphysical system. It is far wiser to make one's worldview explicit and thereby open to criticism and improvement than to deceive oneself with antimetaphysical rhetoric.

• The Impasse •

After years of exploration and experimentation, my quest for a satisfying hermeneutic brought me to an impasse—an impasse encountered by others in the field of biblical studies as well. There were elements of each approach that seemed useful, even essential, for the theological and ethical appropriation of the Bible. For example, in spite of its reductionism, the historical-critical method, especially as refined by the newer social-scientific approaches and when used in a nonpositivist manner, seems to be an indispensable facet in an overall interpretation of a text. Classical liberalism's evolutionary view of spirituality struck me as a helpful criterion in evaluating the theological and ethical significance of proposed readings. With the biblical theologians, I longed to be able to speak of the activity of God, but in the absence of any clear understanding of the relationship between God, history, and revelation, I found myself agreeing with Bultmann's statement that all theology is actually anthropology. Is it possible to speak of God meaningfully? I was beginning to have my doubts.

I was convinced by Bultmann's argument that some philosophical system is inescapable and therefore the interpreter should be self-critical and seek the "right" system. I also found his emphasis on existential decision and self-creation helpful, albeit too individualistic. His students made certain advances in his thought which expanded my thinking at several points, such as their adoption of the later Heidegger's understanding of being as a happening or an event rather than a static concept. Their understanding of language was more sophisticated than Bultmann's as well, though it lacked "literary depth."

After struggling with the reductionist readings of historicism and the intricacies of existential interpretation, my exploration of literary criticism came as a badly needed breath of fresh air. The ability of the various literary methodologies (for example, rhetorical criticism, structuralism, narratological criticism) to make a text immediately available for theological reflection and their attention to the neglected dimensions of imagination and creativity set them apart from other approaches I had considered. Equally helpful was reader-response criticism's focus on the role of the reader in the creation of meaning, a meaning which is open-ended. And in the section immediately above I mentioned several of the aspects of deconstructionist criticism which I find helpful.

Each hermeneutical approach offered something worth pondering if not adopting, but I did not find any one method that I could embrace completely; consequently, I found myself engaged in "tool box raiding." Although my eclecticism was frowned upon by methodological purists, I found it inescapable. Nevertheless, I was uncomfortable with it myself because my use of these divergent tools was entirely ad hoc. The various hermeneutical approaches from which I borrowed were based on diverse, even conflicting perspectives and presuppositions; I had no undergirding methodological rationalization for my eclecticism. I was at an impasse.

• A Process Hermeneutic •

A few years after graduate school, I began to study process thought. Although my first explorations were confined to theological and philosophical matters (for example, God and the problem of evil), I soon discovered that process thought had exciting implications for the development of a hermeneutic. To my surprise, Whitehead's understanding of language—an aspect of his thought which obviously has direct relevance to biblical studies—had until recently received little treatment by process theologians. The publication of Lyman Lundeen's *Risk and Rhetoric in Religion: Whitehead's*

Theory of Language and the Discourse of Faith (1972) opened new avenues of discussion between process theology and biblical studies. In 1974, a conference on Process Philosophy and Biblical Theology was sponsored by Christian Theological Seminary in Indianapolis. The discussion has continued at national AAR/SBL meetings in such working groups as the Process Hermeneutic and Biblical Exegesis Group (1974–1983), the Process and Biblical Theologies Consultation (1986–1987), and frequently in the Bible and Contemporary Theologies Group (1988–present). Moreover, relating process thought and biblical studies was one of the first projects undertaken with the establishment of the Center for Process Studies at Claremont in 1972.[100] The result of this dialogue between process theologians and biblical scholars is an expanding body of literature, as reflected in the bibliography, below.

An examination of this body of literature reveals that it can be divided into two distinct categories.[101] Writings in the first category seek to discover similarities between the biblical text and process theology; that is, process thought is used to illuminate the biblical text, and the theological results of traditional exegesis are expressed in process categories. Gerald Janzen's proposal is representative of this group of writings:

> I am not proposing that we attempt a simple and complete correlation between biblical and Process notions. Nor am I suggesting that biblical notions should be, or are capable of being, subsumed directly and completely under those of Process thought. What I do suggest is that, in general and unavoidably, our explicit or implicit metaphysical perspectives enter into our perceptions, assessments, and evaluations. Further, I suggest that certain fundamental notions and related basic imagery, developed in the sixteenth and seventeenth centuries and still prevalent in the modern world, may be rendering us incapable of taking seriously

---

[100]John B. Cobb, Jr., with David J. Lull and Barry A. Woodbridge, "Introduction: Process Thought and New Testament Exegesis," *Journal of the American Academy of Religion* 47 (1979): 22-23; and Russell Pregeant, *Christology Beyond Dogma: Matthew's Christ in Process Hermeneutic* (Philadelphia/Missoula MT: Fortress Press/Scholars Press, 1978) 11-12.

[101]See David H. Kelsey, "The Theological Use of Scripture in Process Hermeneutics," *Process Studies* 13 (1983): 181-88.

the biblical witness to reality; and that they may even tend to distort our perceptions of that witness, precisely when we are attempting to practice the utmost objectivity and philosophical and scientific integrity. The chief value of Process thought for biblical theology may be its provision of a new fundamental imagery, and fresh categories of thought and expressions, faithful to contemporary knowledge empirically derived and rationally organized, and yet in surprisingly close rapport at many points with the biblical witness. This new imagery, and these new categories, should make possible both a keener sensitivity to what the Bible actually attests, and a renewed readiness to take its attestations seriously.[102]

Writings in the second category use a process understanding of language to develop a method for reading texts. Russell Pregeant's proposal is representative of this group of writings: "What I should like to propose in terms of a process hermeneutic is not the direct translation of New Testament categories into those of process metaphysics, but simply that Whitehead's view of language be used to inform our appreciation of the nature of the text."[103]

Writings in both categories may with some legitimacy lay claim to the designation "process hermeneutic" in that all of them make use of process thought; nevertheless, in a more technical sense the term refers primarily to writings in the second category. Although the hermeneutic formulated in part two and applied in part three has certain points of contact with Janzen's proposal, it is based primarily upon Whitehead's understanding of language.

Almost all of the literature to date is in the form of essays or journal articles. As might be expected, then, most presentations of a process hermeneutic are either too technical or too brief (or both) to help those unacquainted with process thought and terminology. Clearly, a comprehensive introduction is needed if a process hermeneutic is to experience widespread dissemination. This book attempts to fill that need. I will not attempt to survey various formulations of a process hermeneutic; the formulation set forth is mine, with indebtedness indicated by footnotes. Before describing

---

[102]Janzen, "The Old Testament in 'Process' Perspective," 497-98.
[103]Pregeant, *Christology Beyond Dogma*, 43.

the major features of a process hermeneutic (part two) and applying it to biblical texts (part three), the important relationship between language, worldview, and the hermeneutical enterprise will be explored briefly in chapter 2.

Chapter 2

Language, Worldview, and the Hermeneutical Enterprise

Two important aspects of the hermeneutical impasse disclosed in chapter 1 merit special attention: language and worldview. Biblical scholars have grown comfortable talking about how the interpreter's conception of language is related to the hermeneutical enterprise, but they remain suspicious of interpreters who openly reveal their worldview. The assumption seems to be that interpreters who openly acknowledge their metaphysical commitments will misconstrue texts to fit their worldview. Therefore, a few general remarks about the relationship between worldview and the hermeneutical enterprise are in order before engaging in a discussion of how the dominant understanding of language and the modern worldview contribute to the current impasse in biblical interpretation.

Each of the hermeneutical systems described in chapter 1 assumes a worldview. Biblical interpretation is never carried out in a vacuum but rather is in dialog, consciously or unconsciously, with the general modes of thought prevailing at the time. "In general and unavoidably, [one's] explicit or implicit metaphysical perspectives enter into [one's] perceptions, assessments, and evaluations." One's view of reality aids in the hermeneutical enterprise by providing the interpreter with general ideas and terms for the analysis and explication of the Bible. Moreover, a worldview provides "critical control on inconsistencies, apparent or real, between basic metaphors, tradition complexes, and theological trajectories in the Bible." But the relationship between one's worldview and the Bible is two way. The Bible constitutes a part of the total evidence for which a worldview must account. As part of the total evidence, the Bible operates as a critic whenever a worldview "is in danger of becoming shallowly empirical and so tends to overlook some of the evidence in favor of a thin consistency." Thus, one's worldview and the Bible "stand in a reciprocally constructive and critical relation to one another."[1]

• The Four Phases of Language •

Northrop Frye has distinguished four phases of language in the Western tradition.[2] Of course, there are always several types of language in use during any historical period; what Frye attempted to identify by means of these successive phases was "the culturally ascendant language, a language that . . . is accorded a special authority by its society."[3]

The first phase of language, which Frye labeled the *metaphorical* phase,[4] is reflected in Greek literature before Plato, the prebiblical cultures of the Near East, and much of the Bible.[5] In this phase, "there is relatively little emphasis on a clear separation of subject and object: the emphasis falls rather on the feeling that subject and object are linked by a common power or energy." This sense of

---

[1]Janzen, "The Old Testament in 'Process' Perspective" 497-98, 484-85.

[2]Northrop Frye, *The Great Code: The Bible and Literature* (New York: Harcourt Brace Jovanovich, 1982) esp. 3-30. In distinguishing four phases of language, Frye was not asserting that there was no overlapping between successive phases or that characteristics of an earlier phase were not to be found in later historical periods. E.g., poetry, a dominant literary form of the earliest phase, occurs in all four phases.

[3]Frye, *The Great Code: The Bible and Literature*, 7.

[4]Frye (6) also referred to this phase as poetic or hieroglyphic, "not in the sense of sign-writing, but in the sense of using words as particular kinds of signs."

[5]The language of the Bible cannot be *equated* with any one of Frye's phases. As McKnight (*Postmodern Use of the Bible*, 199-200) noted, "it certainly cannot be equated with the descriptive phase [see below], but the Platonic and Neoplatonic view of the second phase [see below] is also inappropriate, for the biblical God is not divorced from the world to be discerned only in a reflective process. The poetic phase of language as such is inappropriate for appreciating the Bible, since, for the Bible, God is not simply to be *identified* with the world. It was through his Word that God created the world. . . . Yet, there is a parallel between the poetic phase and biblical language. In biblical language, there is a power in the words."

identity between humans and nature is embodied in the divine.[6] Frye noted that even today many "primitive" societies

> have words expressing this common energy of human personality and natural environment, which are untranslatable into our normal categories of thought but are very pervasive in theirs: the best known is the Melanesian word *mana*. The articulating of words may bring this common power into being; hence a magic develops in which verbal elements, 'spell,' and 'charm,' and the like, play a central role. A corollary of this principle is that there may be a potential magic in any use of words.[7]

In the metaphorical phase, then, words are words of power. Frye offered the following examples, several of which occur in the Bible:

> knowing the name of a god or elemental spirit may give the knower some control over it; puns and popular etymologies involved in the naming of people and places affect the character of whatever thing or person is given the name. Warriors begin battles with boasts that may be words of power for them; boasting is most objectionable to the gods for a corresponding reason: the possibility of man's acquiring through his words the power that he clearly wants. The vow that cannot be broken . . . again expresses the sense of quasi-physical power released by the utterance of words. When a sacrosanct myth is read at a religious ritual . . . some kind of magical energy is clearly being released.[8]

Uttering certain words, then, is a sort of "verbal magic" which works by means of the energy common to words and things, energy which is embodied in and can be controlled by words.

The period from Plato until the Enlightenment is Frye's second or *metonymic* phase of language. In this phase "language is more

---

[6]"What this means from the critical point of view is that while Homer's conceptions would not have been metaphorical to him . . . , they have to be metaphorical to us. As we think of words, it is only metaphor that can express in language the sense of an energy common to subject and object. The central expression of metaphor is the 'god,' the being who, as sun-god, war-god, sea-god, or whatever, identifies a form of personality with an aspect of nature." Frye, *The Great Code: The Bible and Literature*, 7.

[7]Frye, *The Great Code: The Bible and Literature*, 6.

[8]Frye, *The Great Code: The Bible and Literature*, 6.

individualized, and words become primarily the outward expression of inner thoughts or ideas." Subject and object become more consistently separated, and reflection becomes a prominent feature. "The intellectual operations of the mind become distinguishable from the emotional operations; hence abstraction becomes possible, and the sense that there are valid and invalid ways of thinking . . . develops into the conception of logic." Whereas in the metaphorical phase the basis of language lay in the sense of the *identity* of life or power or energy between humankind and nature ("this is that"), in the second phase the basis lay in a *metonymic* relationship ("this is put for that").

> Specifically, words are "put for" thoughts, and are the outward expressions of an inner reality. But this reality is not merely "inside." Thoughts indicate the existence of a transcendent order "above," which only thinking can communicate with and which only words can express. Thus metonymic language is, or tends to become, analogical language, a verbal imitation of a reality beyond itself that can be conveyed most directly by words.[9]

In the metaphorical phase of language the central conception unifying human thought and imagination was "the conception of a plurality of gods, or embodiments of the identity of personality and nature." In the metonymic phase this unifying conception became "a monotheistic 'God,' a transcendent reality or perfect being that all verbal analogy points to."[10]

According to the metonymic view of language, then, a text is not to be interpreted with a view to the particulars but to the universals behind the particulars. Thus, when Christians in the ancient and medieval church interpreted the Bible, they gave attention to the words of the Bible for the purpose of understanding the thoughts of the authors. Yet because it was believed that the authors wrote in accordance to the will of God, the ultimate goal of interpreters was to understand the mind of God. Therefore, if the allegorical approach (one of the leading methods of interpretation during that period) discovers more than one meaning in a

---

[9]Frye, *The Great Code: The Bible and Literature*, 7-8.
[10]Frye, *The Great Code: The Bible and Literature*, 9.

text, including meanings not intended by the human author, this is not a shortcoming. On the contrary, if an interpreter discovers a meaning which is consistent with the Bible as a whole though not intended by the human author, that meaning may be thought of as intended by God, the ultimate author of the entire Bible.[11]

In the earlier metaphorical phase a sort of verbal magic was possible because of the energy common to words and things; in the metonyic phase

> this sense of verbal magic is sublimated into a quasi-magic inherent in sequence or linear ordering. Hence the medieval fascination with the syllogism and the great medieval dream of deducing all knowledge from the premises of revelation. . . . Analogical language thus came to be thought of as sacramental language, a verbal response to God's own verbal revelation. Some form of analogy was essential, otherwise there would be no reality that human language is "put for," and no one would maintain that human language was fully adequate to conveying such a reality.[12]

The third phase of language, which began during the sixteenth century and attained cultural ascendancy by the eighteenth century, Frye labeled the *descriptive* view. This new phase began as a dissatisfaction with certain elements in the preceding phase. For example, syllogistic reasoning—so widely used during the second phase—actually leads to nothing genuinely new because its conclusions are already contained within its premises. Moreover, the metonymic view of language appeared to have no criteria for distinguishing what really exists from what does not. "Grammatically, logically, and syntactically, there is no difference between a lion and a unicorn . . . the difference can be established only by criteria external to words, and the first of these criteria has to be that of 'things,' or objects in nature." In the descriptive phase there is

> a clear separation of subject and object, in which the subject exposes itself, in sense experience, to the impact of an objective world. The objective world is the order of nature; thinking or reflection follows the suggestions of sense experience, and words

---

[11]Augustine, *On Christian Doctrine* 3.27.38.
[12]Frye, *The Great Code: The Bible and Literature*, 11-12.

are the servomechanisms of reflection. . . . deductive procedures are increasingly subordinated to a primary inductive and fact-gathering process.[13]

Since the time of Descartes, who canonized the subject-object split implicit in the logic of late antiquity, everything has had to give an account of itself to the investigating subject. Language in the third phase primarily describes the "objective" natural world.[14] The accompanying criterion of truth is, understandably, "correspondence" (that is, do words correspond to what they purport to describe?) rather than the inner consistency of an argument.

Two points especially pertinent for the present study should be noted. (1) Although there is a return to a direct relationship between words and the world of nature, as in the metaphorical phase, there is also a sharp distinction between them as well. Words are not words of power, but mere descriptions of objects in the world of nature. (2) In contrast to the metonymic view, the descriptive view of language leaves no room for anything outside of or transcending the world of nature. This model of language cannot conceive of God because there is no external source of validation.[15] Thus, as descriptive language achieved cultural ascendancy, biblical scholarship arrived at an impasse. When employed consistently, the descriptive understanding of language renders all God-talk meaningless and metaphysics impossible.

Frye suggested that there is at present some evidence of a transition to a fourth phase of language.[16] Examples of this evi-

---

[13]Frye, *The Great Code: The Bible and Literature*, 13.

[14]Objective belongs in quotation marks because the "objective" world is actually viewed from the point of view of the subject; thus, the "objective view of the world" is in fact a most subjective view. This point will be expanded below.

[15]"Mythological space became separated from scientific space with the new astronomy of the seventeenth century, and mythological time from scientific time with nineteenth-century geology and biology. Both developments helped to push the conception of God out of the world of time and space, even as a hypothesis." Frye, *The Great Code: The Bible and Literature*, 15-16.

[16]Frye, *The Great Code: The Bible and Literature*, 15. Frye did not name this emergent fourth phase; McKnight (203) proposed calling it "postmodern." Although this term is accurate, it is not of the same class as metaphorical, metonymic, and descriptive.

dence include (1) the obvious shift from the separation of subject and object necessary for pre-Einsteinian physics and the historical-critical approach of the modern period, to the interrelationship of subject and object presupposed by contemporary physics and post-modern forms of criticism such as McKnight's radical reader-response criticism and deconstruction; and (2) the rebirth of interest in metaphorical language not as mere ornament but as language of power, language capable of expressing verbally the energy common to subject and object.[17] The evidence seems to indicate that this fourth phase of language is somewhat parallel to the first (metaphorical) phase, but it is clearly a new phase rather than a return to the first phase. In the opinion of Frye, entry into such a phase of language would enable scholarship once again to speak of God.

The word God is a noun and so falls into the category of objects. This was not a problem for the first two phases of language. However, according to the third (descriptive) phase of language which classified objects as existing and nonexisting based on sense perception, God had to be classified as nonexisting. But what if "noun-thinking" is a fallacy on the order of Alfred North Whitehead's fallacy of misplaced concreteness?[18] Frye offered the following illustration:

> In Exodus 3:14, though God also gives himself a name, he defines himself . . . as "I am that I am," which . . . is more accurately rendered "I will be what I will be." That is, we might come closer to what is meant in the Bible by the word "God" if we understood it as a verb, and not a verb of simple asserted existence but a verb implying a process accomplishing itself. This would involve trying to think our way back to a conception of language in which words were words of power, conveying primarily the sense of forces and energies rather than analogues of physical bodies. To some extent this would be a reversion to the metaphorical language of primitive communities, as our earlier refer-

---

[17]See Frye, *The Great Code: The Bible and Literature*, 15-22 and McKnight, *Postmodern Use of the Bible*, 24, 199-210.

[18]See Alfred North Whitehead, *Process and Reality: An Essay in Cosmology*, corrected edition, ed. David Ray Griffin and Donald W. Shearburne (New York: Free Press, 1978; original: New York: Macmillan, 1929) 7-8.

ences to a cycle of language and the "primitive" word *mana* suggested. But it would also be oddly contemporary with post-Einsteinian physics, where atoms and electrons are no longer thought of as things but rather as traces of processes. God may have lost [the] function [of serving] as the subject or object of a predicate, but *may not be so much dead as entombed in a dead language.*[19]

This fourth phase of language would not involve a return to the first phase of language and to the understanding of the divine as identified with or totally immanent in the world (pantheism). Neither would it mean a return to the second phase of language and to the conception of God as divorced from or totally transcending the world (classical theism). Rather, it would involve a new conception of language and a new understanding of God. God and the world would be conceived of as interrelated but not identical; God would affect the world and vice versa (panentheism).

The understanding of language undergirding the process hermeneutic (developed in part two) is an excellent example of Frye's emerging fourth phase of language, and hence holds forth the promise of moving us beyond the current impasse in biblical interpretation. Before turning to part two, however, a brief discussion of the emerging worldview associated with this fourth phase of language is in order.

• The Emerging Worldview:
From Substance Thinking to Event Thinking •

Although the worldviews undergirding the various hermeneutical approaches described in chapter 1 are by no means identical, they are all—with the exception of deconstruction[20] and McKnight's radical reader-response criticism—variations of the modern Western scientific worldview, although the existential

---

[19]Frye, *The Great Code: The Bible and Literature*, 17-18; emphasis added.

[20]David Ray Griffin (*God & Religion in the Postmodern World* [Albany: SUNY Press, 1989] x, 8, 20) has argued that deconstruction might be more accurately thought of as modernism pushed to its extreme limits: "mostmodern" not postmodern.

approaches show considerable dissatisfaction with it. Emerging during the seventeenth century, modernism quickly became the dominant worldview. The twentieth century, however, has witnessed a growing sense of dissatisfaction with modernity which has manifested itself in a widespread conceptual revolution in most fields of human activity, from physics and biology to philosophy and religion. In order to understand this revolution, one must first sketch the modern Western scientific worldview which is being overthrown.

From the time of the ancient Greek philosophers, the paradigms that have dominated Western thinking have all conceived of reality in terms of substantial[21] and enduring objects. For example, the pre-Socratic philosopher Democritus suggested that reality is composed of tiny, indestructible, unchanging, and indivisible elements he called "atoms" which combine, separate, and recombine in various ways to produce the more complex objects of the sensible world. And a long line of philosophers and scientists have continued to analyze the enduring objects of everyday experience—rocks, trees, animals, and people—into smaller and smaller parts in order to arrive at these atoms.[22] The goal of this analysis has been to explain the qualitative changes in the world of every day experience in terms of the movements of substantial entities which in their own nature do not change.

Substance thinking is a mechanistic model of reality. Just as the gears and levers that make up a machine are not thought of as affected by the changing operations of the machine, so also the substantial entities comprising the universe are not affected by the changes involved in their interaction with one another. This mechanistic model of the universe also implies that this gigantic machine operates according to laws which science can discover. The mechanistic model, then, is thoroughly deterministic.

---

[21]An entity is "substantial" if it is independent, unchanging, and can exist by itself. In traditional metaphysics, substance is the same as "ultimate reality."

[22]When modern scientists arrived at what they thought was the ultimate, indivisible class of substances they named them atoms. When later scientists split the atom, it became apparent that this class of entities had been misnamed (philosophically speaking).

Although René Descartes, the father of modern philosophy, subscribed to the theory that the physical world could be explained in terms of matter in motion, he felt that this explanation could not account for human thought. This exception to the mechanistic model led him to view reality as composed of two substances, matter (which is spatially extended) and mind.[23] The physical universe, including the human body, is composed of matter in motion operating according to established laws, but the human mind is not part of this mechanistic model. Thus, in the first stage of the modern worldview, the existence of a trancendent Creator and the specialness of the human psyche or soul was still assumed.[24]

Although Descartes' dualism allowed human thinking, feeling, and willing to escape the determinism of the mechanistic model, it raised the question of how two totally independent substances can be related. How can a happening in the mind (such as the decision to turn a page in a book) have an effect on the body (the finger turns the page)? Or how can a happening in the body (such as a paper cut on the finger) produce an effect in the mind (pain)? This problem, known as the mind-body problem, has haunted all who have adopt Cartesian dualism.

Many subsequent thinkers, known as materialists, have sought to avoid the problem inherent in dualism by viewing the human mind as part of the physical world. They assert that there is only one substance: matter. The discovery that the mental processes occur in the brain, a part of the physical body, only served to strengthen this conviction. Mental processes and human behavior are determined by the "mechanical" operation of the brain. Thus, "the idea of the human soul as an alien ghost in a machine soon led to mechanistic materialism, largely because of the problem of understanding how an immaterial, personal soul could interact

---

[23]Actually he thought there were three substances, matter, mind, and God who created the other two substances.

[24]Indeed, Descartes was seeking a compromise between science, with its mechanistic, deterministic laws of matter in motion, and the church, with its dogmas of a perfect, infinite spiritual Being who created human beings as finite, imperfect spiritual beings living in a material habitat. By means of this "Cartesian compromise" both scientists and the church had their own jurisdictions.

with a material, impersonal, machine-like body." Likewise, "the idea of God as an omnipotent personal being, totally determining the structure and events of the world, soon led to atheism, partly because of the problem of evil, partly because the idea that the world is a machine made God's action in it difficult to conceive."[25]

But thoroughgoing, mechanistic materialism has its own problems, as the empirical analysis of David Hume demonstrated. Hume's analysis revealed that human beings actually experience only a flux of sensory impressions or phenomena, not the objective world of nature itself. All that humans have access to are sense impressions and memories of these impressions; there is no way to know if these impressions correspond to an objective material world "out there." Even causal relations, so important to scientific knowledge (indeed, to all knowledge), cannot be demonstrated. All the observer of an assumed causal relationship—for example, one ball colliding with another ball "causing" it to move—actually sees is two events. The observer sees the movement of the first ball and the movement of the second ball, but not the supposed "cause." In fact, unless the two events are regularly found together, the observer will not postulate that a causal relation exists between them. Thus, cause and effect and all scientific laws are merely generalizations from repeated sense impressions, merely habits or customs of the mind. And in demonstrating the inadequacy of scientific claims to knowledge Hume also undercut all metaphysical speculation.

Descartes' mental substance fared no better in Hume's phenomenalism for in the analysis of his own experiences he could not find a permanent (that is, continuously the same) self underlying the flux of impressions. Indeed, he did not find any permanent and invariable impressions; all he found was a cluster of experiences and ideas. The notion of the permanent self results from the connection of separate ideas and experiences through the process of memory. Descartes' thinking self is really just a collection of thoughts; instead of saying "I think" Descartes should have said, "There are thoughts." It is not legitimate to say that because there are thoughts there must be a thinker.

---

[25]Griffin, *God & Religion in the Postmodern World*, 22.

Immanuel Kant undertook the task of responding to both materialism and Hume's phenomenalism. Although Kant recognized the force of Hume's arguments, he saw that the logical outcome of radical empiricism (the belief that all knowledge, except for certain logical truths and the principles of mathematics, comes from experience) is absolute skepticism. Kant agreed that there is an empirical component to knowledge (knowledge through the senses) but felt that there is also a rational component. In contrast to radical empiricism, he argued that the mind is not a "blank tablet" or an "empty cupboard" but is equipped with certain concepts or categories by means of which it organizes the flux of sense impressions. These "pure categories of the understanding" include, among others, substances with qualities and quantities, and relations such as cause and effect.

Kant's categories should not be confused with Descartes' innate ideas. According to Descartes, innate ideas, such as "everything has a cause," are imprinted by God and correspond to the structures of the objective material world; therefore, humans can know the true nature of reality. Kant, however, did not claim that the categories correspond to the objective world; they are merely the way in which humans understand reality. The categories do not reveal what things in the objective world are like in and of themselves; humans can only know appearances (phenomena), that is, things as they appear to the mind by means of the categories.[26] Nor should Kant's categories be confused with Plato's forms. For Plato, the forms are themselves ultimate reality; things in the world of flux are but shadowy copies of these eternal forms. But for Kant, the categories are merely the structures of the human mind, not the structures of ultimate reality.

One should note that in saving knowledge—including scientific knowledge—from Hume's skepticism, Kant made knowledge dependent upon the categories of the mind. That is, the laws of science, for example, are not found in or derived from the objective world but rather are found in or derived from the mind. Thus, the mind is not so much a part of nature as nature is a construct of the

---

[26]Thus, Kant agreed with Hume that metaphysics is impossible; the true nature of reality is unknowable.

mind! This does not mean that he doubted the reality of the objective material world; rather, he held that nothing more can be known about it in itself than that it exists. One should also note that Kant believed that humans live in two separate but equal realms. When humans are involved in the pursuit of knowledge, as in scientific study, the world is perceived from the standpoint of one set of rules (which includes determinism). But when they are involved in practical living and religion—that is, involved in everyday decisions, actions, and beliefs—the world is perceived from the standpoint of another set of rules (which includes freedom).

With Kant's idealism philosophy turned a corner. All subsequent thinkers acknowledge the role of the mind in shaping what is known. As a result, philosophy turned its attention to the human knower rather than the objective world. Most nineteenth- and twentieth-century philosophies emphasize the impossibility of explaining the human knower in terms of the objects of knowledge (in contrast to materialist and phenomenalist reductionism). For example, although existentialism replaced idealism's concentration on human thought with attention to human decision, it followed idealism in separating humanity from nature. In fact, the mode of thinking that distinguishes between humanity and nature is deeply ingrained in the academic disciplines, resulting in the sharp distinction between the humanities and the natural sciences. "A deep-seated impression is communicated that the two sides of the educational curriculum have little bearing on each other, that human meaning is not bound up with the worldview suggested by the natural sciences."[27]

As has been noted, one of the results of the growing dissatisfaction with the materialistic Western scientific worldview is that metaphysics, in the sense of speculative philosophy, has fallen out of vogue. Indeed, many philosophers and theologians revel in deconstructing any and all systems of thought. They maintain that all attempts to characterize reality are doomed to fail; in place of laboring to construct a metaphysical system they stress the need

---

[27]Charles Birch and John B. Cobb, Jr., *The Liberation of Life: From the Cell to the Community* (Cambridge: Cambridge University Press, 1981) 102.

to learn to live without any "grand scheme." Certainly one can never hope to formulate general metaphysical principles with finality. "Weakness of insight and deficiencies of language stand in the way inexorably."[28] Nevertheless, refusal to engage in constructive thought exposes one to the dangers of inconsistency in thought and life. Everyone lives out of basic presuppositions which form a type of implicit, though frequently unacknowledged, metaphysical system. It is far wiser to make one's worldview explicit and thereby open to criticism and improvement.

Perhaps a major reason many philosophers hesitate to revive metaphysics is that they feel the only alternative to some form of idealism (such as existentialism) is deterministic materialism with its attending dehumanizing reduction of human beings to mere cogs in a colossal machine. But an increasing number of postmodern thinkers are advocating a metaphysical model for conceptualizing reality which avoids materialistic reductionism. Rather than beginning with the assumption that the world is composed of substantial entities (matter or mind or both), they begin with the idea that reality is composed of events. Of course substance thinking recognizes the occurrences of events, but it explains them in terms of substances, that is, events happen to substances. In the sentence, "The student is reading," the event termed "reading" is viewed as happening to the substantial entity "the student." The student happens to be reading, but this is incidental (that is, accidental not essential) to who the student is; the student could have been walking or eating or sleeping and would still be the same student. In contrast, event thinking recognizes the existence of enduring objects such as rocks, trees, animals, and people, but it explains them in terms of repeated patterns of interrelated events. The student of the preceding example is not viewed as an unchanging substance to whom events such as reading incidentally happen. On the contrary, the student is constituted by her experiences. Reading is one of the events that constitutes the student; moreover, the event of reading is itself composed of "smaller" events such as the visual perception of print on the page, memory, and breathing. The experience the student has in one

---

[28]Whitehead, *Process and Reality*, 4.

hour can be analyzed in terms of the experience she has in each minute. And the experience she has in each minute can be analyzed in terms of the experience she has in each second. This analysis can continue until it reaches a level at which experience cannot be analyzed any further; even the smallest event takes a certain quantum of time. Now the student does not exist apart from her experiences; on the contrary, she is constituted by her experiences. Moreover, the student who experiences the event of reading in the afternoon is not the self-same student who experiences the event of eating that evening. Rather, the notion of the enduring substantial entity called the "self" of the student is an abstraction to be explained in terms of the repeated patterns found in a certain series of interrelated events.

But a dualist might object that the preceding illustration concerns the human mind (or soul); were the illustration to deal with an inanimate object, such as the book the student is reading, it would demonstrate the inadequacy of event thinking. The book is composed of molecules; the molecules, atoms; and the atoms, subatomic particles. Surely this analysis demonstrates the validity of substance thinking. In actuality it does not. For example, atoms are affected by their environment. When two distinct types of atoms, say sodium and chlorine, combine in a certain ratio the resulting combination (sodium chloride, common table salt) evidences certain properties not found in either sodium or chlorine atoms. Substance thinking cannot explain this; because atoms are viewed as unaffected by their relations, the properties of sodium chloride should be discoverable by considering sodium and chlorine atoms individually. Clearly sodium and chlorine atoms are affected by their relation to one another.[29] Furthermore, when scientists split atoms into subatomic particles, they find that these particles do not behave like Greek philosophical "atoms" either. Rather than being a tiny bit of substantial "stuff," an electron appears to be a succession of happenings, a chain of "energy-events." In fact, "field theory, relativity physics and quantum

---

[29]Birch and Cobb, *The Liberation of Life: From the Cell to the Community*, 90-91.

mechanics all point in the direction of event thinking instead of substance thinking."[30]

One way to contrast substance thinking and event thinking is to view the matter in terms of the traditional philosophical distinction between external and internal relations. An external relation is incidental to an entity; whether the relation occurs or does not occur does not affect the essential character of the entity. For example, a book lying on a desk appears to be externally related to the desk in that its constitution seems to be unaffected by its relation to the desk. It would be the same book if it were placed on a shelf or in a briefcase.[31] An internal relation, however, is constitutive of the character and even the existence of an entity. This is most clearly seen at the human level. When the student in the above example is asked to introduce herself on the first day of a graduate seminar, she begins by stating that her name is Maria. She is from Rio de Janeiro and is the daughter of a middle-class, politically minded couple who have always encouraged her to be her own person. Her brother is a priest in the "liberation theology" wing of the Catholic Church. She is working toward a Ph.D. in civil engineering and plans to use her education to improve the lives of the multitudes living in Rio's favelas. When asked about her hobbies, she responds that she enjoys music, dancing, and going to the beach. Apparent at once is that every element in Maria's description of herself is in terms of people and things other than herself; even her name was chosen by her parents. She is constituted by her relationships with her environment; external reality has become internal through these relations. Her present experience or selfhood has arisen from the manner in which she has appropriated, harmonized, modified, and rejected the various environmental influences. Moreover, the line of influence is duo-directional; certainly the environment has influenced Maria, but she also has influenced her environment. Internal relations are not restricted to human beings, however; they pervade the realm of nonliving entities as well, although the significance of the relations

---

[30]Birch and Cobb, *The Liberation of Life: From the Cell to the Community*, 86.
[31]The words "appear" and "seems" occur in this illustration because even nonliving entities are constituted by their "experiences" (see chap. 3).

is seldom as apparent. For example, "field theory in physics shows that the events that make up the field have their existence only as parts of the field. These events cannot exist apart from the field. They are internally related to one another."[32]

According to substance thinking, a substance first exists, in and of itself, and then it enters into relations with other substances. Because the nature of the substance is not changed, these relations are considered external to the substance. Event thinking views relations differently. An event does not first occur and then enter into relations with other events. On the contrary, the event is a synthesis of its relations with other events. And because these relations constitute the event they are considered internal to the event.

Conceptualizing reality in terms of event thinking rather than substance thinking drastically alters the way one approaches the relation of mind and matter. The notion of an energy-event is flexible enough to include events of human thinking as well as unconscious electronic events. Although there are differences between the two types of events, they need not be regarded as belonging to entirely different orders of being.[33] "The older question of the relation of mind to matter becomes the question of the relation of that energy-event which is conscious and in which thinking takes place to those much more elementary ones where there is neither consciousness nor thought."[34]

One may wonder why, with all the evidence against the mechanistic or substantialist model, it continues its dominance in practice. Doubtless, one reason is that for many purposes the model is quite useful. As Birch and Cobb noted, the mechanistic model is illuminating

> to whatever extent the structures studied are relatively independent of environment, such as [a] stone or a metal lever. Since no structure at any level is totally independent of all environmental

---

[32]Birch and Cobb, *The Liberation of Life: From the Cell to the Community*, 88.

[33]Thus, event thinking overcomes the problematic dualism of mind and matter in a way quite different from thorough-going materialism or thoroughgoing idealism. Rather than denying the reality of mind or matter, event thinking affirms a reality which underlies both the subjectivity of mind and the objectivity of matter.

[34]John B. Cobb, Jr., *God and the World* (Philadelphia: Westminster, 1969) 70.

influences, the mechanistic model always involves some abstraction or qualification. But since many phenomena can be studied quite satisfactorily on the basis of such abstractions and qualifications, the mechanical model has a wide range of practical usefulness.[35]

But perhaps the major reason the mechanistic or substantialist model remains dominant has to do with the nature of language. Any given language orders the world in a particular way for those who use that language, and it conceals the aspects of the world that do not fit that order. So subtle is this metaphysical operation most people are not conscious of it. The grammar of the Indo-European languages, which emphasizes nouns, encourages substance thinking. As a result, people in the West tend to think of reality in terms of substantial entities and therefore view events as the interaction of these entities. These languages imply that first there are substantial entities which then incidentally interact. Thus, events tend to be explained in terms of substances instead of the reverse. Perhaps in time a language will be developed that is more appropriate to event thinking. Until then, however, event thinking must struggle against much of the language it must use to express itself.

The effort of many scientists—representing physical, life, and social sciences—to formulate a more appropriate model of reality raises important philosophical questions. Unfortunately most philosophers since Kant have deliberately avoided these questions and so are not prepared to assist scientists in the framing of new models. One notable exception to this generalization is Alfred North Whitehead. The opening chapter of part two sketches the basic contours of Whitehead's process worldview as a foundation for a more detailed discussion of his view of language, which in turn forms the basis for a process hermeneutic.

---

[35]Birch and Cobb, *The Liberation of Life: From the Cell to the Community*, 89-90.

Part Two

Beyond the Impasse

Chapter 3

The Process Worldview

The worldview developed by Alfred North Whitehead is a process worldview. According to the process worldview, what is real is what happens; that is, ultimate reality is composed of events. As was stated in the preceding chapter, people tend to think of an event as happening to "something" that exists before and after the event. In order to promote a new perspective on events, Whitehead developed a specialized and somewhat difficult terminology. The purpose of this chapter is to introduce those aspects of a process worldview and the Whiteheadian terminology (in boldface) which are necessary to undergird the development of a process hermeneutic. A more comprehensive, though by no means exhaustive, overview of Whitehead's metaphysical system can be found in the appendix. From time to time the reader will be referred there for a more detailed discussion of certain points.[1]

---

[1]Introductory descriptions of the process worldview can be found in Cobb, *God and the World*; John B. Cobb, Jr., and David Ray Griffin, *Process Theology: An Introductory Exposition* (Philadelphia: Westminster Press, 1976); and Marjorie Hewitt Suchocki, *God, Christ, Church: A Practical Guide to Process Theology* (New York: Crossroads, 1982). For a detailed analysis of Whitehead's thought, see Ivor Leclerc, *Whitehead's Metaphysics: An Introductory Exposition* (New York: Macmillan, 1958); William A. Christian, *An Interpretation of Whitehead's Metaphysics* (New Haven CT: Yale University Press, 1959; repr.: Westport CT: Greenwood Press, 1977.); Victor Lowe, *Understanding Whitehead* (Baltimore: Johns Hopkins University Press, 1962); and Donald Sherburne, ed., *A Key to Whitehead's Process and Reality* (Chicago: University of Chicago Press, 1966). For an example of how Whiteheadian thought can be used in the development of a natural theology, see John B. Cobb, Jr., *A Christian Natural Theology: Based on the Thought of Alfred North Whitehead* (Philadelphia: Westminster Press, 1965).

Viewing ultimate reality in terms of events or happenings rather than substances means that experiences, not tiny bits of matter, are the building blocks of the universe.[2] These energy-events or occasions of experience Whitehead labeled **actual entities** or **actual occasions**.[3] Under certain circumstances, *groups* of actual entities, termed **societies**, can impinge upon the human sense organs as data in such a manner that they are perceived as the physical objects of ordinary human experience (for example, rocks, trees, animals, and people).[4] *Individual* actual entities are detectable only by means of scientific instruments or intense introspection; they are not observable through ordinary conscious human experience.

Although there are differences between actual entities, one thing that all entities have in common is that they transmit energy from preceding actual entities to succeeding actual entities. In some instances that which is inherited from preceding entities is transmitted to succeeding entities virtually unaltered; in other instances what is inherited is significantly modified before being transmitted. The former occurs in low-grade entities which characterize phenomena typically labeled inorganic; the latter occurs in high-grade entities which characterize phenomena associated with life and consciousness.

The process by which these brief occasion of experience come into being Whitehead labeled **concrescence**, a "growing together" of a diverse "many" into a unified "one."[5] Each becoming occasion inherits, or appropriates as its own, energy or data from past actual occasions. This process of appropriating or "grasping" a

---

[2]The term "experience" can be misleading. Although Whitehead derived the term from human experience, he did not mean that the building blocks of the universe were exactly like human experience. Most occasions of experience lack such things as sense perception, consciousness, and imagination (the term experience does not necessarily imply these things, however; for example, people do speak of unconscious experience).

[3]See the appendix for a more detailed discussion of actual entities/occasions.

[4]Any group of actual occasions interrelated to one another in any way Whitehead termed a **nexus**. A society is a nexus of actual occasions in which members of the nexus depend upon other members for common inherited characteristics. See below for a brief discussion of enduring objects and conscious human occasions of experience; also see the appendix for a more detailed discussion of the macrocosmic world.

[5]See the appendix for a detailed discussion of the phases of concrescence.

datum from a past actual occasion is termed a **prehension** or a **feeling**;[6] each feeling is clothed with a **subjective form** which is "how" the becoming occasion feels that datum, the "tone" of the feeling (examples in human occasions of experience include consciousness, joy, and anger). Clearly, then, the data of the past largely determine what the becoming occasion will be because the past requires of the becoming occasion that it somehow conform to or reenact the past. Yet this determination is never complete, for every actual occasion also exercises some degree of self-determination in its concrescence. *What* an occasion must prehend is determined, but *how* the occasion prehends it is not. In high-grade occasions such as animal or human experience this self-determination may properly be termed freedom; in low-grade occasions such as electronic or molecular experience one should speak rather of indeterminacy because this term does not imply consciousness and the "freedom" exercised by low-grade occasions is negligible.[7] Thus, a becoming occasion selects, harmonizes, and supplements the data of the past, integrating and reintegrating the "many" feelings into "one" final, unified, complex feeling called the **satisfaction** of the actual occasion. This concrescence of feelings is guided by the occasion's **subjective aim** which is a feeling of what the occasion may become. This subjective aim always takes into account (1) the givenness of past occasions, (2) the goal of achieving the greatest intensity of feeling in the becoming occasion, and (3) the goal of the becoming occasion contributing maximally to relevant future occasions.

In its moment of concrescence, every actual entity is a subject, though usually an unconscious one.[8] As a subject, each actual entity presides over its own immediacy of becoming. But upon attain-

---

[6]Technically, only **positive prehensions**—prehensions in which there is the definite inclusion of a datum into positive contribution to the becoming occasion's internal constitution—are referred to as feelings. **Negative prehensions** are the definite exclusion of a datum from positive contribution.

[7]One should note that by means of the notion of the self-determination of actual occasions Whitehead accounted for both human freedom and the indeterminacy revealed in modern physics.

[8]See the appendix for a more accurate description of an occasion as a **subject-superject**.

ing satisfaction, this subjective immediacy passes over into objectivity in the sense of being a datum for prehension by succeeding entities. This aspect of being an object conditioning all concrescences beyond itself as something given is termed the entity's **objective immortality**; it "lives on" in the finite world through its effect on (or its prehension by) succeeding actual entities.[9] Thus, according to the process worldview, the "many" occasions of the past are unified in the "one" becoming occasion; but upon attaining satisfaction, the "one" becomes part of a new "many" which requires unification in a succeeding occasion. This dynamic rhythm of the many and the one is the continuing rhythm of process.

Thus far the discussion has focused on actual occasions as the microscopic building blocks of the universe—for example, electronic and protonic occasions and occasions of "empty" space.[10] However, the discussion can be illustrated more clearly on the macroscopic level of human occasions of experience. After the seminar, Maria, the fictional Brazilian graduate student introduced in chapter 2, sat in a park near the university campus pondering the disbelief several classmates expressed when she mentioned that her reason for pursuing a career in engineering was to improve the lives of people living in the favelas. Apparently she was an anomaly to them, so she began to reflect upon the factors which contributed to her present experience. Growing up in a middle-class family certainly provided her opportunities not available to many of her contemporaries. She always had plenty to eat and nice clothes to wear; she lived in a comfortable house in a safe neighborhood and was able to attend good schools. Her family was very close; moreover, she was deeply influenced by her parents' political and social activism and her brother's liberation theology.

---

[9]One should note that Whitehead overcame one of the destructive dualisms of modern thought: the subject-object split. The subjective and the objective are not opposing realities, as in dualistic thought, nor is either of them unreal, as in materialism and idealism. On the contrary, both are alternating aspects of each actual occasion.

[10]The word *empty* is in quotation marks because this space is not really empty but rather is "occupied" by actual occasions. In these occasions novelty, rather than repetition of the past, predominates to such an extent that no serially ordered society is detectable (as opposed to the space "occupied" by a series of electronic occasions, for example). See the discussion of enduring objects below.

During her undergraduate studies she continually rejected the counsel of numerous friends and teachers to choose a career on the basis of its financial rewards.

In viewing Maria's experience in the park from the perspective of process thought, one could say that her present experience is a concrescence of data from the past unified in accordance with her subjective aim to be the type person who enjoys life and works to enable others to enjoy life also. Her present reflection on her family life involves prehensions of past experiences which are clothed with the subjective forms of gratitude and love; her reflection of the disbelief of her classmates involves prehensions which are clothed with the subjective forms of surprise and disappointment (because she had envisioned North American students to be socially minded). The moments of past experience which she is prehending in the present are "living on" as objectively immortal; these past moments are not continuing into the present as subjects with their own subjective immediacy but rather are functioning as objects conditioning the present moment of her experience. Although Maria's environment determined to a large degree who she would become—for example, growing up in that particular family in that particular country—these factors did not totally determine who she became. She also exercised a degree of freedom or creativity—for example, she rejected the materialistic advice of her friends and teachers, and combined her familial influence with her educational opportunities in a novel way. Thus, the rhythm of process is illustrated in the personal experience of Maria. Many past factors influence Maria, yet they are unified in her present momentary experience. But the rhythm of process will not stop with this unification. This moment in Maria's existence will become one of the many factors which must be unified in all subsequent concrescences. These new concrescences could include a subsequent moment in Maria's own existence, a moment in the life of one of her classmates, or a moment in the common life of a particular favela.

Now if reality is viewed in terms of individual momentary events, how is one to understand the existence of enduring objects[11] such as rocks, trees, animals, and people? As was noted above, large societies of actual occasions sometimes impinge upon the human sense organs in such a fashion that the perception of the physical objects of ordinary human experience occurs: a common pattern of inheritance is perceived over a period of time among a group of actual occasions. Historically, the perception of many "things" as manifesting the same characteristic has been attributed to the notion that the many things all correspond to the same idea or form or universal (as in Platonism). For example, all particular instances of gray are manifestations of the idea gray. Although Whitehead agreed with many of the notions of these idealistic philosophies, he disagreed with others. For example, there is a tendency in such philosophies to consider these unchanging ideas or universals to be more real than the particular temporal manifestations. But for Whitehead, there is nothing more real (that is, more actual) than the particular entities manifesting these ideas; consequently, he avoided the traditional terminology and referred to these ideas or universals as **eternal objects.**[12] Eternal objects are defined as "pure possibilities" which indicate how something might be actual. As "potentialities of definiteness" they are capable of specifying the character of any actual entity, but *in themselves* they refer to no particular actual entity.

A becoming occasion prehends or feels a past occasion by means of one of the past occasion's own prehensions or feelings (for this reason one can speak of the rhythm of process as a "flow of feelings"). Ingredient in each component prehension of the past

---

[11]Although **enduring object** is an technical term for Whitehead, it is used here in a nontechnical sense. As a technical term, an enduring object is a series of occasions, only one of which exists at a time, and each of which inherits its data primarily, though not exclusively, from the immediately preceding occasion in the series (thus, an enduring object is a serially ordered society). In enduring objects repetition of the past, rather than novelty, predominates resulting in stability (e.g., an electron is a series of electronic occasions each of which largely repeats the experience of the preceding occasion). An enduring object in the nontechnical sense (e.g., a rock) is a collection of enduring objects in the technical sense. Whitehead called enduring objects in the nontechnical sense **corpuscular societies** because they are composed of numerous "strands" of enduring objects. See the appendix for a more detailed discussion of enduring objects and the macrocosmic world.

[12]See the appendix for a more detailed discussion of eternal objects.

actual occasion is at least one eternal object. Thus, the becoming occasion's prehension of the past occasion by one of its own prehensions results in the two occasions sharing an eternal object. Although the same eternal object has **ingression**[13] in both actual occasions, "how" the eternal object is felt by the two occasions will not be identical; that is, the subjective forms of the two feelings will differ to some degree ranging from negligible to considerable. Because most actual entities transmit—without *significant* alteration—to succeeding entities the data they have inherited from past entities (that is, the same eternal object has ingression throughout the series and is felt in quite similar ways by each entity in the series), there is order, repetition, and continuity in the universe. Large groups or societies of these low-grade occasions account for the enduring objects of human sense perception.

But if occasions become what they become simply by inheritance from the past, how is one to account for instances of genuine novelty instead of only slight variations within an endless pattern of repetition? Granted, most enduring objects exhibit change—and slight change at that—only over a long period of time (for example, molecules and rocks), but in the case of animals and human beings change can be both rapid and dramatic. The occurrence of genuine novelty means that new possibilities have been actualized. Therefore, eternal objects which were not ingredient in *any* past occasion must somehow be available to new becoming occasions. One could attempt to explain this simply by asserting that the "realm" of eternal objects is available to becoming occasions. A problem immediately arises with this explanation, however. For a novel concrescence to occur, the infinite multiplicity of eternal objects must be ordered in such a manner that *certain* eternal objects which have not been realized in past actual occasions become *relevant* to the situation of the concrescing occasion.[14] The past actual world of the becoming occasion determines which **pure possibilities** are relevant, that is, which pure

---

[13]Other equivalent expressions are realization, participation, exemplification, and illustration.

[14]That is, a "graded relevance" must be established in which unrealized eternal objects are graded on a scale from very relevant to not relevant at all. See below on the initial aim.

possibilities are **real possibilities** for actualization given *that* situation. (For example, one hundred years ago flying to Rio was a pure possibility; today it is a real possibility, at least for those who can afford to purchase an airline ticket.) But how is the vast realm of eternal objects ordered or graded so that certain unrealized eternal objects become relevant to each new concrescing actual entity? As with many thinkers, Whitehead felt that only what is actual has agency.[15] Eternal objects in themselves are abstract not concrete, possibilities not actualities; consequently, agency cannot be attributed to eternal objects in themselves. The eternal objects realized in the past are available to becoming occasions through the agency of past actual occasions; in like manner, eternal objects unrealized in the past must be made available through the agency of some actuality. Thus, because novelty exists there must be an actual entity that so orders the realm of eternal objects with respect to each becoming occasion that certain unrealized eternal objects become relevant to each individual concrescence.

Obviously this entity must differ in certain respects from all other actual entities. (1) Whereas actual occasions in the mode of objective immortality are available only to those occasions which succeed them, this entity must be universally available to all becoming occasions. There can be no occasions which do not prehend it. Furthermore, whereas actual occasions have their moment of subjective immediacy and then perish, this entity must be an everlasting[16] entity (the justification for this statement will become evident below). (2) Although an actual occasion is the realization

---

[15]Whitehead labeled this **the ontological principle**. This principle can also be expressed, "everything must be somewhere; and here 'somewhere' means 'some actual entity.' . . . It is a contradiction in terms to assume that some explanatory fact can float into the actual world out of nonentity. Nonentity is nothingness. Every explanatory fact refers to the decision and to the efficacy of an actual thing" (*Process and Reality*, 46). Thus, unrealized eternal objects or new possibilities cannot come to a becoming occasion out of "nowhere."

[16]Everlasting, not eternal, is the appropriate term to describe this entity for if the entity were eternal it would be totally separate from time. As the following discussion reveals, this entity is related to all finite, temporal actual entities. Occasionally Whitehead referred to this entity as nontemporal, but this expression is misleading because it applies to only one aspect of this entity (see the discussion of the primordial nature below).

of only a limited number of eternal objects, this entity must envisage the entire realm of eternal objects, for apart from their envisagement in one actuality eternal objects would not be available for ingression in other actual entities. (3) For particular, finite actualities to exist there must be some limitation on possibility; because it orders the realm of eternal objects with respect to each becoming occasion, this entity serves as the necessary "principle of limitation." (4) Moreover, the very existence of particular, finite actualities requires that this envisagement of the realm of eternal objects be primordial in nature. Unless this act were primordial, there could be no particular actualities, absolutely none. Thus, the ordered envisagement of the realm of eternal objects by this entity is prior to and presupposed by all other actual entities.

Whitehead named this entity **God**; the primordial envisagement of the realm of eternal objects, the **primordial nature** of God; and the ordering of possibilities offered to each becoming occasion, the **initial aim**.[17] The initial aim God supplies each becoming occasion is the initial phase of the development of that occasion's subjective aim. Although the initial aim contains that possibility which is the optimum way to unify the many into a novel one—that is, if adopted it will guide the concrescence in such a way as to result in the richest, most intense unification of feelings possible in light of the past and the relevant future—the occasion is not bound to implement that possibility. Because the initial aim offers a graded relevance of possibilities,[18] there is room for the becoming occasion to accept, modify, or reject the optimum possibility in the development of the subjective aim which will guide its concrescence. According to the process worldview, then, God's power is persuasive rather than coercive. God seeks to lure each occasion toward that ideal way of becoming which is in keeping with God's own subjective aim of promoting intensity of harmonious feeling in the world.

---

[17]See the appendix for a more detailed discussion of God. One should note that Whitehead's introduction of God was not religiously motivated; he introduced God in order to give a philosophical explanation of the world.

[18]The initial aim is the envisagement of a *set* of related, relevant possibilities for actualization; the becoming occasion "chooses" from among them.

Although God's primordial nature is timeless and thus in this respect God can be described as a *nontemporal* actual entity, God is an *actual entity* and so must meet the basic requirements for actuality. In a manner similar to the way in which every occasion of experience influences succeeding occasions and is influenced by preceding occasions, God also both influences and is influenced by the temporal world. Thus, God cannot be described as nontemporal without qualification. Although the primordial envisagement of the realm of eternal objects was unconditioned by any preceding actualities and thus is timeless, every subsequent act of divine concrescence is influenced by whatever actualities have come into being. With respect to God, the rhythm of process may be summarized as follows. God supplies the initial aim to "begin" each new actual occasion. After the occasion achieves its satisfaction God prehends it in its totality, saving everlastingly what has been accomplished in the divine **consequent nature**.[19] What has been accomplished in the temporal world (preserved everlastingly in the consequent nature) is then integrated with the divine envisagement of eternal objects (the primordial nature) in such a way that the divine satisfaction results in relevant initial aims for prehension by the next generation of occasions. According to the process worldview, then, temporal actualities *matter*; they matter both to succeeding temporal occasions of experience *and* to the divine experience.

To illustrate, Maria's decision to dedicate herself to improving the living conditions of the poor in her city can be seen as a response to God's initial aim for her. This aim grew out of her past actual world, God's envisagement of what could be (given her circumstances), and God's own aim of creating intensity of harmonious feeling in the world. Although this initial aim could have been hidden under layers of insensitivity, ignored because of apathy, or

---

[19]Whitehead's description of God in terms of the primordial and consequent natures should not be understood as implying that God can be "divided" into two natures in the usual sense of the term. Rather, these expressions refer to two functions of one reality. The primordial nature is the aspect or dimension of God typically discussed in Western philosophies (God as eternal, unchanging, infinite, and so forth). It is to Whitehead's credit that he also emphasized the neglected dimension of God.

rejected out of hostility—and thus remained unrealized—Maria's sensitivity to God's lure enabled her to perceive and appropriate this aim. Having adopted this aim, she begins to cocreate with God in developing the knowledge, skills, and values necessary to transform the favelas. Her commitment to the poor not only affects human experience—hers, that of her North American classmates, and the poor (at least it will in the future)—it also affects the divine experience. Certain possibilities God values become actual because of Maria's responsiveness to the initial aim; her actualization of these possibilities thus enriches God as well as the world.

One final aspect of the process worldview remains to be introduced: conscious human experience. One of the ways a theology based on Whiteheadian thought differs from many contemporary theologies is that God's purpose and concern is viewed as extending to all of reality rather than focusing exclusively or even primarily upon human beings. Nevertheless, because the concern of this book is to develop a process hermeneutic, the focus is upon the human experience of reading texts. In light of this fact, a brief account of conscious human experience is necessary.[20]

Several terms defined above should be recalled. (1) A "society" is a group of actual occasions in which members of the group depend upon other members for common inherited characteristics. (2) An "enduring object," in the technical sense of the term, is a series of occasions, only one of which exists at a time; although each occasion in an enduring object prehends all past occasions, its most significant inheritance is from the occasion immediately preceding it in the serially ordered society which forms that enduring object. Thus, the occasions of an enduring object tend to repeat the feelings of their immediate predecessor giving rise to stability. (3) The "enduring objects of ordinary human sense perception," enduring objects in the nontechnical sense of the term, are composed of many strands of enduring objects in the technical sense of the term.

In light of these definitions, a human being in his or her totality is a collection of many enduring objects. That is, a human

---

[20]See the discussion of the macrocosmic world in the appendix for a more detailed treatment of conscious human occasions of experience.

being is composed of an immense number of societies and societies of societies. Yet there is within human beings (and in most animals, for that matter) a single center of control and spontaneity typically spoken of as the self or soul.[21] Although one experiences this self as continuously existing (that is, as a "substantial" self), the self is actually composed of a series of individual occasions of experience.[22] This serially ordered society is the dominant or presiding society within a human being. At any given moment the dominant or presiding occasion within this society inherits from (1) all past occasions in that serially ordered society (the ability to inherit from occasions other than the one immediately preceding is nontechnically referred to as "memory"[23]), (2) all of the occasions composing the human body (primarily, though not exclusively, through the brain and nervous system), and (3) all of the occasions of the past actual world of the human being (primarily, though not exclusively, through the sense organs).

The human self or soul is a remarkable type of society. Whereas the occasions composing most serially ordered societies (or enduring objects) are unconscious, the occasions of the human self contain some prehensions whose subjective form includes consciousness. These dominant occasions are capable of such high level experience due in large part to the complex organization of the human body (especially the central nervous system) which insures a constant flow of novelty from the various body parts to the brain. Thus, novelty rather than repetition characterizes the occasions forming this remarkable society.

This brief account of conscious human occasions of experience will be expanded in the next chapter in relation to Whitehead's theories of perception and language.

---

[21]For an excellent discussion of the human soul see Cobb, *A Christian Natural Theology*, 47-91.

[22]This dominant occasion is the occasion humans are aware of most directly through conscious introspection.

[23]The prehension of these past, noncontiguous occasions is by means of **hybrid physical prehensions** (see the appendix of a discussion of these prehensions). Not all of the past occasions in the series will be prehended consciously at any given time, but all are potentially available for "recall."

Chapter 4

Process Hermeneutic: The Nature of Language

Occasionally, a new hermeneutical model will develop new exegetical methods (for example, structuralism). Generally, however, existing methods are used from a new hermeneutical perspective. The process hermeneutic has not developed any new exegetical methods; consequently, its distinctiveness lies in its new perspective rather than any new "process" exegetical tools.

Most of the current hermeneutical options are reductionistic or exclusive when it comes to the act of interpretation. For example, some use structuralist methods whereas others use historical-critical methods; some focus on sociological data whereas others focus on ideas; some locate meaning in the internal world of the text whereas others locate meaning in the external reality to which it refers, or in the author's intention, or in the reader's response. Of course, every hermeneutic is exclusive in *practice*, but the process hermeneutic is not reductionistic in its *theory* of interpretation. Consequently, a process hermeneutic is open to all existing methods of exegesis with the conviction that when carried far enough the various methods will illuminate one another. This methodological inclusiveness is not ad hoc but rather is derived from its theory of perception-as-interpretation.[1]

---

[1]David J. Lull, "What Is 'Process Hermeneutics'?" *Process Studies* 13 (1983): 189-90; and Kent Harold Richards, "Beyond Bruxism," in *Society of Biblical Literature 1976 Seminar Papers* (Missoula MT: Scholars Press, 1976) 469, quoting William A. Beardslee, "Notes on a Whiteheadian Hermeneutic" (unpublished paper).

• Whitehead's Theory of Perception •

According to Whitehead, the fundamental error of Western epistemology lies in its identification of sense data as the basis of all perception.[2] Whitehead affirmed the soundness of Western philosophy's foundational principles: that philosophical generalizations must be based upon the primary elements in actual experience, and that all knowledge is grounded in perception. He disagreed, however, with the traditional analysis of perception. Ordinary human perception (sense perception) occurs at the level of conscious experience. But because consciousness arises only in the fourth phase of concrescence, it can illuminate the more primitive aspects of experience—that is, prehensions in earlier phases—only in so far as they are elements in the integrations of later phases.[3] Thus,

> those elements of our experience which stand out clearly and distinctly in our consciousness are not its basic facts . . . The consequences of the neglect of this law, that the late derivative elements are more clearly illuminated by consciousness than the primitive elements, have been fatal to the proper analysis of an experient occasion. In fact, most of the difficulties of philosophy are produced by it. Experience has been explained in a thoroughly topsy-turvy fashion, the wrong end first.[4]

Ordinary human perception—which Whitehead termed "perception in the mode of **symbolic reference**"—is actually a mixed or composite mode of perception. Careful analysis of symbolic refer-

---

[2]Whitehead, *Process and Reality*, 130-84, and *Adventures of Ideas* (New York: Free Press, 1967; New York: Macmillan, 1933) 175-90.

[3]See the appendix for a discussion of the phases of concrescence.

[4]Whitehead, *Process and Reality*, 162. Similarly, in *Symbolism: Its Meaning and Effect* (New York: Fordham University Press, 1985; New York: Macmillan, 1927) Whitehead noted that Western philosophy has assumed that "presentational immediacy is primitive, and that causal efficacy is the sophisticated derivative. This is a complete inversion of the evidence" (52). The assumption that presentational immediacy is foundational has led to the explanation of causal efficacy as a habit of thought (Hume) or a category of thought (Kant). ("Presentational immediacy" and "causal efficacy" are explained immediately below.)

ence reveals that it is composed of two more primitive modes: "perception in the mode of **causal efficacy**" and "perception in the mode of **presentational immediacy**." (See fig. 4-1, below, p. 100.) According to Whitehead, the traditional analysis of perception errs in that this composite nature is not discerned, especially the mode of causal efficacy.

Perception in the mode of causal efficacy is a primal awareness of one's relationship to the causal nexus in which one exists. This type of perception is not restricted to humans and other higher levels of actuality, but rather is an ubiquitous feature of all reality. The character of causal efficacy is inheritance from the past. As evidence of this "nonsensuous" mode of perception, Whitehead pointed to two aspects of human experience: memory of one's own immediate past state of consciousness—"that portion of our past lying between a tenth of a second and a half a second ago. It is gone, and yet it is here"—and a vague awareness of one's own body as part of a causal nexus moving from past to present to future.[5] In general, however, causal efficacy is largely unconscious in human experience due to the dominance of perception in the mode of presentational immediacy.

Whereas causal efficacy arises in the first phase of the concrescence of an actual entity, presentational immediacy is a product of later phases of concrescence. As a result, "presentational immediacy is an important factor in the experience of only a few high-grade organisms, . . . for the others it is embryonic or entirely negligible."[6] Whereas causal efficacy is vague, direct, massive,

---

[5]Whitehead, *Adventures of Ideas*, 180-84, and *Process and Reality*, 176-78. Cf. Cobb, *God and the World*, 75: "Consider, for example, the belief in any given moment that there were preceding moments and that there will be future ones. It is doubtful that anyone can ever succeed in radically doubting the reality of past and future. Yet sense experience as such provides absolutely no evidence for either. It is in any moment simply what it is, wholly silent with respect to antecedents or consequences. . . . Neither memory nor anticipation is a sensory relation. . . . Not only our awareness of our past and future, but also our conviction that there is a real world which exists quite independently of our experience of it witnesses to the presence of nonsensory experience."

[6]Whitehead, *Symbolism*, 23. "Thus, we must assign the mode of causal efficacy to the fundamental constitution of an occasion so that in germ this mode belongs even to organisms of the lowest grade; while the mode of presentational immediacy requires the more sophistical activity of the later stages of process, so

inarticulate, and produces a sense of derivation from the past and of passage to the future, presentational immediacy is clear, indirect, sophisticated, articulate, and produces a sense of immediate enjoyment. Causal efficacy is the objectification of the past external world; presentational immediacy is the objectification of "a contemporary region of space as illustrating specific geometrical, extensive relationships."[7]

The ability to distinguish one contemporary spatial region from any other contemporary region rests on the perception of an eternal object (or objects)—such as the color "gray"—residing in that contemporary spatial region. At this point it is imperative to recall that contemporary actual entities are causally independent of each other; that is, whereas an actual entity prehends past actual entities, it cannot prehend contemporary actual entities. (See fig. 4-2, below, p. 100.) The immediate present[8] is perceived as an extensive continuum potentially divisible into regions, but the actual entities occupying these regions cannot be prehended. Thus, the eternal object—such as "gray"—is not actually prehended from the contemporary region; rather, it is prehended from the past actual world perceived in the mode of causal efficacy and "projected"[9] onto the contemporary spatial region. (See fig. 4-3, below, p. 101.) Perception in the mode of presentational immediacy results in a flashing awareness of "gray-there"; the contemporary spatial region is "illustrated" by the medium of the eternal object "gray."[10]

---

as to belong only to organisms of a relatively high grade. So far as we can judge, such high-grade organisms are relatively few, in comparison with the whole number of organisms in our immediate environment" (Whitehead, *Process and Reality*, 172).

[7]Sherburne, *A Key to Whitehead's Process and Reality*, 99.

[8]The notion of the immediate present will be examined in more detail below in relation to the term "presented duration."

[9]As Whitehead (*Process and Reality*, 172-73) noted, this terminology is misleading. Both the eternal object and the location in the immediate present are derived from causal efficacy. Presentational immediacy, which occurs in a supplemental phase of concrescence, is simply the enhancement of the relationship between the eternal object and the location vaguely perceived in the first phase of concrescence.

[10]Christian commented that "if presentational immediacy were the *only* mode of perception, then Whitehead's theory would be purely and simply phenomenalistic. The percipient would be restricted to purely private data. No datum would

Presentational immediacy in itself obviously does not describe ordinary human perception (it does, however, describe classical empiricism's (for example, Hume's) idea of sense perception). In presentational immediacy there is clear, distinct consciousness of the extensive relations of the world, but the regions of the world thus perceived are isolated, cut off, self-contained temporally. There is no information as to the past or the future; this mode merely defines a barren cross section of the universe. To describe ordinary human perception, the two primitive modes must be combined in the mixed mode of symbolic reference. Whereas presentational immediacy merely presupposes causal efficacy, symbolic reference integrates the two modes so that there is both clear location in a contemporary region (presentational immediacy) and the power of continuity with the past and an efficacy for the future (causal efficacy). This is Whitehead's description of ordinary human perception of an enduring object, such as a "gray stone." The word "stone" has a reference to the past, for a stone has a history and probably a future as well. Thus, the mixed mode of symbolic reference perceives the "stone" both as clearly located in a contemporary region of space, illustrated by the eternal object "gray," and also as an enduring entity with a past and an efficacy for the future.[11] Because symbolic reference takes place without conscious effort or reflection, its composite nature is not normally noticed in human experience, and the fundamental error of Western epistemology arises.

The integration of causal efficacy and presentational immediacy in symbolic reference (which occurs in a late phase of concrescence) is possible due to two elements of common ground the more primitive modes of perception share. One common element is the **presented duration** or presented locus (location), that duration which conforms to the commonsense notion of "the immediate present condition of the world at some epoch."[12] Although the past

---

give information of any concretely actual thing other than the percipient subject itself" (128, emphasis added).

[11]"We shall find that generally—though not always—the adjectival words express information derived from the mode of immediacy, while the substantives convey our dim percepts in the mode of efficacy." Whitehead, *Process and Reality*, 179.

[12]Whitehead, *Process and Reality*, 125. The presented duration includes *all* of the

actual worlds of the perceiving occasion and its contemporaries are not identical, they are practically identical. Thus, in the mode of causal efficacy the perceiving occasion *directly* perceives those past occasions which are causally efficacious for both itself and the occasions forming its presented duration. "The percipient therefore, under the limitation of its own perspective, prehends the causal influences to which the presented locus [presented duration] in its important regions is subjected." This amounts to an *indirect* perception of the presented duration itself. In the mode of presentational immediacy there is an inversion of what is perceived directly and indirectly: "The presented locus [presented duration] is *directly* illustrated by the sensa [eternal objects]; while the causal past, the causal future, and the other contemporary events, are only *indirectly* perceived by means of their extensive relations to the presented locus."[13] Thus, the presented duration supplies one element of common ground enabling perception in the mode of symbolic reference to occur; it is perceived directly and distinctly in the mode of presentational immediacy and indirectly and indistinctly in the mode of causal efficacy.

The second element shared by causal efficacy and presentational immediacy is a common ingredient eternal object. The eternal object "projected" upon the presented duration in presentational immediacy is derived from the earlier mode of perception, causal efficacy. Thus, the identical eternal object ingredient in both primitive modes of perception supplies a second element of common ground allowing perception in the mode of symbolic reference to occur.

A deeper appreciation of symbolic reference can be gained by means of a brief examination of Whitehead's general notion of

---

percipient occasion's immediate present. But as is explained in the appendix, each occasion lies in many durations; each of these durations includes portions of this presented duration. "In the case of human perception practically all the important portions are thus included; also in human experience the relationship to such durations is what we express by the notion of 'movement'" (125).

[13]Whitehead, *Process and Reality*, 169; emphasis added. Of course, "the causal future" and "the other contemporary events" which are perceived indirectly in the mode of presentational immediacy are also perceived indirectly in the mode of causal efficacy.

symbolism.[14] Symbolic functioning occurs whenever one set of components of a subject's experience elicit another set of components of its experience; the first set are the "symbols" and the second set are the "meanings" of the symbols. The first set elicits the second because the two sets share some "common ground." The subject determines which set of components will function as symbols and which set will serve as meanings for the symbols.[15] Generally stated, then, "'symbolic reference' is the process of transference from a symbol to its meaning."[16] Relating this understanding of symbolic reference to the modes of perception, "presentational immediacy *refers to* causal efficacy; the latter places the former in a context of meaning."[17]

Now to say that one is aware of being internally related to a larger causal nexus—perception in the mode of causal efficacy—is to affirm that one's perceptions are *based upon* data external to oneself. One is aware of a causal past distinct from one's immediate subjectivity. Yet the Whiteheadian understanding of perception also makes it clear that no experience can take place apart from the appropriation of causal forces *in terms of* one's own subjective immediacy which defines their meanings. Because one perceives data only in relation to the significance the data have for oneself,

---

[14]William A. Beardslee ("Recent Hermeneutics and Process Thought," *Process Studies* 12 [1982]: 69, 71) noted that Whitehead "separated what in other schools is broadly the topic of symbolism into two parts: his theory of symbols, which deals with important aspects of perception, and his theory of propositions, which deals with the use of perception in the total act of self-realization or self-creation. . . . The imaginative and creative dimensions of 'symbolism' appear in Whitehead's thought under the rubric of the theory of propositions, in contrast to symbols which appear in the context of prehension." (Whitehead's theory of propositions is set forth below.)

[15]Whitehead (*Process and Reality*, 181) noted that "in this way there can be symbolic reference between two species in the same perceptive mode: but the chief example of symbolism, upon which is based a great portion of the lives of all high-grade animals, is that between the two perceptive modes." Although it can work both ways in complex human experience, symbolic reference "is chiefly to be thought of as the elucidation of percepta in the mode of causal efficacy by the fluctuating intervention of percepta in the mode of presentational immediacy." Whitehead, *Process and Reality*, 178.

[16]Michael L. Harrington, "Whitehead's Theory of Propositions," (Ph.D. diss., Emory University, 1972) 177. See Whitehead, *Symbolism*, 7-13.

[17]Pregeant, *Christology Beyond Dogma*, 34.

perception is always perspectival. (It will be recalled that the prehension of past occasions involves negative prehensions—the elimination of data—as well as positive prehensions; moreover, these positive prehensions are clothed with subjective forms which are to some degree unique to the prehending occasion.) Thus, perception implies a world of real causal relations which is experienced through subjective participation and valuation.[18]

Although symbolic reference produces a sense of the external world, it is not infallible. One must acknowledge the possibility of error in relating perception in the mode of causal efficacy and perception in the mode of presentational immediacy—for example, common human sense perception errors. Perception in the mode of presentational immediacy is essentially the projection on to the presented duration of eternal objects the percipient inherited from the past actual world. But it is possible that the occasions occupying the presented duration did not inherit these eternal objects (that is, these eternal objects were negatively prehended by the occasions occupying the presented duration). Consequently, the perception of these eternal objects as ingredient in the presented duration is erroneous. Moreover, because the perceiver does not prehend the contemporary world but rather projects the immediate past world on to the present, the greater the distance between the perceiver and the nexus being observed, the greater the chance for error. For example, were Maria, the Brazilian graduate student of our earlier example, to visit the park on a clear night, she might observe the light of a star that perished millions of years ago. Furthermore, ordinary human perception is dependent upon the state of the body in general and the brain in particular. Numerous factors can affect bodily functioning; for example, drugs can cause hallucinations, color blindness can prevent the perception of certain colors, and optical illusions such as those produced by mirrors can deceive the sense organs. Yet in spite of the possibility that error can occur, real knowledge of external data is possible because the two modes of perception share a common eternal object as well

---

[18]Valuation is the subjective form of conceptual feelings (see the appendix for a discussion of conceptual feelings and valuation). This is the most primitive type of creative response open to an entity: valuation up or down.

as a common present duration. Therefore, contrary to the idealism of Kant, one can know about the world as it is, in spite of the contributions of one's mind in shaping one's perception; contrary to the skeptical empiricism of Hume, the notion of cause and effect can be restored; and contrary to the rationalism of Descartes, knowledge begins with experience rather than innate ideas.[19]

Whitehead's theory of perception as presented thus far can be described as a complex, integrated process of interpretation of data from the past actual world and projection onto the contemporary world. For the purpose at hand, one more aspect of perception must be discussed. Perception in its broadest sense also includes the process of the interpretation of **propositions** about the past actual world germane to its possible future states.

One of Whitehead's most significant contributions to modern thought is his understanding of propositions, entities he also termed "concrete possibilities," "theories," or "proposals." The rise of a proposition occurs in the following manner: an actual entity or nexus—the *logical subject* of the proposition—is abstracted from experience to the point of being a mere "it," and some eternal object (or group of eternal objects)—the *predicate* of the proposition—is predicated of it.[20] A proposition, then, is a proposal, a predication of an abstract possibility upon an actual entity or nexus already known in a subject's experience. Moreover, because the eternal object predicated of the logical subject may differ to some degree from that which is actually ingredient in the logical subject (the technical explanation of which would take us far afield[21]), an important function of propositions is to serve as "the indispensable vehicle of imagination which reaches out from that which has already been experienced toward possibilities as yet un-

---

[19]See, Pregeant, *Christology Beyond Dogma*, 35, and William A. Beardslee, "Whitehead and Hermeneutic" *Journal of the American Academy of Religion* 47 (1979): 32-33.

[20]See the appendix for an extended discussion of propositions (figs. A-7 and A-8).

[21]See the appendix for a discussion of how propositions may arise through **conceptual reversion** rather than **conceptual reproduction** (fig. A-7) and how the **indicative feeling** and the **physical recognition** may be derived from different physical feelings (fig. A-8).

realized."[22] In fact, "transformation of 'the way things *are*,' for better or worse, depends on entertaining proposals about 'how things *could be*.'"[23]

Whitehead adopted the term "proposition" from logic; to avoid possible misunderstandings of his use of the term, three points should be noted. (1) Most propositions do not function at the conscious level. Consciousness is the subjective form of **intellectual feelings** which arise in the fourth phase of concrescence.[24] Because propositional feelings arise in the third phase of concrescence, only those which function as component feelings in the more complex intellectual feelings enter into consciousness. (2) Because propositions arise in the third phase of concrescence, they are prelinguistic. Only those which become component feelings in intellectual feelings are capable of linguistic expression. (3) It is more important that propositions be interesting than that they be true; the importance of truth is that it tends to add to interest.[25]

What, then, is the primary function of a proposition? A proposition is a datum for feeling that awaits a subject to feel it. Therefore, the primary function of a proposition is to serve as a "lure for feeling"; that is, a proposition lures the subject to feel a past datum in a particular way in the subject's process of self-creation. A given proposition can be felt by many subjects and in many ways, that is, the subjective form varies from subject to subject (for example, it can be felt as hopeful or dreadful, interesting or dull, attractive or repulsive, true or false, and so forth). The main point to observe is that propositions grow out of the past actual world (because of the logical subject) and pave the way for the advance into novelty as lures for creative emergence in the future (because of the predicate). Thus, propositions combine "imaginative freedom with grounding in reality."[26]

---

[22]Beardslee, "Whitehead and Hermeneutic," 34. This is Whitehead's explanation of creative imagination.

[23]Lull, "What Is 'Process Hermeneutics'?" 190; emphasis added.

[24]See the appendix for a discusson of intellectual feelings (figs. A-9 and A-10).

[25]Whitehead, *Process and Reality*, 259. See the appendix for Whitehead's criticism of those whom he labeled "overintellectualized philosophers."

[26]Beardslee, "Recent Hermeneutics and Process Thought," 72.

The logical subject of a particular proposition may not lie in the past actual world of a particular actual entity; when this is the case that proposition is nonexistent for that actual entity. For example, the proposition "the airplane is silver"[27] did not exist until this century; for such a proposition to exist, it had to await the emergence of its logical subject. Thus, not only do propositions pave the way for the advance into novelty in the future; new propositions themselves come into existence with the creative advance of the world.[28]

In summary, whereas symbolic reference focuses on the external world in its pastness or actuality—that is, symbolic reference focuses on the *receptive* aspect of perception—propositional feelings focus on a future or potential world as well as a past actual one—that is, propositional feelings focus on the *imaginative* and *creative* aspects of perception. Perception, then, "is a complex process of interpretation of 'data from the real [past] world' as well as of 'proposals' about the past actual world germane to its possible future states."[29] Thus, *perception is interpretation.*

• Whitehead's Theory of Language •

Language is nothing more than a set of definite sounds or marks on paper. A unit of language becomes meaningful only when it is associated with some particular thing; expressed in terms of symbolic reference, the unit of language is the "symbol" and the thing associated, the "meaning" of that symbol. Thus, language is humankind's "most obvious and elaborate symbolic system."[30]

Expressed in terms of process metaphysics, what language does is: (1) to arouse in a thinking subject a **physical prehension**[31] of

---

[27]The notion of a proposition should not be equated with a sentence, for a sentence may be a bundle of propositions. (See below.)

[28]Whitehead, *Process and Reality*, 188.

[29]Lull, "What Is 'Process Hermeneutics'?" 191.

[30]Beardslee, "Whitehead and Hermeneutic," 33.

[31]A prehension whose datum is an actual entity is termed a physical prehension in distinction from a conceptual prehension whose datum is an eternal object. A physical prehension involves an eternal object, but an eternal object as immanent, as ingredient in a particular actual entity (e.g., gray ingredient in a particular actual occasion). In contrast, a conceptual prehension is the feeling of

those entities which are "meanings" and are to be logical subjects for the emerging proposition; (2) to promote the development of a **conceptual prehension** of the eternal objects which are to be the predicate for the emerging proposition[32]; and (3) to encourage the integration of the physical and conceptual prehensions into a **propositional prehension** whose datum is the proposition. "Words and phrases are thus efficacious in indicating to a thinker which actual entities and eternal objects should be prehended, so that a propositional prehension can be originated involving the proposition expressed by the sentence."[33]

Language, then, is a tool facilitating the recall and communication of propositions. But it is by no means a perfect tool. Whitehead called attention to the fact that "every proposition refers to a universe exhibiting some general systematic metaphysical character"; and he further noted the "impossibility of tearing a proposition from its systematic context in the actual world."[34] The reason for this is that the logical subjects of a proposition are actual entities. Now each actual entity has a definite internal bond (either positive or negative) with every actuality in its universe; the entire universe is ingredient in the actual entity. Therefore, a proposition cannot be abstracted from this set of complex and dynamic relationships. But language attempts to do just that; it attempts to express a proposition without reference to its system of relations, its "concrete connectedness." The fallacy of misplaced concreteness is mistaking the clear and distinct impressions which arise in the conscious phase of concrescence for the most concrete and basic elements of experience. But as Gerald Janzen noted, "we experience more than we know, and we know more than we can think; and we think more than we can say; and language therefore lags behind the intuitions of immediate experience."[35] Consequently,

---

an eternal object without reference to any particular actual entity, a feeling of the eternal object "in itself" (e.g., grayness nowhere in particular).

[32]See the appendix for a discussion of the development of conceptual prehensions.

[33]Harrington, "Whitehead's Theory of Propositions," 179.

[34]Whitehead, *Process and Reality*, 11.

[35]Janzen, "The Old Testament in 'Process' Perspective," 492. Similarly, Bernard E. Meland ("Response to Paper by Professor Beardslee," *Encounter* 36 [1975]: 340)

Whitehead asserted that "it is merely credulous to accept verbal phrases as adequate statements of propositions."[36] Language can only approximate the full meaning of a proposition; language is always incomplete and fragmentary.

Process metaphysics of necessity, then, understands language to be analogical, indeterminate, imprecise, and value laden. Because reality is a fluid environment composed of myriads of internally related causal nexuses rather than a world of discrete objects, it is obvious that words can never be understood in a univocal sense, as if they referred to absolutely definite and discrete objects. The application of a name to an object requires that *some* aspects of an actuality be lifted out of the complex and dynamic set of relationships within which it occurs (its concrete connectedness) and that *other* aspects of the actuality be ignored. Consequently, language is always abstract[37]—an imprecise, incomplete, and indeterminate representation of concrete actuality. Moreover, "the process of abstraction necessary for the formation of a word is anything but a cold and unfeeling activity. It takes place only because a *felt value* is already at work in the very act of discriminating an object for naming."[38] Thus, the act of naming—both on the part of a speaker/author and a hearer/reader—involves an element of creativity.

The plurisignificant nature of language so conceived is obvious. Due to the "elliptical" character of language, each word is potentially capable of designating a whole host of things; no word can indicate precisely one singular and individual thing. A sentence, therefore, is capable of eliciting an indefinite number of related propositions which fit its verbal form; each of these propositions becomes a possible meaning for the sentence. Moreover, no sentence or similar verbal unit merely *enunciates* a proposition.

---

noted that "we live more deeply than we can think. . . . There are vast dimensions of experienced reality which must remain unavailable to conceptual formulation which, nevertheless, have important bearing upon our thinking."

[36]Whitehead, *Process and Reality*, 11.

[37]"The essence of language is that it utilizes those elements in experience most easily abstracted for conscious entertainment, and most easily reproduced in experience" (Whitehead, *Modes of Thought*, 34).

[38]Pregeant, *Christology Beyond Dogma*, 37; emphasis added.

Inherent in all statements, written as well as oral, is some *incitement* for entertaining a proposition in a given way. For example, the tone of voice, the choice of words, and even the book (for example, an "authoritative" book such as the Bible or a text book) in which the words occur can convey particular incitement.[39]

Whitehead was aware that people often ignore the fact that words are analogical, imprecise, and value laden, and treat the objects so designated as if they were self-contained, self-defined, valueless entities. As Janzen remarked:

> The language of the special sciences, logic, mathematics, and rational philosophy have as their ideal the development of terms that are univalent, conceptually focused, precisely defined. These languages—examples of what Philip Wheelwright calls *steno-languages*—are enormously useful for the formulation of rational explanations, and for exercising control over the world for specific purposes. But these 'definitive' languages constitute a high abstraction from, and therefore a quite limited representation of, the concrete totality of the world as experienced.[40]

Therefore, to assume that steno-language is the most adequate language for the attempt to understand and report empirical reality is to commit the fallacy of misplaced concreteness because the assumption arises from a failure to acknowledge the degree of abstraction involved in the formation of words. But however much elements of steno-language "be stabilized as technicalities, they remain metaphors mutely appealing for an imaginative leap."[41]

For Whitehead, "the deeper truths must be adumbrated by myths" and poetry[42]—what Wheelwright called *tensive language*. "Employing multivalent words laden with innumerable associational and valuational and emotional ligatures, this mode of language conveys the essential connectedness and concrete particulari-

---

[39]Harrington, "Whitehead's Theory of Propositions," 180-81, 184.

[40]Janzen, "The Old Testament in 'Process' Perspective," 492-93. Janzen referred to Philip Wheelwright, *The Burning Fountain: A Study in the Language of Symbolism*, rev. ed. (Bloomington: Indiana University Press, 1968). See also Wheelwright's *Metaphor and Reality* (Bloomington: Indiana University Press, 1962).

[41]Whitehead, *Process and Reality*, 4.

[42]Whitehead, *Modes of Thought*, 10.

ty of things." These features render tensive language incapable of serving the *limited* functional purposes of the special sciences, but these same features "enable it to report the empirical world most richly and concretely for human understanding. And indeed, such language not only reports, but in some sense conveys, or reenacts, what it reports." Thus, contrary to common assumption, "the most concretely historical mode of language is the poetic, while the definitive languages of the sciences, including that of historical scholarship, are, for all their enormous utility, only in a secondary and abstract sense historical."[43]

If one may describe steno-language as the language of rational discourse, and tensive language as the language of empirical expression, then "it can readily be appreciated that, for Whitehead's rational empiricism, neither mode has exclusive, or even preponderant, claims to credence."[44] Rather, each is indispensable. The two forms of language merely differ with respect to the degree of indeterminacy each possesses. All language is relatively (in)determinate; each instance of language can be located on a spectrum ranging from one hypothetical extreme—completely determinate—to the other hypothetical extreme—completely indeterminate. (See fig. 4-4, below, p. 101.)

Whitehead's understanding of language means that religious language (and other manifestations of tensive language) can be valued positively. "Because words never refer to absolutely definite and discrete objects, but point analogically to elements abstracted from a continuous flow of experience, every assertion ultimately presupposes and points toward a larger whole, an encompassing process that embraces all experience." To be sure, religious language is subjective and value laden, but the same is also true

---

[43]Janzen, "The Old Testament in 'Process' Perspective," 493. Cf. D. Lynn Holt, "Metaphors as Imaginative Propositions," *Process Studies* 12 (1982): 253: "One normally thinks of abstraction in terms of higher and vaguer generalizations: 'cow' is more abstract than 'Bossie,' 'mammal' is more abstract than 'cow.' But what a verbal abstraction from a proposition omits is the general systematic character of the proposition, not the particular details. In this sense, the more 'abstract' a statement is, the less it exhibits generality. Thus, 'Bossie' is more abstract than 'cow,' 'cow' is more abstract than 'mammal,' etc. This notion of the inverted abstraction of language has important implications for metaphorical expression."

[44]Janzen, "The Old Testament in 'Process' Perspective," 493.

in some measure of all language—even that which claims the highest objectivity. But the unique value of religious language is that it, like metaphysical language, makes "explicit what is merely implicit in all other modes of speech: an understanding of and a commitment to a particular vision of the ultimate nature of things."[45]

As with all types of language, religious language can be misleading. The problem occurs when an interpreter takes any form of language to be literal rather than analogical. With respect to religious language, this occurs when an interpreter understands religious statements "as dogmas, as denoting the content of faith in a direct, precise, literal fashion. . . . Properly understood, religious statements (like all statements) are primarily lures for feeling."[46] Moreover, whereas the *descriptive* and *metonymic* views of language understand religious language as objective assertions about the world of nature and the transcendent realm (respectively) which

---

[45]Pregeant, *Christology Beyond Dogma*, 38.

[46]Pregeant, *Christology Beyond Dogma*, 39. The following quotations from Alfred North Whitehead's *Religion in the Making* (New York: Macmillan, 1926) illustrate the significance of Pregeant's point.

A dogma is the expression of a fact as it appears within a certain sphere of thought. . . . You cannot claim absolute finality for a dogma without claiming a commensurate finality for the sphere of thought within which it arose. . . . A dogma . . . can never be final; it can only be adequate. (125-26)

Thus an ill-balanced zeal for the propagation of dogma bears witness to a certain coarseness of aesthetic sensitiveness. It shows a strain of indifference—due perhaps to arrogance, perhaps to rashness, perhaps to mere ignorance—a strain of indifference to the fact that others may require a proportion of formulation different from that suitable for ourselves. (123-24)

The intolerant use of religious dogmas has practically destroyed their utility for a great, if not the greater part, of the civilized world. (132)

Religions commit suicide when they find their inspirations in their dogmas. The inspiration of religion lies in the history of religion. By this I mean that it is to be found in the primary expressions of the intuitions of the finest types of religious lives. The sources of religious belief are always growing, though some supreme expressions may lie in the past. Records of these sources are not formulae. They elicit in us intuitive response which pierces beyond dogma. (138-39)

A system of dogmas may be the ark within which the Church floats safely down the flood tide of history. But the Church will perish unless it opens its window and lets out the dove to search for an olive branch. Sometimes even it will do well to disembark on Mount Ararat and build a new altar to the divine Spirit. (140)

Idolatry is the necessary product of static dogmas. (142)

are to be grasped by an externally related subject (that is, subject and object are distinct from one another), the *Whiteheadian* view of language understands religious language as donations of propositions for feeling in the self-creation of an internally related subject (that is, subject and object are inseparable). Thus, the process understanding of language is evidence of the dawning of the fourth phase of language mentioned in chapter 2.

The process understanding of the nature of language based, upon Whitehead's theory of perception and especially his notion of propositions, gives rise to a distinctive understanding of the nature of texts, to which we now turn.

Figure 4-1

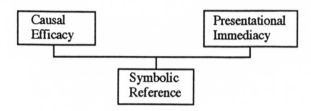

Perception in the mode of symbolic reference is a mixed mode composed of perception in the mode of causal efficacy and perception in the mode of presentational immediacy.

Figure 4-2[47]

Each square in this figure represents an actual entity, arrows represent prehensions (or perception in the mode of causal efficacy), and time moves to the right. Whereas an actual entity (the middle square) prehends past actual entities and is prehended by subsequent entities, it cannot prehend contemporary actual entities; contemporary actual entities are causally independent.

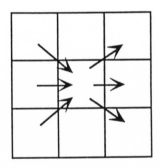

---

[47]Process thinkers cringe when they are asked to illustrate process thought, responding that diagrams are inherently misleading. For example, diagrams inevitably place datum occasions *outside* the becoming occasion whereas one of the basis tenets of process thought is that relations are internal not external. Similarly, spatializing time is quite misleading. These and other misleading aspects of diagrams notwithstanding, I have opted to "resort" to diagrams for I feel that they can be helpful heuristic devices in an initial attempt to understand Whitehead's thought.

Figure 4-3

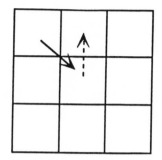

The solid arrow represents a prehension, and the broken arrow represents a projection onto a contemporary entity. In perception in the mode of presentational immediacy, an eternal object is prehended from the past actual world perceived in the mode of causal efficacy and then "projected" onto the contemporary spatial region.

Figure 4-4[48]

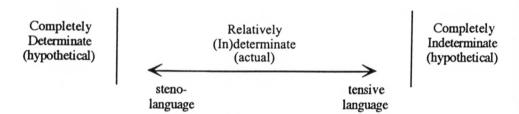

Completely Determinate (hypothetical)	Relatively (In)determinate (actual)	Completely Indeterminate (hypothetical)
	steno-language tensive language	

Examples of steno-language include precise scientific language, ordinary discursive language, and rational argumentation. Such language occurs toward the left on this spectrum. Examples of tensive language include analogical language, intuitive language, imaginative language, and symbolic or metaphorical language. Such language occurs toward the right on this spectrum. All language is relatively (in)determinate; no language is completely determinate or completely indeterminate.

---

[48]Adapted from Pregeant, "Where is the Meaning? Metaphysical Criticism and the Problem of Indeterminacy," *The Journal of Religion* 63 (1983): 111.

Chapter 5

Process Hermeneutic: The Nature of Texts

In light of the preceding discussion, it is apparent that all texts are proposals, clusters of propositions. As lures for feeling, propositions grow out of objective events in the actual world (including events in the personal experience of the author and events to which his or her writing refers) and concern possibilities for the future (the future of subsequent as well as the original readers). This view of the text relates it to historical events on the one hand and to creative, alternative ways of constituting one's self with regard to those past events on the other.[1]

Three observations should be noted: (1) a text is always the partial, inexact expression of an author's original vision of propositions; (2) a text will of necessity evoke propositions not entertained by the author; and (3) the propositions entertained by one reader will never be exactly the same as those felt by another reader.[2] (See fig. 5-1, below, p. 107.) Thus, only to the degree that *some* of the same propositions entertained by the author are felt by the original and subsequent readers is one justified saying that the author, the original readers, and subsequent readers all have to do with "the same text."

There are at least three reasons for this "evolutionary nature"[3]

---

[1]Barry A. Woodbridge, "An Assessment and Prospectus for a Process Hermeneutic" *Journal of the American Academy of Religion* 47 (1979): 123.

[2]See Barry A Woodbridge, "Process Hermeneutic: An Approach to Biblical Texts," in *Society of Biblical Literature 1977 Seminar Papers* (Missoula MT: Scholars Press, 1977) 79-82.

[3]Woodbridge, "An Assessment and Prospectus for a Process Hermeneutic,"

of texts. First, the imprecision of language affects both authorial expression and reader interpretation. Words cannot express exhaustively or precisely that which they seek to convey. Not only do words merely approximate a given proposition, but they also evoke an indefinite number of related propositions. Second, even if the same proposition is felt by the author and a reader, or by two different readers, or by one reader at two different times, the proposition will not be felt the same way. The subjective forms of the feelings will differ to some degree. A third reason for the evolutionary nature of texts is that a proposition presupposes a general nexus which includes not only that nexus of actual entities forming the logical subject of the proposition, but also that nexus of entities which, as prehending subjects, can entertain that proposition. Now it is apparent that the perspectives and actual worlds of author and reader—or of two different readers, or of the same reader at two different times—differ. Consequently, these differences change the range of propositions which may be entertained by a reader and evoked by a text. Thus, as was noted in chapter 4, "new propositions come into being with the creative advance of the world."[4]

Most hermeneutical models have assumed that the present meaning of a text must be expressed in terms similar to what it meant when it was composed. In the eyes of many interpreters, "what the text historically meant has become an essence from which its present meaning can only deviate within narrow confines." But if the text inevitably evokes new propositions during the course of time, "what the text might come to mean can theoretically be more important than anything the text has meant in the past." One could say that "potential meanings of the text remain encoded in its total capacity to elicit lures for feeling until the kairotic moment arrives." At the opportune moment, the givenness of a particular past, the contingencies of a particular present, and the possibilities for the future converge in the reading of a text, and a new meaning emerges.[5] Thus, according to a process herme-

---

124.

[4]Whitehead, *Process and Reality*, 259.

[5]Woodbridge, "An Assessment and Prospectus for a Process Hermeneutic,"

neutical model the meaning of a text consists of the totality of propositions it can evoke. The meaning of a text is open-ended, evolving with the creative advance of the world.

Interpreting a text from the standpoint of a process hermeneutic requires what Russell Pregeant called "a bifocal approach to the text." First, because language is analogical, imprecise, and value-laden, "the interpreter must work through the discursive implications of the text back to the complex of feelings toward which it lures the reader."[6] In this way the interpreter identifies the major lures (propositions) at work in the text. Second, it was noted earlier that all language "ultimately presupposes and points toward a larger whole, an encompassing process that embraces all experience." Moreover, the unique value of religious language was said to be that it, like metaphysical language, makes "explicit what is merely implicit in all other modes of speech: an understanding of and a commitment to a particular vision of the ultimate nature of things."[7] Therefore, in addition to the more obvious lures, the biblical interpreter must trace "the broadest presuppositions of the address embodied in the text" to arrive at *the basal lures* underlying the other lures at work in the text. These basal lures reveal "a fundamental disposition toward reality itself," the presupposed metaphysical commitments of the language of the text.[8]

Pregeant referred to this search for basal lures as "metaphysical criticism." Being sensitive to the metaphysical implications of the text does not mean that the interpreter "must begin with rigid metaphysical commitments."[9] On the contrary, because all lan-

---

124. Because these new meanings stand in genetic continuity with past meanings, it is possible to trace the history of the transmission and development of a particular tradition. This will be discussed in chap. 6 in connection with "historic routes of living occasions."

[6]Pregeant, *Christology Beyond Dogma*, 44.

[7]Pregeant, *Christology Beyond Dogma*, 38.

[8]Pregeant, *Christology Beyond Dogma*, 44.

[9]Pregeant, *Christology Beyond Dogma*, 44. Pregeant ("Where Is the Meaning?" 116) acknowledged that "the traditional wariness, on the part of both literary and biblical scholars, of metaphysically oriented interpretations is well founded. The process of reading a text through the eyes of a system can easily suppress tensive elements which are the sources of evocative power, strip a text of all its concreteness, and even turn a text completely against itself."

guage is incomplete and fragmentary, a final, univocally-understood metaphysic is impossible. Moreover, "metaphysical reflection is not, for Whitehead, the construction of a system closed to new insights; metaphysics itself, and hence any critical method based upon it, must be seen as ongoing activities which are themselves checks upon subjectivity." Thus, metaphysical criticism should not be understood as "the imposition of a foreign ideology on the text but rather as an open-ended process by which certain fundamental metaphysical insights are employed in the working out of a standpoint from which the text can be clarified."[10]

Metaphysical criticism so conceived results in viewing the understanding of reality implicit in the text as a proposition, a proposal, a possible way to understand existence. And it is important to note that in some texts this implicit metaphysical understanding may function in a manner quite at odds with a univocal reading of language of the text; in such instances one may speak of this basal lure as an "undercurrent." The importance of detecting these undercurrents will be illustrated in chapter 8.[11]

One final aspect of a process hermeneutic needs to be described: its understanding of what constitutes a valid reading of a text. For this we turn to chapter 6.

---

[10]Pregeant, "Where Is the Meaning?" 116-17.

[11]See also Russell Pregeant, "The Matthean Undercurrent: Process Hermeneutic and the 'Parable of the Last Judgment,'" in *Society of Biblical Literature 1975 Seminar Papers* (Missoula MT: Scholars Press, 1975) 143-59, and "Matthew's 'Undercurrent' and Ogden's Christology" *Process Studies* 6 (1976): 181-94. These papers culminated in Pregeant's *Christology Beyond Dogma*; see especially part IV, "The Undercurrent: An Incipient Universalism."

Figure 5-1[12]

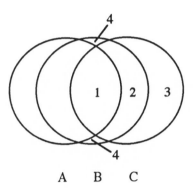

Circle A represents the propositions originally entertained by the author; circle B represents the propositions frequently elicited in the experience of the original readers; and circle C represents the propositions felt by a later reader. Number 1 represents the propositions entertained by author, original readers, and a later reader; thus the possibility of genuine communication exists. Numbers 2, 3, and 4 represent the "growing edges" of a living tradition, i.e., propositions beyond those entertained by the author (due to the indeterminacy of language).

---

[12]Adapted from Woodbridge, "Process Hermeneutic: An Approach to Biblical Texts," 81. Variations of the diagram appear in Barry Woodbridge, "The Role of Text and Emergent Possibilities in the Interpretation of Christian Tradition: A Process Hermeneutic in Response to the German Hermeneutical Discussion" (Ph.D. diss., Claremont Graduate School, 1976).

Chapter 6

Process Hermeneutic: Validity in Interpretation and Theological Norms

According to a process hermeneutic, novel meanings of a text are to be anticipated not rejected a priori as if only the original meaning were valid. This feature of a process hermeneutic obviously raises questions concerning validity in interpretation and theological norms.

The emphasis on texts as proposals could lead one to assume that the cluster of propositions in a biblical text is what is normative for theological and ethical reflection.[1] David Lull noted three problems with this approach to theological norms, however. First, "the propositions in question are not simply properties of a *text*; text *and* interpretation participate in the creation of a given proposition, so that it is as much 'in *interpretation*' as it is 'in *Scripture*.'" Thus, propositions are found in Scripture-as-interpreted. Second,

> the term "proposition" itself does not set material limits to what belongs to its general class. It therefore neither states nor implies the criterion/criteria by which a proposal can be judged appropriate to Christian theology. For appropriateness entails a judgment *about* a certain text-as-interpreted, within which "propositions" reside; it is not a judgment made *in* the interpretation of a text.[2]

---

[1] E.g., Kelsey, "The Theological Use of Scripture in Process Hermeneutics," 181-88.

[2] Lull, "What Is 'Process Hermeneutics'?" 194.

Third, a proposition has no "force" in and of itself. The subjective form (*how* the proposition is felt) is supplied by the interpreter. Thus, although a process hermeneutic proposes that an interpreter attend to the propositions evoked by a text, this does not answer the questions: What constitutes a valid interpretation? What is normative for theology?

Process interpreters approach these important questions primarily through two Whiteheadian concepts: **historic routes of living occasions** and God's work of **creative transformation**. A distinctive understanding of the authority of the Bible emerges from these concepts. A third notion relevant to these questions is the role of "the community of interpretation," a feature not unique to a process hermeneutic.

• Historic Routes of Living Occasions •

As was observed in chapter 3, an actual occasion prehends all of the occasions in its past actual world. But although the becoming occasion inherits from all past occasions, certain of these occasions are more important with respect to what the concrescing occasion becomes. When these more important occasions exhibit serial order, they are termed "an historic route of occasions." Because the becoming occasion's inheritance from these occasions is especially important to its self-creation, it may be said to belong to that route. As a superject, it transmits what it inherited from this historic route to succeeding occasions; it also transmits some element of novelty due to its creative response to the past. Now if this route of occasions contains living occasions, then it is termed "an historic route of living occasions"; and with living occasions the note of novelty is heightened considerably.

When Whitehead's notion of an historic route of living occasions is applied to the interpretation of texts, one notices a striking similarity to what Hans Georg Gadamer called "effective history." Contrary to most hermeneuticians, Gadamer did not view the temporal distance between interpreter and text as an empty chasm needing to be bridged. This temporal distance "is not a yawning abyss, but is filled with the continuity of custom and tradition, in the light of which all that is handed down presents itself to us."[3] The term effective history refers to the effect a text has upon generation after generation as the text is interpreted in light of new events and new events are interpreted in light of the text. Thus, the modern interpreter does not encounter the text alone, but the text and its effective history. In process terminology, the interpreter, as a member of this historic route, is internally related not only to the text but also to the tradition of interpretation associated with the text. For example, Augustine's interpretation influenced Luther's; Augustine's and Luther's interpretations influenced Schleiermacher's; and so on down to the present interpreter. This does not mean that the present interpreter has "no immediate access to the lures elicited by reading the text itself," but it does mean that the kind of lures the interpreter feels "have been socially conditioned by prior feelings of the text's lures."[4]

Similarities also exist between Whitehead's concept of an historic route of living occasions and James Robinson's call to replace the term "tradition"—in the sense of the *transmission* of traditions—with "trajectory."[5] For Robinson, "tradition" defines the continuity involved in the process of transmission too much by the *content* of what is transmitted. The more important level of *existential meaning* is not conveyed by the term. In spite of the similarities between Whitehead's concept and that of Robinson, John Cobb enumerated four important differences—differences which actually clarify and strengthen the point Robinson was making.[6]

---

[3]Hans Georg Gadamer, *Truth and Method*, trans. Garrett Barden and John Comming (New York: Seabury Press, 1975) 264.

[4]Woodbridge, "Process Hermeneutic: An Approach to Biblical Texts," 84-85. See also Clark M. Williamson, "Process Hermeneutics and Christianity's Post-Holocaust Reinterpretation of Itself," *Process Studies* 12 (1982): 79-82. The point made in this paragraph will be expanded below in relation to "creative transformation" and "the community of interpretation."

[5]James M. Robinson, "Introduction: The Dismantling and Reassembling of the Categories of New Testament Scholarship," in *Trajectories through Early Christianity*, with Helmut Koester (Philadelphia: Fortress Press, 1971) 1-19.

[6]John B. Cobb, Jr., "Trajectories and Historic Routes," *Semeia* 24 (1982): 92-93. Cobb's criticism of Robinson's suggestion is based upon the image evoked by the term trajectory—"a substantial entity moving through time with only external relations to the rest of the world" (91). Such an image contrasts sharply with the process understanding of reality as composed of actual entities (events, not substances) internally related to the rest of the world.

(1) Robinson's trajectory image suggests that individual trajectories "are so formed by the initiating impetus and the situational field that they can be described in mutual independence of one another as quite distinct and discrete entities." (See the top diagram in fig. 6-1, below, p. 119.) It is important to note that this was not Robinson's intention. In an historic route of occasions, however, the individual historic routes "influence one another by constituting part of the situational field for one another"; consequently, "their distinctness is a matter of emphasis or degree." (See the bottom diagram in fig. 6-1, below, p. 119.) Cobb noted that "in some cases the extent to which one event is shaped by a particular series of past events is so dominant that it may be considered as a member of that series and as relatively separable from other factors in its environment. But more commonly an event is shaped by multiple factors such that it can be viewed as a member of more than one historic route."

(2) Another inadequacy of Robinson's trajectory image is that it "fails to highlight the elements of creative novelty in the events that make up the trajectory." Because trajectories are usually bits of matter, it is all too easy "to think of the trajectory as determined exhaustively by the impetus of the past and the force of the field through which the entity passes." But the historic routes Robinson is concerned to trace, Cobb pointed out, "are self-determining as well as externally caused."

(3) "Normally in a trajectory the direct cause of the locus at any given point is found in the impetus transmitted by the preceding point on the trajectory together with the new field which has been entered." (See the top diagram in fig. 6-2, below, p. 119.) But in religious trajectories a major factor in each event is the "reencountering of the originating events, that is, the reading of sacred texts, the proclamation of their meaning, and the reenactment of sacred rites. Hence, in addition to the originating impetus of those events, their conscious reconsideration is an important factor in forming the trajectory." This conscious reconsideration of originating events is better depicted by an historic route of living occasions because each occasion in the route "takes account not only of immediate past members of the route but also, in memory, of more distant ones." (See the bottom diagram in fig. 6-2, p. 119.)

(4) In contrast to the trajectory image, the image of an historic route "does not conjure up so strongly the image of a single all-decisive originative impetus." (See the top diagram in fig. 6-3, below, p. 120.) Rather, "it allows for the recognition that several streams of events may have flowed together to constitute the route and that, however important a particular past event was as a distinctive impetus, it was itself part of an historic route and not its absolute beginning." (See the bottom diagram in fig. 6-3.)

A most important feature of applying Whitehead's historic route of living occasions to the interpretation of religious texts is that it does not promote the idea of a self-identical "essence" of a religion. (See fig. 5-1, above, p. 107.) That is, the unity of the historic route is not found in a common essence at all points along the route. Instead, the unity is a causal continuity which allows for change. What happens in later occasions of the route is deeply affected by what happened in earlier occasions, but it is not simply repetitive. No feature of earlier occasions need be repeated unchanged in later occasions. What is distinctive about life is novelty. Identity through time for living occasions is not achieved by the endless repetition of a particular form; in fact, identity achieved through endless repetition is a form of decay because intensity of feeling and zest continually diminish from the levels present in earlier occasions of the route. On the contrary, for living occasions "identity through time is maintained when successors include, transform, and build upon what they have received. . . . The past is more resource for new and creative response to opportunities and challenges than pattern to be reiterated or preserved." Thus, the identity of an historic route of living occasions is found "more in the form of its change than in its unchanged preservation of particular forms."[7]

---

[7]Cobb, "Trajectories and Historic Routes," 94-95. In another essay ("The Authority of the Bible," in *Hermeneutics and the Worldliness of Faith: A Festschrift in Memory of Carl Michalson*, ed. Charles Courtney, Olin M. Ivey, and Gordon E. Michalson [*The Drew Gateway* 45 (1974–1975)] 194) Cobb made the following provocative statement: "Much theology is devoted to seeking an unchanging essence of Christian faith in the midst of obviously changing beliefs and social patterns. But what if there is no such essence? What if Christian faith is instead a force released in history through Jesus that can be traced only by its continuity—not by

In considerations of validity in interpretation and theological norms, therefore, what is needed is a way of discerning when change is the appropriate novel expression continuing an historic route and when it is betrayal breaking away from an historic route. Cobb suggested the following criteria:

> Change is appropriate development or healthy growth when central elements in the historic route encourage the emergence of novel forms capable at once of enlivening much of the content of that route and of appropriating potential contributions from other sources. Change is betrayal when, for the sake of appropriating elements foreign to the historic route, the continuing contribution of that route is curtailed or blocked.[8]

• Creative Transformation •

In order to appreciate fully this discussion of change verses repetition, one must view it in light of Whitehead's understanding of God's work of "creative transformation." In process thought, God is not simply the foundation of order but is also the goad toward novelty. Order and novelty are instruments in God's overall aim of creating intensity of harmonious feeling in the universe.[9]

---

its self-identity? Then the attempt to produce today the same effect originally achieved might be unresponsive to the claim that faith now makes upon us."

[8]Cobb, "Trajectories and Historic Routes," 95. It should be noted that the process understanding of historical development differs from both traditional Protestant and modern Catholic understandings. Protestants have tended to view the historical development of Christianity as a perversion of or a deviation from the normative essence, i.e., the first expression of Christianity. In an effort to avoid this negative evaluation of historical development, Catholics have viewed development as the unfolding of what is implicit in the normative essence; the full meaning of the first expression of Christianity becomes clear only through later development (e.g., later developments are read back into the New Testament as implied meanings). The Protestant understanding denigrates development, and the Catholic understanding robs the past of its ability to encounter the present as something foreign (past and present have been assimilated).

[9]Whitehead distinguished between "order as the condition for excellence, and order as stifling the freshness of living. . . . The art of progress is to preserve order amid change, and to preserve change amid order. Life refuses to be embalmed alive. The more prolonged the halt in some unrelieved system of order, the greater the crash of the dead society. . . . In either alternative of excess,

Growth—on the microcosmic or macrocosmic level—is not achieved simply by adding together the various discordant elements in the actual world of a concrescing subject. Discordant elements cannot be united in a single experience simply by addition. The easiest way to achieve a new synthesis is by blocking out the discordant elements (by means of negative prehensions). The trivial harmony which results lacks intensity of feeling, however. Whitehead labeled this approach "anaesthesia."[10] There is another approach. Although the various discordant elements cannot be brought into harmony as they stand, there may be a larger, more inclusive novel pattern which can contain the discordant elements in such a manner that the **contrast**[11] between them contributes to the intensity of the whole. This new pattern is not part of the world; rather, it comes from God (the initial aim). To the extent that the subject appropriates this new pattern, it experiences creative transformation.[12]

Because God works in the world through the process of creative transformation, the process interpreter will pay special attention to the way in which the Bible contributes toward this end. The propositions in Scripture-as-interpreted—that is, proposals of how events or reality might be viewed—are set alongside alternative propositions, from the Bible and from other sources.[13] But instead of immediately choosing between the disparate propo-

---

whether the past be lost, or be dominant, the present is enfeebled" (*Process and Reality*, 338-39).

[10]Whitehead, *Adventures of Ideas*, 256, 259, 275.

[11]A contrast is the unity had by the many components in a complex datum (e.g., holding many colors in a unified pattern, as in a kaleidoscope, as opposed to a single color). Contrast is the opposite of incompatibility, for incompatibility results in the exclusion of one or more elements to achieve (a more trivial) harmony. The more a subject holds the items of its experience in contrasts and contrasts of contrasts, the more it elicits depth and intensity of experience. (See the appendix for a more detailed discussion.)

[12]See Cobb and Griffin, *Process Theology: An Introductory Exposition*, 99.

[13]As Lyman Lundeen observed ("The Authority of the Word in a Process Perspective," *Encounter* 36 (1975): 298), for process thought "pluralism, the availability of alternatives, is not basically a problem but an opportunity. If freedom counts, then people need alternatives. In changing circumstances we need new options. A helpful sense of authority ought to free us to change." The process understanding of authority will be discussed below.

sitions, the process interpreter will seek to create a harmonious contrast of the propositions through a novel, more inclusive pattern, and thereby experience creative transformation.[14] Because creative transformation is the theological norm, Christians can be open to insights from other historic routes without breaking away from their own. This theological norm encourages interpreters to seek inclusion, to attempt to shed new light on old propositions by relating them to new propositions, to explore the possibility that propositions once experienced as (or assumed to be) incompatible may actually complement one another. A process hermeneutic does not presuppose that *all* propositions can be brought into harmonious contrasts. Nor does it presuppose that every transformation is creative; for transformation to be creative it must manifest openness toward other sources of meaning without abandoning previous sources, thereby resulting in an enlargement of perspective. Nevertheless, a process hermeneutic clearly aims at a goal quite different from that of most hermeneutical models.[15]

As Barry Woodbridge observed, interpreters may not sense the arrival of a kairotic moment for creative transformation of a text if they have not attended to its history of interpretation. "This is not to suggest that only historical scholars of scripture will be attuned to its new possibilities for feeling. But it may be that those who have attended to its function in the community where it is read and proclaimed find themselves in a better position to feel its relevance for the present hour."[16]

Yet one may ask why process theologians bother with the Bible. Process theology can stand on its own without biblical warrant. In fact, one can even argue that the Bible is not necessary for Christian existence.[17] Christian existence is genetically indebted

---

[14]The experience of creative transformation in the process of interpreting a text is similar to Gadamer's fusion of horizons. See Williamson, "Process Hermeneutics and Christianity's Post-Holocaust Reinterpretation of Itself," 82-85, for a comparison.

[15]David Lull ("What Is 'Process Hermeneutics'?" 194-96) has argued persuasively that the process notion of "creative transformation" is central to the biblical witness to the reality of God and to the uses of tradition within the Bible.

[16]Woodbridge, "An Assessment and Prospectus for a Process Hermeneutic," 124-25.

[17]As Augustine (*On Christian Doctrine* 1.39.43) noted, a person "supported by

to the events of its emergence in the first century CE,[18] but it is not dependent upon conscious knowledge of those events or conscious beliefs about them. "The indebtedness of a particular mode of existence to the past is largely on a preconscious level; thus, while knowledge and conscious beliefs about the Christian past are important, they are not all-controlling."[19]

Nevertheless, if one's theology is to *remain* Christian, i.e., is to maintain continuity with the Christian tradition, one must attend to the Bible. Conscious knowledge and beliefs do increase the effectiveness of the past in shaping one's present existence; consequently, attention to the Bible is important because the Bible records and interprets those events surrounding the first appearance of Christian existence. That this does not mean the mere repetition of some "essence" should, by now, be obvious. As John Cobb wrote:

> Rather than seeking an essential form of faith identical with that witnessed to in Scriptures, we must seek to discern the present movement of the spirit that is continuous with a movement begun in primitive Christianity.
>
> Even so the Bible remains authoritative. We can discriminate the process of faith within the present only as a trajectory whose early states are already discernible in the New Testament. Without attention to the origins, we cannot make reliable judgments in the present.[20]

This "process view" of biblical authority enables one to live from the past, in the present, toward the future.[21] That this description parallels the concrescence of an actual occasion is significant.

---

faith, hope, and charity, with an unshaken hold upon them, does not need the Scriptures except for the instruction of others. And many live by these three things in solitude without books."

[18]Cobb ('The Authority of the Bible," 198) affirmed that "wherever Christian existence is found we may assume some historical connection with Jesus Christ."

[19]Lull, "What Is 'Process Hermeneutics'?" 197.

[20]Cobb, "The Authority of the Bible," 201.

[21]See Norman Pittenger, *The Christian Church as Social Process* (Philadelphia: Westminster Press, 1971).

• The Community of Interpretation •

As was noted above, a process hermeneutic attributes a great deal of importance to the history of a religious tradition and the influence of the community upon the individual interpreter. Of course, other hermeneutical systems acknowledge the importance of this "community of interpretation"; but because process thought asserts that interpreters are internally related to their environment, the significance of the community is heightened. Thus, the community to which an interpreter belongs—for example, a particular faith group or the scholarly guild—determines to a considerable degree what he or she "sees" in a text.

But the significance of the community goes beyond simply influencing what the interpreter sees in a text. The individual's interpretation finds its confirmation *in part* within the community.[22] The individual's interpretation may either enhance the growth of the community or contribute to its decay. For a process hermeneutic, then, one criterion for a valid interpretation is that it results in the creative transformation of the interpreter's community.[23]

With this discussion of validity in interpretation and theological norms, the description of a process hermeneutic is complete. What now remains is an assessment of the hermeneutical theory (chapter 7) and an application of the hermeneutic to actual texts (part three).

---

[22]As Whitehead (*Process and Reality*, 151) observed, "the creative process is rhythmic: it swings from the publicity of many things to the individual privacy; and it swings back from the private individual to the publicity of the objectified individual."

[23]Woodbridge, "Process Hermeneutic: An Approach to Biblical Texts," 85, and Woodbridge, "An Assessment and Prospectus for a Process Hermeneutic," 126-27. In the words of Lyman T. Lundeen ("The Authority of the Word in a Process Perspective," 298), "Interpretations are . . . proposals for testing in experience."

Figure 6-1

Robinson's trajectory image (top diagram) implies the independence of trajectories A, B, and C.

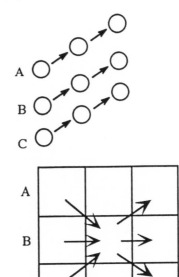

Whitehead's historic route of living occasions stresses the interrelationship of historic routes A, B, and C. (The interrelationship the bottom diagram shows of B is true also of A and C.)

Figure 6-2

The broken arrows in the top diagram represent the influence of the situational field through which the trajectory passes. The solid arrows represent the influence of past points on the trajectory.

The solid arrows in the bottom diagram represent prehensions of past occasions, including prehensions of the distant past both as mediated by the immediate past occasion and as prehended directly.

Robinson

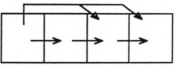

Whitehead

Figure 6-3

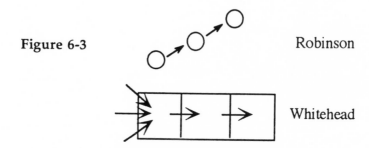

Robinson

Whitehead

Robinson's trajectory image (top diagram) implies that there is a single all-decisive originative impetus to the trajectory.

The arrows in the bottom diagram represent prehensions of past occasions. The occasion which initiates the historic route identified for study is itself part of an earlier historic route (or routes) and not its absolute beginning.

Chapter 7

Process Hermeneutic: An Assessment

The process hermeneutic described in the preceding chapters makes a number of contributions to the field of hermeneutical studies. Indeed, these contributions are substantial enough to enable the process-informed interpreter to move beyond the current hermeneutical impasse described in part one, as the following representative summary demonstrates.

• Author Intent or Indeterminate Meaning? •

Most recent hermeneutical options have challenged one of the most sacred canons of modern biblical scholarship: that the meaning of a text is to be found through reconstruction of the life situation of the author and original readers of a text, thereby enabling one to determine the author's intent. Although each has its own distinctive approach, many of these contemporary hermeneutical options affirm the indeterminacy of a text. Meaning is "open-ended, taking specific form only insofar as a reader makes a contribution to it."[1] Although these hermeneutical models acknowledge indeterminacy, a process hermeneutic renders the concept intelligible by grounding it in the general nature of reality. The abstraction necessary for the formation of words means that language can only approximate that to which it refers. Even those types of language that lie closest to the hypothetical point of complete determinacy manifest some degree of indeterminacy. (See

---

[1]Pregeant, "Where Is the Meaning?" 107.

fig. 4-4.) As a result, authors always say more than they intend. Moreover, the meaning of a text will change as it is experienced by different readers in different contexts. (See fig. 5-1.) Meaning resides "neither in the author's mind nor the text itself nor the reader alone in any simplistic sense; it rather comes to be in every moment of interaction between reader and text, wherein certain parameters of meaning—embodied in a text through an author's intentionality and the influence of language—are delivered to a reader who finally shapes *a* meaning for himself or herself in a particular moment."[2]

Although a process hermeneutic views the language of a text as indeterminate and its meaning as open-ended, it nevertheless restores the quest for the author as a legitimate, though elusive, focus of inquiry (contrary to many contemporary hermeneutical theories). Because language is capable of *some* degree of determinacy, authorial intention can be known to some extent. Thus, the quest for the author is a legitimate aspect of a process interpreter's task. (This legitimation of the quest for authorial intention, however, does not prevent an interpreter from approaching a text as an autonomous aesthetic object as well.)

• The Value of Religious Language •

Individuals with a positivistic bent discount religious language as meaningless; proponents of the New Hermeneutic sharply distinguish between discursive, everyday language and evocative, authentically religious language. In marked contrast, process interpreters relativize these distinctions because they recognize that all language is relatively (in)determinate, subjective, and value-laden. As a result, process interpreters value religious language as much as scientific language, although they recognize the difference between the two. However, process interpreters avoid the linguistic solipsism inherent when the distinction between religious language and everyday language is exaggerated as it is in the New Hermeneutic. Because no language, even religious language, is

---

[2]Pregeant, "Where Is the Meaning?" 112.

completely indeterminate, the possibility exists for genuine communication.

On a related note, one of the most attractive aspects of process thought is its ability to overcome the split between the natural sciences and the humanities. Throughout the modern period humanists have been threatened by the encroachment of the scientific mode of knowledge and understanding (with its attending reductionism, positivism, and determinism). As Beardslee remarked, "the close connection between hermeneutics and phenomenology is no accident." Only the analysis of consciousness, it was thought, could preserve the distinctively human. In overcoming Kantian dualism (see chapter 2), Whitehead brought scientific and humanistic understanding and knowledge into a comprehensive frame of discourse where they can interact, yet in a manner which recognizes the value of both methods. Whitehead demonstrated that "there is a continuum of methods of knowing reality" and in the process reduced "the reductionism, positivism, and determinism of empirical methods by showing that these methods, useful and necessary as they are, are relative."[3] As a result, the two ways of knowing can relate to one another in fruitful ways.

• The Excision of Problematic Elements •

Because they focus on logical truth or falsity, existential authenticity or inauthenticity, or contemporary relevance or irrelevance, most hermeneutical approaches can only commend a narrow portion of most biblical texts to the modern reader. In contrast, a process hermeneutic commends far more of the content of a text for the following reasons. First, because the propositions evoked by a text are rooted in objective events in the past actual world of the author and reader (by means of the propositions' logical subjects) and presuppose a universe exhibiting some general systematic metaphysical character, a text's "subject matter" cannot be confined to the realm of existential self-understanding. A text may be legitimately viewed as concerned with the natural world and God

---

[3]Beardslee, "Whitehead and Hermeneutic," 32, and Beardslee, "Recent Hermeneutics and Process Thought," 69.

as well as with the human situation.[4] Second, the propositions evoked by a text are viewed as lures for feeling whose interest is far more important than their truth or falsity. Thus, process interpreters will not remove "problematic" elements of a text—e.g., demythologizing aspects of a text failing to conform to the interpreters' worldview—because such a priori excisions or "translations" eliminate propositions whose interest might lead to novel interpretations. Third, process interpreters also seek to avoid either/or choices. When faced with binary opposites, paradoxes, or tensions, process interpreters approach the situation not as demanding an immediate either/or choice but rather as providing the opportunity of formulating a more inclusive contrast. Fourth, the greater an entity's ability to hold diverse elements of its experience in the harmony of a contrast, the greater is its intensity of experience. This suggests that interpreters who seek to eliminate the problematic features of a text or who too quickly make an either/or choice reduce the level of contrasts within their interpretive experience, whereas those who retain these features actually intensify the aesthetic value of their experience. Thus, as Barry Woodbridge noted, a process hermeneutic can

> rescue from Jeffersonian excision . . . texts whose cosmology or psychology or theology runs counter to our modern sensibilities. They may not be "true" in the sense of conforming to our grasp

---

[4]Lewis S. Ford commented:
Without question existential emphases upon risk, subjective appropriation, and decision must be affirmed, and the call to authentic openness may be appreciated . . . but as a total context existential philosophy is methodologically too restrictive. If faith can only be expressed in terms of human encounter, such that we are precluded from using any cosmological framework in expressing our understanding of God, then we have no way of appreciating God's activity and manifestation of concern toward the rest of the created order. We are in danger of succumbing to a global *anthropocentricity* in our existential preoccupation, precisely at a time when members of the scientific community are reckoning with the strong probability of intelligent life inhabiting other worlds within our universe.
"Biblical Recital and Process Philosophy: Some Whiteheadian Suggestions for Old Testament Hermeneutics," *Interpretation* 26 (1972): 200; emphasis added. To Ford's comment I would add that anthropocentricity is totally inappropriate at a time when human actions are threatening the very life of the planet.

of reality, but they may nevertheless be very interesting (inspiring) as a lure for feeling about how the world . . . *might be.* . . . By holding our attention to texts which may seem neither true or relevant, a process exegesis may allow biblical texts to critique our presuppositions about reality, thereby executing more fully the New Hermeneutic's insistence that the text address us, not vice versa. . . .[5]

This entertainment of problematic elements in a text includes ideas opposed to process thought.[6] Contrary to many hermeneutical models, a process hermeneutic encourages special attention to those dimensions of a text opposed to its own worldview. There are two reasons for this. First, the entertainment of lures foreign to the interpreter's sensibilities can result in the emergence of a novel pattern large enough to include both the foreign and the familiar in a harmonious contrast. When this occurs, the interpreter's perspective is creatively transformed. Second, "process thought and categories can never be adequately expressed and must always be subject to correction and revision." This acknowledgement means that a process hermeneutic must be able to transcend its present formulation, but this is possible only if it is open to ideas that oppose it.[7]

• The Essentialist vs the Evolutionary Approach •

Many hermeneutical theories—even some of those which acknowledge the indeterminacy of language (for example, Bultmann)—have as their goal the extraction of the "essence" of the

---

[5]Barry Woodbridge, "An Assessment and Prospectus for a Process Hermeneutic," 123. See also Beardslee, "Whitehead and Hermeneutic," 35-36. The New Hermeneutic's assertion that the text interprets the reader, not vice versa, reflects a theme common to many current hermeneutical models. A process hermeneutic, however, does not need to hypostatize the text to account for the vigor of the reader's response. The vigor is due to the reader entertaining the propositions evoked by the text in the process of his or her self-creation. Thus, the reader, not the text, is the active agent.

[6]Although some process-informed readings of biblical texts (see bibliography) have focused mainly or exclusively on aspects of texts compatible with process categories, this limited focus is not a feature of a process hermeneutic per se.

[7]Woodbridge, "An Assessment and Prospectus for a Process Hermeneutic," 127; and idem, "Process Hermeneutic: An Approach to Biblical Texts," 84.

text from its historical and cultural garb and its restatement in modern terms. The present meaning of the text can only deviate within narrow confines from what it originally meant. In contrast to this "essentialist" approach, a process hermeneutic affirms an "evolutionary" or "trajectory" approach. As has been demonstrated, there is a growing edge to tradition. (See fig. 5-1.) Three points follow from this notion. First, as was noted above, what a text might come to mean can be more important than anything it has meant in the past. Thus, the Bible can be seen as a *living* Word. Second, the search for the "center" or "unity" of the Hebrew Bible, New Testament, or the Bible as a whole is misguided. Rather than seeking this center—with its implication that other aspects are peripheral—the process interpreter would view the individual Testaments and the Bible as being composed of continuously developing and interacting historic routes. And third, "if the evolutionary nature of texts calls for continuous and disciplined exposure to them, then a process hermeneutic may well contribute to a renewed theology of proclamation and spirituality."[8] Preaching and Bible reading are seen in a new light if meaning is not exhausted at any one time.[9] Therefore, repeated exposure to the Bible does not entail the mere repetition of previous perceptions but rather provides the opportunity for adventures of novelty and creative transformation.

• The Nature of Authority •

The perspectival nature of all human experience creates a problem with regard to the notion of biblical authority. For many people the idea of authority, biblical or otherwise, is incompatible with partial perspectives and freedom. (Of course, the reason some people desire absolute authority is that it removes the risk and

---

[8]Woodbridge, "An Assessment and Prospectus for a Process Hermeneutic," 124-25.

[9]For a process view of preaching see William A. Beardslee, John B. Cobb, Jr., David J. Lull, Russell Pregeant, Theodore J. Weeden, Sr., and Barry A. Woodbridge, *Biblical Preaching on the Death of Jesus* (Nashville: Abingdon Press, 1989); and Clark M. Williamson and Ronald J. Allen, *A Credible and Timely Word: Process Theology and Preaching* (St. Louis: Chalice Press, 1991).

ambiguity involved in decision making; it provides an unchanging foundation for knowledge and action.) Philosophers and theologians have wrestled with this problem for centuries, but in recent years society in general has come to experience the crisis provoked by the absence of final authorities. No authorities presently command widespread assent. As long as partial perspectives and freedom are perceived to be incompatible with the notion of authority, the crisis will be unresolvable. But because process metaphysics conceives of knowledge and reality in more dynamic and open-ended terms—relativity and evolution are important categories in process thought—the notion of authority is conceived in terms which not only allow but require partial perspectives and freedom. Moreover, the nature of authority arising from a process view of reality is persuasive[10] rather than coercive: "it is the attraction of an invitation, the appeal of intrinsic worth or the motivating vision of possibility." And because of the creative advance of the world, "all authoritative factors require new interpretation and reappropriation in changing circumstances. They not only allow but require further development."[11] In the process model, then, authority is adequate, not absolute. Because partial knowledge and partial truth are all that is available, dogmatic claims on any subject are entirely inappropriate.

---

[10]Indeed, Whitehead described God, the ultimate authority, as "the poet of the world, with tender patience leading it by his vision of truth, beauty, and goodness" (*Process and Reality*, 346). And as William A. Beardslee observed:

Central as persuasion is to process thinking, it may often be tacitly identified with discursive, coherent, logical persuasion when the category is transferred into the religious sphere. That persuasion as it functions most deeply in faith often takes place by reversal, paradox, or hyperbole is an insight that needs to be worked out more thoroughly in process interpretation of faith.

"Narrative Form in the New Testament and Process Theology" *Encounter* 36 (1975): 312.

[11]Lundeen, "The Authority of the Word in a Process Perspective," 291, 296. Lundeen concluded (299):

The appeal to experience . . . allows us to be pragmatic about authorities. That's honest because in the long run no one follows authorities that do not somehow provide a satisfying and helpful approach to life itself. . . . The authority of the [Bible] is its experienced sufficiency not necessity.

• History, Freedom, and Divine Activity •

Process thought allows an interpreter to have a new appreciation of history. During the modern period history had come to be viewed as a closed system of cause and effect thereby eliminating human freedom (apart from some form of idealistic philosophy such as existentialism). According to process metaphysics, however, history contains both conditioning or determining factors (the past actual world) and freedom (the initial aim and the becoming occasion's self-creativity). Moreover, contrary to the modern view of history, the process view does not exclude God from acting in history—although God's activity is largely confined to the preconscious level of temporal concrescence (the initial aim), God's power is persuasive not coercive, and God's potential influence as "the ground of novelty" is much more significant with respect to high-grade occasions such as those constituting animal and human psyches (because these occasions have a greater capacity for self-creation). One can again speak of God as an important causal factor in history legitimately and without recourse to Kantian dualism.[12]

• Symbolism •

A process hermeneutic has the potential of making significant contributions to the current discussion of symbolism. Although phenomenological interpreters such as Paul Ricoeur "are concerned to analyze layers of experience which lie behind what is clearly experienced in consciousness," they do not "make affirmations about what lies beyond the scope of that which the mind forms." One contribution of process thought lies in its understanding of the composite nature of symbolic reference. Because presentational immediacy refers to causal efficacy, there is a real link to the external world in symbolism (although process thought remains critical of any naïve correspondence view). This extralinguistic aspect of symbolism means that no longer is the interpreter

---

[12]For an excellent discussion of this matter see David R. Griffin, "Relativism, Divine Causation, and Biblical Theology," *Encounter* 36 (1975): 342-60.

"locked into a language-limited universe." Moreover, because the initial aim of God is a lure guiding the concrescence of an actual occasion, the formation of symbols is also linked to God. Thus, a process hermeneutic offers two substantial contributions to the current discussion of symbolism.[13]

• Narrative and Myth •

A process hermeneutic also holds the promise of contributing to the contemporary discussion concerning narrative. In a narrative, events are ushered into some sort of meaningful succession through the interpretive lens of an organizing vision or myth of what life is intended to be. Although in most ancient narratives this organizing myth is fixed, many recent narratives operate with a changing myth, one moving "in the direction of more inclusiveness, as it is enriched by its interaction with experience."[14] Process thought certainly has affinity with this newer notion, but its contribution to the discussion of narrative is not limited to this.

One of the issues debated today is "how symbols become so related that they present us with an ordered sequence, so that a complex of symbolic density can become an orienting myth." One explanation is the structural analysis of myth associated with Claude Lévi-Strauss. According to this view, experience offers "sets of oppositions between contrasting and perhaps often irreconcilable elements which have none the less to be brought into some kind of relation." In this view, "the emphasis is not on any final resolution of the tension between opposites, but on the alternation and tension between insistently contrasting elements in experience." Although a process hermeneutic acknowledges that tension often arises between elements of experience, process thought encourages transforming the apparently irreconcilable elements into members of a contrast by means of a novel, more inclusive pattern. Thus, in contrast to the structural analysis of myth which emphasizes binary opposites or contradictions in human experi-

---

[13]Beardslee, "Narrative Form in the New Testament and Process Theology," 303-304, and Beardslee, "Whitehead and Hermeneutic," 34.

[14]Beardslee, "Narrative Form in the New Testament and Process Theology," 302.

ence, the process analysis underscores the unity and integrity of existence. Moreover, because "Whitehead took the actual succession of experiences far more seriously than most modern philosophers have done," the process analysis of myth places more emphasis on successiveness than does nontemporal structural analysis.[15] Of course, this successiveness is open to novel happenings which disrupt the expected sequence.

• Confessionalism or Public Discussion? •

Although faith may be a legitimate goal of biblical studies, "it cannot be the starting point unless the circle of conversation is limited to a closed group of believers, in isolation from society at large."[16] Thus John Collins voiced his agreement with the common complaint that today there is a widespread drift toward confessionalism, as attested to by such approaches as canonical criticism. Because a process hermeneutic is undergirded by an explicit metaphysical system which is available for public discussion, a process interpreter can affirm that biblical studies *can and should* have a public character as well as address the needs of faith communities.

• The Role of the Interpreter's Community •

Because the process view of reality is social in nature, it emphasizes the importance of community (as opposed to pure individualism) for the hermeneutical enterprise. The interpreter's community of interpretation—be it the scholarly guild or a particular faith community (both are historic routes of living occasions)—influences *to a degree* one's interpretation of a biblical text, and one's interpretation finds its confirmation *in part* within that community. This dimension of process interpretation promises to restore to biblical studies the sociopolitical relevance lost in the more individualistic existential interpretation and demanded by liberation theology.[17]

---

[15]Beardslee, "Narrative Form in the New Testament and Process Theology," 304.

[16]John J. Collins, "Process Hermeneutic: Promise and Problems," *Semeia* 24 (1982): 107-108, 115.

[17]Woodbridge, "Process Hermeneutic: An Approach to Biblical Texts," 85; and

• New Categories for Interpretation •

Several biblical scholars have remarked that the categories of process thought have enabled them to articulate more adequately certain biblical ideas and concepts which are not readily express-ible in substance-thinking terminology. For example, Kent Harold Richards testified that the historic route of living occasions enabled him better to explain "both the common forms transmitted in a tradition as well as the transmission or canalization of novelty."[18] Thus, one can view a process hermeneutic as an attempt to meet the call of James Robinson and Helmut Koester for the develop-ment of new categories for biblical interpretation.[19] And because a process hermeneutic is based on a well-defined metaphysical system, doubtless its dissemination will make interpreters more aware of their own metaphysical assumptions, even if they do not adopt a process hermeneutic.

• A Descriptive or Hermeneutical Task? •

The customary distinction between what a text "meant" and what it "means," with the accompanying designation of the former as "descriptive" and the latter as "hermeneutical," is transcended in a process hermeneutic. The entire process is viewed as herme-neutical; "purely descriptive" methodologies are not so pure as they were once believed.

• Inspiration and Revelation •

Finally, the traditional concepts of inspiration (or illumination) and revelation can be accounted for in a process hermeneutic. In the initial phase of concrescence, each occasion prehends God's initial aim for it, that lure for feeling which leads to the highest degree of self-actualization possible at that moment. This initial

---

idem, "An Assessment and Prospectus for a Process Hermeneutic," 127.

[18]Richards, "Beyond Bruxism," 471.

[19]See James M. Robinson and Helmut Koester, *Trajectories through Early Christianity* (Philadelphia: Fortress Press, 1971).

aim is God's act of "inspiration."[20] Insofar as an occasion's final subjective aim is in accord with the initial aim, the efficient causation of God is maximized. When this accord is great, it may be consciously felt as God's initiative, and "revelation" occurs. Clearly, this understanding of revelation parallels aspects of existential theology, for God initiates the relationship and demands a human response of self-creation. The process understanding, however, is not hampered by a worldview which excludes divine activity.[21]

All too often books dealing with hermeneutics are entirely theoretical in nature and hence conclude at this point. Part three of the present book, however, attempts to overcome this shortcoming by applying the process hermeneutic developed in part two to several well-known exegetical difficulties. I have chosen to work with the Apocalypse to John because many contemporary interpreters think that there is little of theological or ethical value in the Apocalypse. What will the application of a process hermeneutic reveal?

---

[20]Thus God is involved in both the writing and interpretation of a text.

[21]See Jerry D. Korsmeyer, "A Resonance Model for Revelation," *Process Studies* 6 (1976): 195-96; and Whitehead, *Religion in the Making*.

Part Three

Process Hermeneutic Applied

Chapter 8

The Lamb and the Beast: The Apocalypse of Power

Revelation 4–5 in Process Hermeneutic[*]

In this chapter the process hermeneutic formulated in part two will be used to undergird the interpretation of a biblical text. As the title intimates,[1] this study will focus on the understanding of power—divine and human—in the Apocalypse to John. In order to set the stage for this adventure in interpretation, two notions of power must be contrasted.

• Two Conceptions of Power •

The view of God expressed in classical theism[2] has dominated the Western world. Two aspects of this portrait are important for

---

[*]An earlier version of this chapter appeared as "Divine Power in the Apocalypse to John: Revelation 4–5 in Process Hermeneutic," in *Society of Biblical Literature 1993 Seminar Papers*, ed. Eugene H. Lovering, Jr. (Atlanta: Scholars Press, 1993).

[1]The word "apocalypse" means an unveiling, a revelation. In the chapter title the term performs a double duty: it refers to the Apocalypse to John, and it refers to the fact that a particular notion of power—divine and human—is unveiled in the Apocalypse to John.

[2]Classical theism refers to medieval scholarship (and its present day remnants) which Charles Hartshorne characterized as "a compromise between a not-very-well-understood Greek philosophy and a not-very-scholarly interpretation of sacred writings." *Omnipotence and other Theological Mistakes* (Albany: SUNY Press, 1984) 43.

understanding what has become the dominant conception of divine power. First, God is viewed as omnipotent in the sense of determining or controlling all that happens. All talk of genuine creaturely freedom or decision making is double-talk.[3] Second, God is completely impassive, incapable of feeling the feelings of others. God influences all things, but nothing influences God; God's power is unilateral. To be sure, God is viewed as a God of love, but the word love is emptied of a most essential element, the element of sympathy, of feeling the feelings of others. Thus, divine love—frequently termed agape—is merely beneficence, totally unmoved by creaturely sufferings or joy.

Process thinkers have criticized the classical view of divine power on several points. First, this definition of divine power results in the notoriously insoluble problem of evil. Second, this understanding of omnipotence is not asserted unambiguously by either Greek philosophy or the Judeo-Christian Scriptures. And third, process metaphysics suggests a different understanding of divine power, one which is found in Greek philosophy and the

---

[3]Of course, classical theologians speak of human free will, but such talk is misleading. Hartshorne (*Omnipotence and Other Theological Mistakes*, 11-12) simply labeled it "double-talk": God decides that a person shall perform a certain act, but the divine decision is that the act shall be performed "freely."

David Ray Griffin ("Faith and Spiritual Discipline: A Comparison of Augustinian and Process Theologies," *Faith and Philosophy* 3 [1986]: 59-61, 65) suggested that the confusion results from a failure to recognize a threefold distinction in human freedom: cosmological freedom (freedom in relation to other finite things in the cosmos), theological freedom (freedom in relation to God), and axiological freedom (the ability to actualize desired ideas or values). For example, in the Augustinian-Pelagian debate, both parties affirmed what Griffin labeled cosmological freedom. But in denying the Pelagian assertion that divine grace was not needed for living the Christian life (axiological freedom), Augustine failed to distinguish between axiological freedom and theological freedom; God's (irresistible) grace (unilaterally) provides faith (predestination) as well as the possibility of living the Christian life. According to Griffin, Augustine may have been closer to the truth in regard to axiological freedom, but the Pelagians were closer in regard to theological freedom. According to process thought, "prevenient grace consists in the provision of possibilities that free us from the necessity of being simply determined by the past. Accordingly, it is precisely *God's causal influence on us that provides us with both cosmological freedom and the possibility of axiological freedom.* And yet this divine causal influence works in such a way that *we also have theological freedom*" (65).

Bible. For the purpose at hand, the process conception of power can be divided into two aspects.

The first aspect of the process definition is that *divine power is persuasive and all-influencing rather than coercive and all-controlling.* God does influence every actual occasion, but this operation of divine power is not determinative. God seeks to lure or persuade each actual occasion toward the optimum mode for its development, but each occasion is genuinely free[4] to choose the degree to which it follows the divine aim in its concrescence. Thus, rather than God's power being coercive and all-controlling, it is persuasive and all-influencing.

The second aspect of the process definition is that *divine power is relational rather than unilateral.* Upon completion of its concrescence, each actual occasion is prehended or felt by God in the consequent nature. This feeling is then integrated with God's feelings of the entire world within the primordial nature of harmonized possibilities; thus, what each actual occasion becomes influences the divine concrescence. Therefore, if unilateral power is the ability to produce effects in others and is essentially one-directional in its workings—that is, the capacity to influence others without being influenced—and if relational power is the ability both to produce and to undergo an effect—that is, the capacity to influence others and to be influenced by others[5]—then it is obvious that according to the process model God's power is relational not unilateral.[6]

Because the initial aim of God is for the welfare of the actual occasion, and because the power of God is relational, one might be tempted to refer to the process understanding of divine power as "love." Caution must be exercised at this point, however. Because classical theism views God as completely impassive, incapable of feeling the feelings of others, it therefore understands God's

---

[4]In process thought, there are degrees of freedom ranging from negligible (e.g., subatomic particles) to considerable (e.g., human beings).

[5]Cf. Bernard Loomer, "Two Conceptions of Power," *Process Studies* 6 (1976): 5-21.

[6]Although this paragraph and the preceding paragraph have discussed the relation of divine power on the microcosmic level, the basic principles apply to the macrocosmic world of enduring objects, animals, and people.

love—agape—to be unilateral. According to the process model, however, God's love is not only creative (influencing others), it is also responsive (capable of being influenced). Consequently, process theologians John Cobb and David Griffin use the phrase "creative-responsive love" to refer to God's power;[7] process-feminist theologian Rita Nakashima Brock prefers the expression "erotic power."[8]

Now a person's conception of divine power greatly influences his or her understanding of power on the human level; in fact, one's view of human power differs from one's understanding of divine power only in quantity, not quality. Therefore, if God's power is viewed as coercive, all-controlling, and unilateral, the corresponding human power will be understood as "the capacity to influence, guide, adjust, manipulate, shape, control, or transform the human or natural environment in order to advance one's purpose."[9] Seven consequences of this understanding of human power should be noted.

(1) This view of power operates so as to make the other a function of one's own ends, even when one's aims include what is thought to be the good of the other. (2) One's size or stature and self-worth are correlative to one's place in the scale of the inevitable inequalities of existence. A gain in power by the other is experienced as a loss of one's own power; consequently, one's size and self-worth are diminished. (3) Accordingly, the other is often perceived as a threat; being influenced by the other is experienced as weakness; and dependence on another is a reflection of personal inadequacy. (4) If individuals are emergents from their relationships, as the social sciences and process thought affirm, then the practice of unilateral power blocks the full flow of energy that could be productive of the emergence of greater-sized individuals. (5) This understanding of power results in wearing the blinders of specialized concerns. One tends to deal only with those aspects of the human or natural environment that are relevant to one's

---

[7]Cobb and Griffin, *Process Theology*, 41-62.

[8]Rita Nakashima Brock, *Journeys by Heart: A Christology of Erotic Power* (New York: Crossroad, 1988).

[9]Loomer, "Two Conceptions of Power," 8. The following analysis of coercive, controlling, unilateral human power is based upon Loomer, 8-16.

narrowly defined purposes. The gross inadequacy of this understanding is vividly revealed in recent liberation movements among women, blacks, the aged, and third-world nations as well as in the ecological crisis. (6) Because the continued practice of this form of power breeds an insensitivity to the presence of others, it is antithetical to many of the deeper dimensions of the religious life. One becomes insensitive not only to other people and the environment but to the presence and will of God as well. (7) Although this understanding of power has dominated the Western world—for example, political and economic systems; the ordering of society; many educational philosophies and methods; the relationship between the sexes, races, and generations; and the reshaping and exploiting of the environment—there have always been those who sought to counteract its destructiveness by means of love. Unfortunately, love has been understood in terms of classical theism also—that is, concern for the good of the other with no concern for self, as well as not allowing the self to be influenced by the other.

But if one views God's power as persuasive, all-influencing, and relational, the corresponding understanding of human power will be radically different. Five consequences of this understanding of human power should be noted.[10] (1) The ability to absorb an influence will be viewed as much a mark of power as the strength involved in exerting an influence. Receiving an influence requires active openness rather than unresponsive passivity. (2) One's reception of the other indicates that one is, or will become, large enough to make room for the other within oneself. Size, then, is dependent upon the extent to which one can be influenced by another without loosing one's own identity and freedom. (3) Humans are communal individuals; one lives in society, and society quite literally lives in oneself. To a large extent, one's life is a gift from those who make up the societal context in which one lives. This relational view of the self stands in sharp contrast to the substantive view which posits that the self has its inner being within itself. According to the substantive view, the self has relationships, but its essential being is not composed of these

---

[10]The following analysis of persuasive, influencing, relational human power is based upon Loomer, "Two Conceptions of Power," 17-31.

relationships; the self has experiences, but the self is to be distinguished from these experiences. The process or relational view of the self posits just the opposite. The self is composed of its relationships; the self is its experiences. (4) Thus, power is viewed as the creation and enhancement of mutually internal relationships, relationships in which all participating members are transformed into individuals of greater size. Creating and sustaining such relationships requires an openness to being influenced as well as to influencing others. (5) The cost involved in sustaining and enhancing such relationships can be enormous: patience, emotional strength, trust, hope, and above all the willingness to suffer. When power is exercised in terms of classical theism, the inescapable inequalities of life lead to the stronger dominating the weaker and claiming a disproportionate share of the world's resources. Conversely, when power is exercised in terms of process theology, those of greater size must undergo greater suffering and bear a greater burden in sustaining these relationships—for as Jesus said, "from everyone who has been given much, much will be required" (Luke 12:48).

In light of the preceding discussion of two conceptions of power, doubtless many will think that I have chosen to apply a process hermeneutic to one of the least promising genres of biblical literature. After all, many New Testament scholars quote with approval D. H. Lawrence's estimation of the Apocalypse to John. He felt there were two kinds of Christianity: one focused on Jesus and the love command; the other focused on the Apocalypse with its sanctification of the will to power and envy. Thus for him, Revelation is the "Judas" of the New Testament.[11] Whitehead himself called the Apocalypse "barbaric" in that its notion of "the absolute despot" leads to "the undoing of Christian intuition" (that is, the doctrine of grace).[12] Yet two factors make sense of my choice of text. First, the process hermeneutic formulated in part two claims to be applicable to all texts, not just those which evoke propositions compatible with process thought. Second, recent developments in the study of early Christian apocalyptic literature

---

[11]D. H. Lawrence, *Apocalypse* (Harmondsworth UK: Penguin, 1974) 14-15.
[12]Whitehead, *Adventures of Ideas*, 170.

have made new understandings of the Apocalypse to John possible.

• Recent Study in Early Christian Apocalypticism and the Apocalypse to John •

For many years early Christian apocalypticism was not the subject of comprehensive study. This neglect was largely due to the conviction that early Christian apocalyptic texts were expressions of Jewish apocalypticism rather than an independent phenomenon. In recent years Jewish apocalypticism, and consequently Christian apocalypticism as well, have come to be viewed as peculiar expressions within the development of Hellenistic syncretism. The result of this new approach is that although the continuity of Christian apocalypticism with Jewish apocalypticism is still affirmed, scholars now maintain that it has its own distinct perspective.

Through the work of various groups[13] considerable light has been shed on the distinct perspective of early Christian apocalypticism in general and the Apocalypse to John in particular. A thorough discussion of this perspective would take us far afield, but several aspects of this early Christian perspective have definite bearing on the subject at hand and so warrant review. For ease of presentation, recent scholarly findings will be organized under three rubrics: genre analysis; sociohistorical analysis; and literary analysis.

---

[13]Most notably the Apocalypse Group of the SBL Genres Project (*Apocalypse: The Morphology of a Genre*, ed. John J. Collins, *Semeia* 14 [Missoula MT: Scholars Press, 1979]); the 1979 Louvain Colloquium on the Book of Revelation (J. Lambrecht, ed., *L'Apocalypse johannique et l'Apocalyptique dans le Nouveau Testament* [Leuven: Leuven University Press, 1980]); the International Colloquium on Apocalypticism at Uppsala in 1979 (*Apocalypticism in the Mediterranean World and the Near East*, ed. David Hellholm [Tübingen: J. C. B. Mohr, 1983]); the SBL Early Christian Apocalypticism Seminar (*Early Christian Apocalypticism: Genre and Social Setting*, ed. Adela Yarbro Collins, *Semeia* 36 [Decatur, GA: Scholars Press, 1986]); and the current SBL Reading the Apocalypse: the Intersection of Literary and Social Methods Seminar.

• Genre Analysis •

Characteristic of Christian—but not Jewish—apocalypses is an emphasis on paraenesis. The extensive use of paraenesis and the fact that Revelation claims to be prophecy[14] have led several scholars to conclude that early Christian apocalyptic is an expression of early Christian prophecy.[15] Consequently, the alternative, either prophetic or apocalyptic, derived from the discussion of Jewish apocalyptic origins, should not be applied to early Christian apocalyptic in general or the Book of Revelation in particular.

The observation that Revelation is not a thoroughgoing apocalypse but rather uses apocalyptic language and imagery within the context of prophecy is significant. Like prophecy, process thought views the future as organically growing out of the past by means of the lure of God; the divine lure does not cancel out genuine creaturely freedom. Process thought differs sharply with thoroughgoing apocalyptic expectation because such expectation is based upon divine determinism and cataclysmic interruption.[16]

• Sociohistorical Analysis •

For centuries interpreters of Revelation have assumed that the crisis which occasioned the book was official, government-sponsored persecution under Domitian. Recent studies, however, have cast doubt on this widely held hypothesis.[17] Evidence for a Domitianic persecution of Christians is quite slim; in fact, there is

---

[14]Rev 1:3; 22:7, 10, 18, 19. Cf. Rev 10:7, 11; 11:3, 6, 10, 18; 16:6; 18:20, 24; 19:10; 22:6, 9.

[15]E.g., Elisabeth Schüssler Fiorenza, "The Phenomenon of Early Christian Apocalyptic," in *Apocalypticism in the Mediterranean World and the Near East*, ed. David Hellholm (Tübingen: J. C. B. Mohr, 1983) 300; and "Apokalypsis and Propheteia: The Book of Revelation in the Context of Early Christian Prophecy," in *L'Apocalypse johannique et l'Apocalyptique dans le Nouveau Testament*, ed. J. Lambrecht (Leuven: Leuven University Press, 1980). See also M. Eugene Boring, "The Theology of Revelation: 'The Lord Our God the Almighty Reigns,'" *Interpretation* 40 (1986): 257-69, esp. n. 9.

[16]Lewis S. Ford, *The Lure of God: A Biblical Background for Process Theism* (Philadelphia: Fortress Press, 1978) 24, 31.

[17]E.g., Adela Yarbro Collins, *Crisis & Catharsis: The Power of the Apocalypse* (Philadelphia: Westminster Press, 1984); and Leonard Thompson, "A Sociological Analysis of Tribulation in the Apocalypse of John," *Semeia* 36 (1986): 147-74.

no reliable evidence clearly supporting the hypothesis. This is not to deny that the readers were experiencing persecution; on the contrary, Revelation gives evidence of persecution, past and present (1:9; 2:13; 6:9-11). What is called into question is the assumption that this persecution resulted from a new government policy aimed at Christians.

Recent sociohistorical studies suggest that the social status of Christians in Asia Minor was being threatened on several fronts. Christians were being ostracized and occasionally accused before the authorities by their Jewish neighbors. Gentiles despised the Christians because of their suspicious beliefs and practices, and, like the Jews, accused them before the magistrates. Moreover, the tension between rich and poor frequently erupted during times of stress and food shortages. The Christians, generally poor and disenfranchised themselves, probably sympathized with the poor in these conflicts, which again brought them into confrontation with the authorities. As a result of these situations, the Roman magistrates increasingly looked with disfavor upon Christians and condemned their endurance as stubborn disobedience. Apparently, one means used to test the loyalty of a person accused before the authorities was willingness to participate in the imperial cult. If they persistently refused to participate, Christians were condemned to death; their endurance was perceived as stubborn disobedience and disloyalty to the state.[18]

Faced with this multifaceted crisis in which their opponents' power was clearly coercive, controlling, and unilateral, Christian

---

[18]Cf. Adela Yarbro Collins, *Crisis and Catharsis: The Power of the Apocalypse*, 84-110, and J. P. M. Sweet, *Revelation*, Westminster Pelican Commentaries, ed. D. E. Nineham (Philadelphia: Westminster Press, 1979) 24-35. Thompson ("A Sociological Analysis of Tribulation in the Apocalypse of John," 169-70) suggested that

if Pliny's correspondence is typical, the populus was more adamant than Roman officials in bringing Christians to trial. . . . Trajan (probably following guidelines from the time of Domitian) directs Pliny not to listen to anonymous accusations and not to initiate prosecution by seeking Christians out. At the same time Christianity is viewed clearly as a social ill to be dealt with, if Christians are brought before a tribunal; for in that case they would probably be killed if, after due opportunity was given to them, they did not confess the religious dimensions of the common, public Roman life.

leaders proposed two quite different responses.[19] One group of leaders—represented in Revelation by the Nicolaitans, the Balaamites, and Jezebel—advocated participation in civic life to counter the antipathy Christians experienced. Such a solution amounted to embracing their opponents' conception of power. The other group of Christian leaders—represented by John—called for a Christian communal life of social radicalism; no accommodation was allowed. As will be demonstrated below, this solution necessitated a rejection of their opponents' conception of power in favor of a radically different understanding of power.

• Literary Analysis •

A significant observation of recent studies is that in early Christian apocalyptic texts, apocalyptic motifs and symbols of salvation are applied not only to future expectations but also to the present and the past of Christ and Christians. Whereas Jewish apocalyptic authors hoped for the imminent intervention of God and eschatological salvation, early Christian apocalyptic writers believed that the end events had already been inaugurated in the person of Jesus the Christ.[20] This conviction found expression in both futuristic *and* realized eschatological language. According to Elisabeth Schüssler Fiorenza, eschatological language can function in two distinct ways. First, by means of eschatological language authors can "provide an alternative vision of the world and its determinative powers in order to encourage alternative community structures and to interpret the Christians' experience of persecution and oppressive reality undermining their faith conviction that Christ is the Lord of the world and God [is] the creator of the cosmos." Or second, authors can "appeal to apocalyptic imagery and eschatological projection in their description of the 'afterlife'

---

[19]David Barr ("The Apocalypse of John as Oral Enactment," *Interpretation* 40 [1986]: 243-56) labeled this "a struggle between prophets." As Boring noted ("The Theology of Revelation," 261-62), *a prophet's ministry is hermeneutical in nature*: a prophet interprets history, especially the contemporary historical situation which has produced "a crisis of meaning."

[20]This explains why early Christian apocalyptic is more positive in its assessment of history than is Jewish apocalyptic. Rather than abandoning history, God accomplishes salvation in history.

in order to control the behavior of the individual Christian and the Christian community in this life."[21]

It is noteworthy that the first function—that of providing an alternative world vision and interpreting present persecution—is characteristic of the earlier Christian apocalyptic texts, whereas the second function—that of controlling the behavior of Christians by vivid descriptions of eschatological punishment—is characteristic of the later Christian apocalypses. Schüssler Fiorenza concluded that this functional shift in language indicates a change in the sociopolitical situation of the Christian community. "It signals a shift from an alternative vision of the world and political power to the rejection of the world for the sake of the afterlife, from a countercultural Christian movement to a church adapted and integrated into its culture and society, from a sociopolitical, religious ethos to an individualized and privatized ethics." Moreover, this shift in function "engenders a shift in apocalyptic language and form, from evocative-mythopoetic symbols and political language"—that is, symbols and language evoking imaginative participation and catharsis—"to allegorical descriptions of eternal punishments and moralistic injunctions against the sins of the individual."[22]

The Book of Revelation belongs to the earlier stage of Christian apocalyptic; consequently, its eschatological vision and paraenesis have the function of providing an alternative vision of the world in order to strengthen the Christians of Asia in their resistance to the oppression and persecution they faced. Leonard Thompson cautioned against one-sidedness in relating the text and social setting, however. Most attempts to date—based upon theories of crisis and deprivation—grant a higher degree of reality to social, institutional entities than to symbolic, literary entities and consequently understand the flow of causality primarily from the former to the latter. Thus, the symbolic universe of the Apocalypse is viewed as an alternative to the social world of everyday life—an ephemeral world John and his readers participate in "so as to

---

[21]Schüssler Fiorenza, "The Phenomenon of Early Christian Apocalyptic," 313.
[22]Schüssler Fiorenza, "The Phenomenon of Early Christian Apocalyptic," 313-14.

experience momentarily the reality of their hopes, to gain strength and courage to face social oppression, and to resolve tensions experienced between their faith and their social experience." Themes such as hope, salvation, and vindication "function as compensations for Christians who feel deprived in their social situation."[23] John's symbolism, then, evokes an "emotional catharsis," a release of pent-up, disquieting emotions such as fear, powerlessness, and aggression by projecting them into cosmic categories.[24]

In opposing the understanding of Revelation based on theories of crisis and deprivation, Thompson argued for an alternative approach—one based upon theories of replication, homologues, and proportions. Whereas the former approach understands the flow of causality primarily from social, institutional entities to symbolic, literary entities, Thompson's approach recognizes causal forces as feedback loops so that everything affects everything intrinsically, not just externally.[25] Thus, rather than viewing Revelation's symbolic universe as an ephemeral world separate from the "real social world," Thompson proposed that John's symbolic world be understood as a comprehensive and coherent replication of reality—"comprehensive in that John offers his symbolic structure as an all-inclusive world embracing the whole of Christian existence including social, political exchanges in everyday life" and "coherent in that, if appropriated, it integrates human experience and makes Christian existence whole." Rather than viewing the "real social world" and Revelation's symbolic world as "separate circles," John's symbolics should be understood "as a grid or an overlay that orders all experience." Thus, conflict in the Apocalypse is not between elements of Christian existence (for example, faith versus sociopolitical realities)[26] but between two

---

[23]Thompson, "A Sociological Analysis of Tribulation in the Apocalypse of John," 163-67.

[24]Cf. Adela Yarbro Collins, *Crisis & Catharsis: The Power of the Apocalypse*, 141-63.

[25]Thompson's suggestion that "everything affects everything intrinsically" agrees with process metaphysics.

[26]Thompson, "A Sociological Analysis of Tribulation in the Apocalypse of John," 168-69:

Most crisis theories assume that the Apocalypse and life experience reflected in it are filled with conflicting oppositions. Most of them also,

comprehensive and coherent worlds or interpretations of reality, one set forth by John and one embodied in the Roman Empire (which John judged to be false).[27]

In a similar manner, David Barr has argued that one should not view the mythic world portrayed in the Book of Revelation as "ephemeral" in contrast to the "real world" of persecution. On the contrary, "myth really does transform reality; it is not just pretend." Myth supplies a language in which what is incomprehensible—for example, the apparent conflict between faith and sociopolitical realities—becomes understandable. Rather than serving as a mere "glimpse of some future day" which is supposed to evoke within the readers "courage to endure present suffering," the myth *transforms* the readers "as they comprehend that it is their suffering witness . . . that brings salvation and judgment to the world, just as the suffering of Jesus was really the overthrow of evil." Thus, John's symbolism should not be reduced to a "pretend world"

---

implicitly or explicitly, draw upon structuralist analyses of myth which assume that a writing such as the Apocalypse mediates binary oppositions or contradictions in human experience. As an alternative sociological approach, I suggest that elements in our thinking and living more often relate as homologues, analogies, and proportions than as binary oppositions. With regard to the Apocalypse of John, proportions and homologues in his literary production disclose the structured processes which guide John's unfolding of Christian existence. . . . Proportions and homologues yield quite a different view of the world from binary oppositions. In terms of the latter, separate forces operate along different lines which create conflict between natural impulses and cultural demands, social disappointments and religious promises, bodily mortality and spiritual hopes of immortality. These conflicts are seen at the most fundamental level of experiencing and understanding life. None of the clever ruses, such as the Apocalypse of John, can long mediate or blur those fundamental conflicts. In contrast, proportions and homologues underscore the unity and integrity of Christian, and more broadly human existence. Such an emphasis affirms that at their most fundamental level, both the world and our experience of it disclose coherence, integrity, and wholeness. The seer of the Apocalypse fundamentally sees the world along those lines.

Thompson's understanding of human existence has parallels to process thought, especially the notion of an actual entity holding the various discordant elements of its experience in the unity of a contrast to elicit depth and intensity for its satisfaction.

[27]Thompson, "A Sociological Analysis of Tribulation in the Apocalypse of John," 166-69.

which evokes an emotional catharsis. This is not to deny the presence of such "emotional therapy" in Revelation, but that is not the chief function of the mythic language. Rather, the catharsis evoked by John's symbolism functions as "'intellectual clarification,' . . . a very complex process which primarily enlightens the audience, giving them a new understanding of their world." Barr summarized:

> This is no ephemeral experience. The hearers are decisively changed. . . . Persecution does not shock them back to reality. They live in a new reality. . . .
> They no longer suffer helplessly at the hands of Rome; they are now in charge of their own destiny and by their voluntary suffering they participate in the overthrow of evil and the establishment of God's kingdom.[28]

A final observation of recent literary studies concerns the *structure* of Revelation. Several structural analyses have noted that the visions of destruction (chapters 6–20) are bracketed by the vision of God the Creator and Redeemer (4–5) who makes all things new (21:1–22:5). Moreover, the whole drama (4:1–22:5) is itself bracketed by exhortations to faithfulness addressed to the readers (1–3 and 22:6-21).[29] Recognition of this series of brackets profoundly affects the interpretation of the book, as will be demonstrated below.

The preceding selective review of recent developments in the study of early Christian apocalypticism and the Book of Revelation indicates a need for significant revision of the common understanding of Revelation. Moreover, it will be demonstrated that close analysis of key passages based upon this revised understanding will demonstrate (a surprisingly) extensive compatibility between the Apocalypse to John and process thought (although there is obviously much which is not compatible). For the purpose at hand—the conception of power—I will confine my analysis pri-

---

[28]David Barr, "The Apocalypse as a Symbolic Transformation of the World: A Literary Analysis," *Interpretation* 38 (1984): 48-50.
[29]Cf. Sweet, *Revelation*, 13, 47, 51, 126. David Barr ("Symbolic Transformation," 46, and "Oral Enactment," 252-56) noted that the setting of the final bracket is the worship of the church, or more specifically, the Eucharist.

marily to Revelation 4–5, with special emphasis on the fifth chapter.

• Analysis of Revelation 4–5 •

Commentators frequently identify the issue of power as one of the deepest theological concerns of Revelation. The drama, set forth in what to modern readers is bizarre symbolism, can be characterized as a clash of powers. The Dragon (Satan), working through his henchman the Beast (the Roman government), wages war against the people of God. The power the Beast exercises is clearly coercive, controlling, and unilateral. That God overcomes the Beast and the Dragon is clear. What many interpreters have failed to perceive, however, is the manner in which God conquers. The question to be answered in the course of this analysis is, What is the nature of God's power?

The main title for God in the Book of Revelation is *pantokrator*, a term variously translated "almighty," "all-powerful," "omnipotent," and "ruler of all things."[30] Although many commentators tone down the classical understanding of omnipotence, they find it difficult to abandon altogether, as the following statement by R. H. Charles illustrates:

> But though omnipotent, His [God's] omnipotence is ethically and not metaphysically conceived. It is not unconditioned force. *That He possesses such absolute power is an axiom of the Christian faith,* but He will not use it, since such use of it would compel the recognition of His sovereignty, not win it, would enslave man, not make him free.[31]

Many commentators have correctly noted that chapters four and five are pivotal to the understanding of the book as a whole and the issue of power in particular. Nevertheless, their inability

---

[30]Of the ten occurrences of the term in the NT, nine are found in Revelation (1:8; 4:8; 11:17; 15:3; 16:7, 14; 19:6, 15; 21:22). In the Septuagint the term frequently translates *Sebaoth* (Hosts) and *Shaddai* (Almighty).

[31]R. H. Charles, *A Critical and Exegetical Commentary on the Revelation of St. John,* 2 vols., International Critical Commentary (Edinburgh: T.&T. Clark; New York: Scribner's, 1920) 1:cx; emphasis added.

to abandon the classical definition of omnipotence has blinded them to the significance of certain lures within these crucial chapters, as the following statement by Leon Morris demonstrates:

> John makes his point that the future belongs not to the Roman emperor, . . . but only to Christ, that Christ who was crucified for the salvation of mankind. He it is who can open the book of human destiny. . . . This peep behind the scenes brings . . . a glimpse of the realities of power. Real power rests with Christ, the Lion. The appearances may be against it for the present. But ultimate reality is not dependent on present appearances. . . . In vision after vision the truth is emphasized that God is supreme and that He brings His purposes to pass in the affairs of men.[32]

Morris's description of Christ as the one "who can open the book of human destiny" indicates that he views chapters four and five as pivotal to understanding Revelation. Yet his assertions that real power rests with Christ "the *Lion*" and that "God is supreme . . . and brings His purposes to pass in the affairs of men" indicate that he—like most commentators—presupposes the classical definition of divine power. The following analysis of these crucial chapters will attempt to demonstrate the inadequacy of this presupposition.

Because the dominate themes of chapters four and five are creation and redemption respectively, Pierre Prigent suggested that John patterned the heavenly worship of this section of the Apocalypse on the Jewish morning liturgy in which the praise of God as Creator was followed by celebration of the Torah and thanksgiving for redemption at the Red Sea.[33] Whether this is the case or not, certainly the experiences of redemption from Egypt and Babylon were seen as repetitions of God's victory at Creation.[34] In like manner, John interprets the ordeal through which his readers are passing as part of the process by which the chaotic world is transformed into the New Creation.[35]

---

[32]Leon Morris, *The Revelation of St. John*, Tyndale New Testament Commentaries (Grand Rapids: Eerdmans, 1969) 20-21.
[33]Pierre Prigent, *Apocalypse et Liturgie* (N.p.: Delachaux et Niestlé, 1964) 61-76.
[34]Exod 15:8-10; Ps 77:16-20; Isa 27:1; 51:9-11.
[35]John makes frequent use of the symbols the primeval sea and the dragon.

In a manner reminiscent of the Old Testament prophets, John is invited to observe the heavenly council where the purpose of God is revealed.[36] In keeping with this prophetic motif, John is admitted to the heavenly throne room in order that he may subsequently reveal to God's people the divine purpose and what part they are to play in implementing it.

Dominating chapter four—indeed, dominating the entire book—is the recurring symbol of the heavenly throne, a symbol of divine sovereignty.[37] Unlike his probable source (Ezek 1:26-28), John refrains from an anthropomorphic description of the one occupying the throne (with the exception of 5:1). Rather, "with evocative language he hints at what is beyond description. Yet the whole chapter is numinous with the divine presence."[38] Clearly the vision depicts God as Creator, the one who is worthy of worship. Moreover, God's holiness, power, eternity, and creative work form the basis for John's assurance of the ultimate triumph of righteousness.[39] What comfort this vision of the heavenly throne must have brought to those who lived under the shadow of another throne!

Chapter 5 opens with a scroll lying on the right[40] palm of the one sitting upon the throne. Although other interpretations have been proposed, most commentators are in general agreement with G. B. Caird: "the scroll is God's redemptive plan, . . . by which he means to assert his sovereignty over a sinful world and so to achieve the purpose of creation."[41] The scroll is sealed (perfect passive participle) with seven seals; hence, the scroll is *securely* sealed. Although the scroll rests in God's open hand, its opening awaits the emergence of a human agent[42] willing and worthy to

---

[36]First Kgs 22:19-23; Amos 3:7; Jer 23:18.

[37]Forty-seven of the sixty-two NT occurrences of the word *thronos* are in Revelation, fourteen of which are found in chap. 4.

[38]G. B. Caird, *A Commentary on the Revelation of St. John the Divine,* Harper's New Testament Commentaries (New York: Harper & Row, 1966) 63.

[39]Cf. Charles, *A Critical and Exegetical Commentary on the Revelation of St. John,* 1:127, 133-34.

[40]God's right hand is the hand of power (Exod 15:6; Ps 44:3) and salvation (Isa 41:10; Ps 138:7).

[41]Caird, *A Commentary on the Revelation of St. John the Divine,* 72.

[42]Examples of God's salvation being contingent upon a human agent include Rom 5:11-21 and Heb 2:5-18.

break the seals, thereby revealing and implementing the content of the scroll. The revelation that no one in *all* creation—in heaven, on earth, or under the earth—was found worthy to open the scroll moves John to uncontrollable weeping. Will God's purpose fail to be revealed and enacted for lack of a worthy agent?

At this point it is instructive to observe the significance of the word "worthy." Whereas the term "throne" is central to chapter four, the word "worthy" is central to chapter five. Many commentators have understood the use of *axios* in this passage to be "the inner ethical presupposition of the ability . . . to open the Book,"[43] but few have dealt with the question *why* a certain worthiness is indispensable if one is to open the scroll. After surveying numerous Hellenistic, Jewish, and Christian parallels involving the entrusting of holy books, mysteries, or revelations to worthy people, W. C. van Unnik concluded that "'worthiness' is not a quality that as such entitles a man to something divine, but it is the right inner attitude, shown forth by deeds which enable him to receive this gift. A severe test has brought this to light."[44]

Thus, anyone who wanted to open the divine scroll must be worthy, must through testing manifest that there is nothing in his or her life to hinder receiving the scroll. That not a single person was found worthy sets in bold relief the announcement of the elder that "the Lion of the Tribe of Judah, the Root of David," has conquered (aorist tense) so that he can open the scroll. That the announcement is couched in the traditional messianic imagery of the Old Testament is noted by all commentators.[45] Less frequently noted is the "martial ring"[46] of both expressions.

In reading Revelation, one is wise to examine the dialectical relationship between what John hears and what he sees. Auditions and visions explain one another. An unfortunate paragraph break between verses 5 and 6 in most Greek editions and English translations can cause the reader to miss the full impact of two

---

[43]Charles, *A Critical and Exegetical Commentary on the Revelation of St. John,* 1:139.

[44]W. C. van Unnik, "'Worthy is the Lamb': The Background of Apoc 5," in *Melanges Bibliques* (Gembloux: J. Duculot, 1970) 457-58.

[45]Gen 49:9-10; Isa 11:1-10.

[46]Caird, *A Commentary on the Revelation of St. John the Divine,* 73.

contrasting images. John looks for the Lion of the audition but sees instead a Lamb. The vision in verse 6 of a Lamb bearing the marks of sacrificial slaughter stands in stark contrast to the militant messianic audition of verse 5.

The most frequent symbol referring to Jesus the Christ in the Apocalypse is the Lamb. Of the thirty New Testament occurrences of the word *arnion*, twenty-nine are in Revelation.[47] Originally the diminutive of *aren* with the significance of "little lamb," *arnion* had lost this force by the first century. The meaning of the term in Revelation is disputed, however. Some commentators argue that in the Apocalypse the term should be translated "ram" due to the depiction of the wrath (6:16-17), and victorious warfare (17:14; cf. 19:11-21) of the *arnion*. Moreover, the *arnion* is depicted with seven horns (5:6) leading some scholars to explain the *arnion* in terms of the ram of the zodiac. Other commentators, however, point out that passages such as Dan 8:3; 1 Enoch 89:42-49; 90:9-16 (cf. T. Joseph 19:8, especially Armenian); and Zech 4:10 could easily account for the seven horns. In any case, "the philological justification of the translation 'ram' is highly doubtful."[48] In Jewish usage—the Septuagint, the Psalms of Solomon, and Josephus, for example—the only significance is "lamb." Indeed, Josephus distinguished between *arnion*, lamb, and *krios*, ram.[49] The only New Testament occurrence of *arnion* outside Revelation, John 21:15, clearly used the term to mean lamb. Moreover, the fact that the *arnion* is depicted as slain[50] (cf. Jer 11:19; Isa 53:7, 10-12) indicates that the symbol should not be separated from the early Christian depiction of Jesus as the sacrificial lamb who suffers patiently, innocently, and representatively (John 1:29, 36; Acts 8:22; 1 Pet 1:19[51]).

---

[47]Twenty-eight times *arnion* refers to Jesus the Christ; once (13:11) it refers to the Earth Beast, a parody of the Christ.

[48]*Theological Dictionary of the New Testament*, s.v. ἀρνίον, by Joachim Jeremias.

[49]*Ant* 3.221.251.

[50]Although *sphazo* can be used for slaughtering one's enemies, its main LXX usage is in sacrificial settings. The sacrificial sense is frequently found in secular Greek as well (*Theological Dictionary of the New Testament*, s.v. σφάζω, by Otto Michel). *Sphazo* is also used of the deaths of Christians in Rev 6:9 and 18:24 thus transforming their murders into sacrifices.

[51]The term *amnos* occurs in these passages.

The Lamb is described *"standing as* having been slain" because in the vision the Lamb is very much alive. The perfect passive participle pictures the sacrifice as having been accomplished, with the marks of slaughter still visible.

Returning to the audition/vision dialectic, the audition (Lion of Judah, Root of David) explains the vision (slain Lamb): the death of Jesus is not weakness and defeat but power and victory. Likewise, the vision explains the audition: God's power and victory lie in suffering, redemptive love. This contrasts sharply with Satan's power: in 13:11, the Earth Beast *looks* like a lamb but *speaks* like a dragon! The Earth Beast is a deliberate parody of the Lamb. Christ's only power is that of the sword which issues from his mouth (1:16; 2:12, 16; 19:15), words which pierce people's souls.[52] The paradox resulting from this dialectical relationship between seeing and hearing is the key both to John's interpretation of the Old Testament and to the symbolism of his apocalypse. God's victory is achieved only through suffering, redemptive love.[53]

In addition to the marks of slaughter, the Lamb has two other striking characteristics: seven horns and seven eyes.[54] Horns frequently symbolize power in Jewish literature. The presence of seven horns indicates that the Lamb is perfect in power. Thus, John asserts that suffering, redemptive love is the most powerful force in the universe. Eyes frequently symbolize wisdom or knowledge; consequently, seven eyes means that the Lamb is perfect in wisdom.[55]

---

[52]Cf. Heb 4:12. As Barr ("Symbolic Transformation," 42) noted, this is a complex symbol. The enemies of God are vanquished by the word of Jesus, which is both "the Word of God" (a title for Christ 19:13) and "the word of his testimony." This latter expression has two referents in Revelation: Jesus' *own* faithful testimony, which is his sacrificial death, and faithful testimony *about* Jesus (1:2, 5, 9; 2:10, 13; 3:14; 6:9; 11:7; 12:11, 17; 17:14; 19:10-11; 20:4).

[53]The expression "suffering, redemptive love" includes both the sacrifice of the Lamb and faithful testimony to that act of love by the Lamb's followers (see below).

[54]Seven horns (power) corresponds to the Lion of Judah (Gen 49:9-10); seven eyes (wisdom), to the Root of David (Isa 11:1-2).

[55]Cf. 1 Cor 1:23-24, "Christ crucified, . . . the power of God and the wisdom of God."

Caird was undoubtedly correct when he stated that by means of this symbolism John redefined omnipotence. In fact, Caird came close to the process definition of divine power when he asserted, "Omnipotence is not to be understood as the power of unlimited coercion, but as the power of infinite persuasion, the invincible power of self-negating, self-sacrificing love."[56] The first portion of his statement clearly indicates that he viewed God's power as persuasive and all-influencing rather than coercive and all-controlling. However, the last part of his statement—"self-negating, self-sacrificing love"—reflects classical theism's understanding of God's love. Recently process, liberationist, black, and especially feminist theologians have called attention to the fact that a self-negating or "no-self" theology—characteristic of patriarchy and paternalism—is destructive to personality, especially for the oppressed and marginalized. Redemptive suffering,[57] which recognizes the interconnectedness of existence, is to be distinguished from self-centeredness and its alter ego self-negation, both of which deny the interconnectedness of existence. Thus, missing from Caird's definition is the relational versus unilateral aspect of God's power. The relational aspect can be discerned in chapter five (and throughout Revelation), however, as the remainder of my analysis demonstrates.

John goes on to state that the horns and the eyes of the Lamb are "the seven spirits of God sent out into all the earth." The Spirit of God in all its fullness ("*seven* spirits") can be sent out only as the horns and eyes of the Lamb. Apparently John has interpreted Isaiah 11 by Zech 3:8–4:10 where seven lamps are "the eyes of the Lord which range through the whole earth," and the point is, "Not by might, nor by power, but by my Spirit." The earlier symbolism of the seven churches as seven lampstands (1:12, 20) would have

---

[56]Caird, *A Commentary on the Revelation of St. John the Divine*, 75. Cf. Barr ("Symbolic Transformation," 41): "a more complete reversal of value would be hard to imagine"; and Boring ("The Theology of Revelation," 266): "as profound a 'rebirth of images' and redefinition of the meaning of 'power' as anything in the history of theology."

[57]The Apocalypse's call for suffering, redemptive love is comparable to Beardslee's and Cobb's notion of self-transcending existence fulfilled in love. See Jack Boozer and William Beardslee, *Faith to Act: An Essay on the Meaning of Christian Existence* (New York/Nashville: Abingdon Press, 1967) and John B. Cobb, Jr., *The Structure of Christian Existence* (Philadelphia: Westminster Press, 1967).

prepared John's readers to understand the seven flaming spirits of God (1:4; 4:5), which are the manifold energies of the Spirit of God, in terms of their own mission and witness.[58] Thus, John asserts that the continued activity of God in the world is contingent on the followers of the Lamb acting as the horns and eyes of the Lamb.[59]

In verse seven the Lamb takes the scroll from the hand of God, and in 6:1 begins opening the seals.[60] Thus, the Lamb becomes the agent through whom God implements the divine purpose. Upon the Lamb's receiving the scroll, the heavenly worship of chapter four is resumed; however, the celebration has changed its focus from creation to redemption.[61] Throughout Revelation, heavenly hymns serve to interpret visions; the hymn of 5:9-14 is no exception. In ever enlarging circles—beginning with the four living creatures and the twenty-four elders and expanding to every creature in heaven, on the earth, under the earth, and in the sea—the Lamb is proclaimed worthy to open the scroll because by his sacrificial death he redeemed to God people from every tribe, tongue, people, and nation. As the hymn indicates, the redeemed are liberated to serve as priests (5:10), with the goal of unifying the cosmos in the worship of God and the Lamb (5:13).

At this point, it is important to refer to the structural analysis of Revelation noted earlier: the visions of destruction (6–20) are bracketed by the vision of God the Creator and Redeemer (4–5) who makes all things new (21:1–22:5). Now if chapters 6–20 stood alone, it would be hard to see them as anything other than a cry for vengeance arising from anger, hatred, and envy—"an attitude poles apart from the love for enemies which Jesus taught"—and a gruesome portrait of divine coercive power. Reading chapters 6–20 in light of this bracketing, however, significantly alters the inter-

---

[58]Cf. John 20:21-22, "As the Father has sent me, even so I send you. . . . Receive the Holy Spirit."

[59]Cf. Eph 3:10, "that *through the church* the manifold wisdom of God might now be made known to the principalities and powers in the heavenly places."

[60]It should be noted that the Lamb opens the seals in conjunction with the prayers of the saints (5:8; 6:10; 8:3-5), another example of relational rather than unilateral power.

[61]The new song (5:9-10) is a song of redemption (cf. 14:2-3; 15:2-4; Ps 33:3; 40:3; 98:1).

pretation of the passage. The wrath and victory of the Lamb (6–20) is to be understood in light of the slain Lamb who redeemed a people to serve as priests with the task of unifying the cosmos in the worship of God (5:1-14). Moreover, the nations and their kings, the victims of the destructions of 6–20, will walk by the light of the New Jerusalem's lamp, which is the Lamb (21:23-27), and the leaves of the tree which grows in the city's street are for the healing of the nations (22:1-3). But this New Creation (21:1) is not accomplished by divine fiat. The whole drama (4:1–22:5) is itself bracketed by exhortations to faithfulness addressed to the readers (1–3; and 22:6-21). For the Word of God to accomplish the New Creation, the followers of the Lamb must bear faithful testimony.[62] Thus, the testimony of the Lamb's followers is not merely *witness* to the reality and nature of God's power; their testimony is also the *instrument* through which the divine power accomplishes its purposes.

An often overlooked aspect of Revelation lends additional support to this interpretation suggested by the bracketing structure: God's ability to implement the divine purpose is contingent upon finding a worthy human agent. An axiom of process thought is that God works with what is to bring about what can be. The failure of a becoming occasion to follow the initial aim influences the nature of the initial aim God is able to supply for the next moment of concrescence. Conversely, the degree to which a becoming occasion actualizes the initial aim influences the nature of the succeeding initial aim. Furthermore, because everything influences everything else in a process universe, the initial aim God is able to supply to one occasion is somewhat dependent upon all other occasions. A similar idea is presented in the Apocalypse. When John wrote that Jesus' sacrificial death enabled God to do what could not be done before—that is, open the scroll—he indicated that God's power is relational not unilateral. The implementation of God's will is contingent upon the response of a human agent.

But John did not limit this interdependent relationship to God and Jesus. In the Apocalypse, the scene continually shifts from

---

[62]Sweet, *Revelation*, 13, 126.

earth to heaven and back. As J. P. M. Sweet noted, in heaven are found "both the origin and the reflection of earthly events, . . . [Moreover,] heaven's will waits on earth's response." Sweet further noted that in worship "the heavenly will is communicated and becomes fruitful in earthly doing and suffering; [then] the earthly victory is registered . . . and becomes effective in new heavenly dispositions."[63] Yet not only are good earthly deeds reflected in heaven—deeds in which the divine will has been accomplished—but also deeds resulting from neglecting the divine will in varying degrees.[64] These bad deeds also are registered and affect new heavenly dispositions. Throughout the Apocalypse, John exhorts his readers to conquer *in the same fashion* as Jesus conquered.[65] Jesus' sacrificial death may have enabled God to inaugurate the divine purpose, but the *continued* implementation of God's purpose is contingent upon the followers of Jesus making his lifestyle their lifestyle. Obviously, this requires a radically new understanding of reality, one in which a slain Lamb conquers and faithful testimony—accompanied by voluntary, redemptive suffering—result in the overthrow of evil and the establishment of the rule of God.

• Hermeneutical Reflections on John's "Undercurrent" •

The preceding analysis of Revelation 4–5 has uncovered a cluster of basal lures in which John provides his readers with a new perspective on power, both divine and human. The power which will triumph—that is, which will result in God's purpose—is persuasive not coercive, influencing not controlling, relational not unilateral. Surprisingly, then, there is an aspect of the Apocalypse, this "undercurrent," which is compatible with process theology in that it portrays ultimate power as the power of creative-responsive love.

---

[63]Sweet, *Revelation*, 113-14.

[64]Examples of evil being reflected in heaven include the sea (4:6), the martyrs under the altar (6:9-11), and the war in heaven (12:7-12).

[65]See the promise to those who "conquer" at the end of each of the seven letters in chaps. 2–3; see also 12:11 and 20:4, 6.

Even if this analysis has proven convincing, undoubtedly some will insist, and rightly so, that it is not the whole picture. That the dominant imagery of the Apocalypse (the surface lures) presents God's power as coercive, all-controlling, and unilateral seems undeniable. Interpreters throughout the ages have felt that the major textual lures operate in this deterministic fashion. As was indicated in part two, propositions are *suggestions* for way things might be appropriated in the process of self-creation. But suggestions are not demands; they may be adopted as they are, or modified, or even rejected. In the course of Christian history, many people have adopted the view of God's power suggested by these deterministic lures; as was noted earlier, classical theism has been the dominant mode of conceptualizing God in the West. But other interpreters have felt compelled to modify this understanding of God, as the quotation from R. H. Charles testifies. And some, D. H. Lawrence for example, have rejected it all together.

Now clearly such a view of divine power is incompatible with process theology.[66] But unlike other hermeneutical models, a process hermeneutic does not excise propositions incompatible with its worldview; on the contrary, it encourages special attention to those dimensions of a text. The entertainment of lures foreign to the interpreter's sensibilities may result in the emergence of a novel pattern large enough to include both the foreign and the familiar in a harmonious contrast. How might this occur with

---

[66]In the opinion of Whitehead (*Process and Reality*, 342-43),
The church gave unto God the attributes which belonged exclusively to Caesar. In the great formative period of theistic philosophy . . . three strains of thought emerge which, amid many variations in detail, respectively fashion God in the image of an imperial ruler, God in the image of a personification of moral energy, God in the image of an ultimate philosophical principle. . . . There is, however, in the Galilean origin of Christianity yet another suggestion which does not fit very well with any of the three main strands of thought. It does not emphasize the ruling Caesar, or the ruthless moralist, or the unmoved mover. It dwells upon the tender elements in the world, which slowly and in quietness operate by love; . . . Love neither rules, nor is it unmoved; also it is a little oblivious as to morals.
In *Religion in the Making* (54-55) Whitehead observed that "the worship of glory arising from power is not only dangerous: it arises from a barbaric conception of God. . . . The glorification of power has broken more hearts than it has healed."

respect to the discordant propositions at hand: that God's power be viewed as coercive, all-controlling, and unilateral (the surface lures) and that God's power be viewed as persuasive, all-influencing, and relational (the basal lures)?

As was noted in part two, the basal lures uncovered by a process hermeneutic may at times operate in a manner quite at odds with the dominant textual lures. Obviously, the preceding analysis has disclosed this to be the case with the Apocalypse to John. Although the dominant "surface" imagery portrays God's power as coercive, all-controlling, and unilateral, the analysis revealed a strong "undercurrent" working against the dominant imagery by means of basal lures suggesting that divine power be understood as persuasive, all-influencing, and relational. Of course, it is a matter of conjecture as to how aware John was of the tension he created by means of this undercurrent. Being a child of the first-century may have prevented him from perceiving what is obvious—obvious at least in light of the preceding analysis—to modern readers operating with a radically different worldview. Thus, it is possible that John was unaware of the problem he created with (1) his insistence on the necessity of a worthy human agent to reveal and implement God's purpose for creation, (2) his image of the slain Lamb as the wisdom and power of God, (3) his call for the Lamb's followers to adopt the Lamb's lifestyle, rather than the lifestyle of the Beast, so that the continuance of God's aim is insured, and (4) his portrayal of earthly events as not only reflected in heaven but also affecting heavenly dispositions. But whether John created this "undercurrent" intentionally or inadvertently, these basal lures nevertheless stand in tension with the deterministic worldview implied by the "surface" lures.

Whether John viewed the deterministic language of the surface lures univocally or imaginatively is also a matter of conjecture. But even if John intended it to be understood univocally, present-day readers may view it imaginatively because all language, especially mythopoetic language, is relatively indeterminate. Moreover, a process hermeneutic proposes that when the basal lures of the text function as an undercurrent to the surface lures, then the surface lures should be read imaginatively rather than univocally. The reason for this hermeneutical proposal is that the basal lures form the deepest metaphysical assumptions undergirding the text as a whole (and thus are the most important lures), even if these implied assumptions were not consciously entertained by the author.

Therefore, when held in the unity of a contrast with the basal lures, John's deterministic language can evoke nondeterministic lures. The deterministic language of the surface lures can evoke the firm conviction that God and God's people will eventually overcome evil, while the nondeterministic language of the undercurrent can evoke the manner: suffering, redemptive love (the basal lure) will eventually triumph (the surface lure); creative-responsive love (the basal lure) is the most powerful force in the universe (the surface lure). Thus, a process hermeneutic enables the Apocalypse to speak powerfully and relevantly to today's reader by issuing a transforming challenge to the modern world's understanding of power.

Chapter 9

Transforming a Paradox: Universal/Limited Salvation in the Apocalypse to John

One of the problems encountered in interpreting the Apocalypse to John concerns the presence of two distinct and irreconcilable conceptions of salvation. Whereas some texts portray or imply limited salvation, others just as clearly portray or imply universal salvation. Some interpreters explain—or better, explain away—one group of texts in light of the other group; that is, they argue that the Apocalypse has only one understanding of salvation, either universal or limited. Other interpreters, however, affirm the need to let the two groups of texts stand as a paradox. (There are others, of course, who see the presence of two conceptions of salvation as simply the product of fuzzy thinking on John's part.)

The present chapter applies the process hermeneutic developed in part two to this interpretative problem. Although the presence of two distinct understandings of salvation is affirmed, a process hermeneutic allows an interpreter to move beyond the impasse implied in viewing the situation as a paradox. Perceiving the two understandings of salvation as a "contrast" of "propositions," the process-informed interpreter is able to move beyond the paradox to "creative transformation."

Before applying a process hermeneutic to the paradox, the evidence typically used to demonstrate that the Apocalypse does, indeed, contain both understandings of salvation will be rehearsed. For the sake of brevity, the presentation of evidence will be limited to a few texts supportive of the respective notions of salvation.

• Limited Salvation in the Apocalypse •

Representative of passages picturing only a limited number of people experiencing salvation are two distinct groups of texts: final judgment texts (14:9-11; 14:14-20; 20:11-15) and exclusion texts (21:8, 27; 22:15).

The first final judgment text to be examined, 14:9-11, draws its vivid imagery from the judgment of Sodom and Gomorrah (Gen 19:24-28) which is echoed in Isaiah's portrait of the judgment of Edom (34:8-10). Those who worship the beast and receive its mark "shall be tormented with fire and sulphur . . . and the smoke of their torment goes up for ever and ever; and they have no rest, day or night."[1] That this text describes everlasting damnation for the followers of the beast—or at least that they do not experience salvation—seems undeniable.[2] The only remarkable feature in this rather typical apocalyptic description of the final state of the wicked is that their torment occurs "in the presence of the holy angels and in the presence of the Lamb." Conspicuously absent are the redeemed who frequently view the torment of the wicked as part of their heavenly bliss (cf. 2 Esdras 7:36; 1 Enoch 27:2-3; 48:9).[3]

---

[1]Contrast their everlasting fate with the unending service and reign of the redeemed (7:15; 22:5) and the four living creatures' ceaseless worship (4:8).

[2]Caird (*A Commentary on the Revelation of St. John the Divine*, 186-87) has argued that the imagery in 14:11 should not be taken to mean that John believed the impenitent would suffer everlasting torment, for in 20:14-15 he stated that those whose names were not written in the book of life were thrown into the lake of fire which is the second death, i.e., extinction and total oblivion. Just as John's attempts to describe the everlasting bliss of heaven push his language to the breaking point on several occasions, so too his attempts to describe the fate of those who miss everlasting life. The imagery of 14:11, then, is meant to describe the privation of life in the presence of God. (One should note that although Caird's interpretation of 14:11 is "more positive" than the common interpretation, it still supports the notion of limited salvation.)

[3]Caird* (187n.1) suggested that "this gruesome idea apparently arose out of a mistranslation of Isa 66:24. The words 'they shall be repulsive to all mankind' were read (e.g., in the LXX) as if they were 'they shall be a spectacle to all mankind.'"

[*Following an initial citation—as for Caird in n. 2 above—frequent references to the commentaries will be by the author's last name only, except where the addition of a short title is necessary to distinguish multiple works cited. See the bibliography for full citations.]

Rather than satisfying a desire for vengeance, the everlasting torment of the wicked serves as a call for "the endurance of the saints" even to the point of martyrdom if need be, for if they "die in the Lord" they will experience the blessed rest denied the wicked (Rev 14:12-13).[4]

The second judgment text listed above, 14:14-20, has spawned numerous interpretations[5]. Some interpreters[6] view both the grain harvest and the winepress as images of the judgment of the wicked. Certainly harvest, sickle, and vintage images are used regularly in the Old Testament as symbols for divine judgment.[7] Other interpreters[8] suggest that whereas the winepress represents judgment, the grain harvest pictures salvation, the ingathering of the redeemed. In support of this interpretation these exegetes note that the gospels frequently use the grain harvest metaphor in this positive way.[9] Moreover, they argue that John prepared the reader for this interpretation in 14:4 by referring to the redeemed as the "first fruits," another grain harvest metaphor. This interpretation claims additional support in the fact that "one like a Son of Man"[10]

---

[4]Although some commentators view 14:12-13 as parenthetical or dislocated—e.g., Charles, *A Critical and Exegetical Commentary on the Revelation of St. John* 2:18, "restored" the verses to their "original position" after 13:15—others detect a close connection between 14:9-11 and 14:12-13. According to Elisabeth Schüssler Fiorenza, (*Invitation to the Book of Revelation* [Garden City NY: Image Books, 1981] 142), "the function of this prophetic announcement is not an invitation for the Christians to gloat over the torture of their enemies but a call for steadfast resistance and loyal endurance." G. B. Caird's interpretation is similar to Schüssler Fiorenza's but expands it by noting that the endurance of the saints includes their witness to a "doomed world": "the speech of the third angel is addressed to the seven churches, not in order that they may gloat over the retribution in store for the ungodly, but in order that they may prevent it from happening."

[5]One should note that Charles (2:18-26) overcame the difficulty this passage presents by excising vv. 15-17 (and "angel" in v. 19) as an interpolation. In his opinion, the remaining verses (14, 18-20) then present a unified picture of the judgment of the wicked in response to the prayers of the martyrs in 6:9-10 (cf. 16:7).

[6]E.g., Adela Yarbro Collins, *The Apocalypse* (Wilmington DE: Michael Glazier, 1979) 102-103; and Morris, *The Revelation of St. John*, 184-86.

[7]E.g., Hos 6:11; Lam 1:15; Jer 51:33; Joel 3:9-14; and Isa 63:1-6.

[8]E.g., William Barclay, *The Revelation of John*, 2 vols., rev. ed. (Philadelphia: Westminster Press, 1976) 2:116; and Schüssler Fiorenza, *Invitation*, 144-46.

[9]E.g., Matt 9:37-38 (‖ Luke 10:2); 13:24-30, 36-43; Mark 4:29; John 4:35-38.

[10]Of course, not all interpreters see this as a reference to Christ (e.g., Morris,

carries out the grain harvest whereas a mere angel gathers the grapes. A third group of interpreters[11] view the grain harvest as a picture of comprehensive judgment, the recompense of the righteous *and* the wicked. In their view, the harvest scene parallels Matt 13:30 which describes wheat and tares being gathered in the same harvest. These interpreters agree, however, that the winepress represents God's wrath on the wicked. According to this reading of the passage, John uses one of his favorite literary devices: a vision of a whole (14:14-16) is followed by a vision of a detail or part of the whole (14:17-20).

In sharp contrast with the preceding interpretations, G. B. Caird has suggested that 14:14-20 presents a radical rebirth of images: traditional images of judgment are transformed into pictures of salvation.[12] Caird argued that the parallelism of the harvest and the vintage is too close to regard them as symbols for contrary notions, as in the second interpretation. Moreover, the phrase "for the hour to reap has come" in 14:15 echoes "for the hour of his judgment has come" in 14:7. Harvest and vintage, then, are variations on the theme of judgment. So far Caird's interpretation agrees with the first interpretation. Having agreed that both images are traditional images of judgment, Caird then argued that both images undergo a rebirth, a transformation, by means of John's creative imagination. As mentioned in the second interpretation, the presence of the word "first fruit" in 14:4 leads the reader to view the grain harvest in terms of the redeemed; likewise, the presence of the word "vine" in 14:18—an common symbol for Israel, the people of God[13]—leads the reader to interpret the vintage as the ingathering of God's people. John observes that the winepress was trodden "outside the city," an expression the early church adopted to describe the death of Jesus and which is used in Hebrews and the Apocalypse as a justification for urging

---

184).

[11]E.g., I. T. Beckwith, *The Apocalypse of John* (New York: Macmillan, 1920) 662-63.

[12]Caird, 191-96. Sweet, *Revelation*, 230-33, is in general agreement with Caird.

[13]See Hos 10:1; Isa 5:1-7; Jer 2:21; Ezek 17:1-8; 19:10-14; Psa 80:8-13; and John 15:1-8. One should also note that the word "vine" does not occur in any of the Old Testament pictures of vintage judgment.

the followers of Jesus to come "outside the city" and share Christ's sufferings.[14] Because the crucifixion took place outside the city, the location becomes the place for martyrdom as well.[15] The suggestion of martyrdom assists in transforming the image of the winepress. Certainly a winepress is used as a symbol for judgment in the Old Testament, but it is also the means by which grapes are crushed into wine. In the judgment of Babylon (14:10; 18:6) she is made to drink the wine of God's wrath. Later, in 17:6, Babylon is portrayed as drunk on the blood of God's people. Thus, "from an earthly point of view it is Babylon that sheds the great river of blood [in 14:20] . . . but to the eyes of faith what is happening is that the cup which will send Babylon reeling to her doom is being prepared in the great winepress of the wrath of God."[16] The cumulative effect of these transformations Caird suggested may now be stated. John used the double image of the harvest and the vintage to assist his readers in interpreting aright the martyrdom to which he calls them throughout the Apocalypse. The mention of "first fruit" in 14:4 leads the reader to transform the traditional image of harvest judgment into an image of the ingathering of the redeemed (as in the gospels); likewise, the mention of "vine" in 14:18 and "outside the city" in 14:20 leads the reader to transform the traditional image of vintage judgment into martyrdom; and when the transformed harvest image is read in conjunction with the transformed vintage image, the defeat and loss of martyrdom are transformed into a victorious homecoming that leads to the overthrow of evil.[17]

---

[14]See the way Matthew and Luke rewrite Mark 12:8 (Matt 21:39; Luke 20:15). See also Heb 13:12-13 and Rev 18:4; cf. 12:6. Other commentators note that the location outside the city could refer to the Jewish expectation that at the end Gentiles would be brought to Jerusalem and judged outside the city (e.g., Joel 3:2, 12).

[15]Moreover, Stephen, the first Christian martyr, died outside the city (Acts 7:58).

[16]Caird, 193. As additional support for this interpretation Caird observed that this river of blood "through which the martyrs have passed in the great vintage . . . becomes [15:2] a heavenly Red Sea, poised after the passage of the true Israel to engulf Israel's persecutors" (196-97).

[17]Compare the similar transformation in Rev 6:9; the violent death of those murdered on earth for the word of God is transformed into "the sacrificial offering of a life in worship and service to God" (Caird, 84). Sweet (232) suggested that the robes of the multitude (who had come out of the great tribulation) which were made white by being washed in the blood of the Lamb

The third final judgment text to be examined is 20:11-15, the great white throne judgment. The scene begins with the present heaven and earth vanishing without a trace. All people, "great and small," stand immediately before the luminous throne; no one is so great as to be exempt, no one is so insignificant as to be ignored.[18] And the books are opened. In typical apocalyptic manner, people are judged on the basis of their deeds as recorded in the books.[19] According to John's picture thus far, human freedom and responsibility are taken quite seriously: people "write" their own judgment. Yet John mentions another book, "the book of life."[20] Failing to have one's name inscribed in this book "before the foundation of the world" (13:8; cf. 17:8) results in being thrown into "the lake of fire" along with the beast, the false prophet, the devil, death, and hades (19:20; 20:10; 20:14-15).[21] Thus, although judgment is based on deeds, final destiny is determined by God's sovereign foreordination.[22]

The final destiny of the wicked portrayed in the great white throne judgment has occasioned some debate. In light of 19:20 and 20:10, many interpreters see the lake of fire as a gruesome portrait of everlasting torment. Eugene Boring, however, has noted a difficulty with this understanding.[23] The lake of fire is the final repository not only of mortal beings but also of transcendent

---

(7:14) had been washed in the winepress outside the city from which flowed the blood of Christ and the martyrs.

[18]According to Charles (2:192-3), John distinguishes between the judgment of the living over which Christ presides (14:14, 18-20) and the judgment of the dead, who were not part of the first resurrection, over which God presides (20:11-15). In Sweet's opinion (293), this judgment only concerns the earth-dwellers ("the dead") because all who had not worshiped the beast had already risen (20:4).

[19]E.g., Dan 7:10; 1 Enoch 90:20; 2 Esdras 6:20; 2 Baruch 24:1.

[20]See Exod 32:32; Psa 69:28; Dan 12:1; Mal 3:16; Luke 10:20; Phil 4:3; Rev 3:5.

[21]If one proved unfaithful one's name could be removed from the book of life (3:5; cf. 21:27). This idea qualifies the absolute determinism reflected in 13:8 and 17:8; although one cannot inscribe one's name in the book of life one can cause it to be erased.

[22]The contrasting notions of human freedom and foreordination present the interpreter with another paradox frequently found in Jewish and Christian writings (e.g., Paul wrote both 1 Thess 2:14-16 and Rom 11:25-29.)

[23]M. Eugene Boring, *Revelation* (Louisville: John Knox Press, 1989) 213; cf. Sweet, 292, 295.

powers like death and abstractions like the beast that can hardly be tortured. Moreover, if death is destroyed in the lake of fire—the usual interpretation of the imagery (cf. 21:4; 1 Cor 15:26)—why are not mortal beings destroyed, also? In a similar fashion, G. B. Caird has argued that although the lake of fire is a place of everlasting torment for the demonic enemies of God—the devil, the beast, and the false prophet—who are apparently incapable of death, it means annihilation for human beings as seen in the phrase "the second death" (20:14; cf. 21:8).[24] But regardless of whether one takes the imagery of the lake of fire as everlasting torment or annihilation, clearly this passage pictures salvation as limited in scope.

In addition to the three final judgment texts discussed above, the notion of limited salvation is also reflected in the Apocalypse's exclusion texts. Several times during the description of the New Jerusalem John lists various categories of people excluded from the city. In 21:8 those consigned to the lake of fire are the *cowardly*, the *faithless*, the *polluted* (or abominable), *murderers, fornicators, sorcerers, idolaters*, and all *liars*; 21:27 adds to the list the *unclean*; in 22:15 *dogs* are also listed as outside the city.[25] Undoubtedly cowards and the unfaithful head the list because the Apocalypse as a whole is a call to heroic faithfulness, even to the point of death. Most of the other terms listed echo the crimes of the beast and the great whore; those who shared in their crimes share in their fate as well.[26] Liars are those who have committed themselves to that fundamental falsity which is the nature of the demonic. And because the city is holy (21:2, 10), nothing unclean (or common) can enter it. The final category John mentions is "dogs." Although the Jewish use of the term can carry the meaning of male prostitute,[27] it was more frequently used as a symbol for something

---

[24]Caird, 248, 260.

[25]Also mentioned in Rev 21:27 are those who practice falsehood; 22:15 repeats from 21:8 *sorcerers, fornicators, murderers, idolaters,* and those *who love and practice falsehood*. That John repeats certain of these categories suggests they were particularly abhorrent to him.

[26]For the polluted (or those who practice *abomination*), see 17:4-5; for *murderers*, 13:15; 17:6; 18:24; 19:2; for *fornicators*, 17:2, 4; 18:3, 9; 19:2; for *sorcerers*, 9:21; 18:23; for *idolaters*, 13:14-15; 14:9, 11; 16:2; 19:20.

[27]Deut 23:18.

malicious, unclean, and disgusting.[28] In the present passage it is clearly the latter idea John has in mind because the term is followed by the same catalog of vices recalling the crimes of the beast and whore.

In reaction to those commentators who view the exclusion texts as predictive descriptions of those who are eternally condemned, Schüssler Fiorenza noted that these texts function as stern warnings or prophetic exhortations to those Christians who are tempted by the ways of the dragon, the beast, and the whore.[29] And Boring noted that

> John does not say . . . that anyone who has ever been guilty of these failings is prohibited from participation in the Holy City, only that no one will bring these sinful practices with him or her into the Holy City. The list serves to characterize life in the city of God, not a limitation on who will finally be there.[30]

Yet even with these and similar qualifications in mind, one can hardly escape the impression that the exclusion texts support the notion of limited salvation.

• Universal Salvation in the Apocalypse •

That one has no difficulty in marshalling texts portraying salvation as limited in scope should come as no surprise given the general tone of apocalyptic writings. What one does not expect to discover in Revelation are many passages which picture salvation as a universal gift.[31] Representative of these passages are three distinct groups of texts: passages echoing prophetic themes of the inclusion of Gentiles in the messianic kingdom and the universal worship of Yahweh (5:13; 15:4; 21:24-26); passages depicting

---

[28]Psa 22:16; Matt 7:6; Phil 3:2. Consequently, Gentiles were called *dogs* (Mark 7:27).

[29]Schüssler Fiorenza, *Invitation*, 197, 214.

[30]Boring, *Revelation*, 217-18.

[31]As Boring remarked: "Finding universal salvation in Revelation is a matter of exegesis, not of the sentimentality of interpreters not tough-minded enough to accept John's pictures of judgment and damnation" (*Revelation*, 229).

repentance of the wicked (1:7; 11:13; 19:15a, 21); and passages describing the renewal of creation (21:5; 22:1-2).

The first group of texts to be examined are those which echo prophetic themes of the inclusion of Gentiles in the messianic kingdom and the universal worship of Yahweh. Although it is true that many Jewish writers looked for the everlasting torment or at least the annihilation of the Gentiles,[32] that was not true of all Jews. The expectation that God would be worshiped by all nations and that their kings would bring gifts to Jerusalem is found in numerous texts as well.[33] Certain passages in the Apocalypse reflect this inclusive vision. In 5:13 "every creature in heaven and on earth and under the earth and in the sea, and all that is in them" join the four living creatures, the twenty-four elders, and an innumerable host of angels in worshiping the one who sits upon the throne and the Lamb. The universality of this verse is undeniable: *every* creature in heaven, earth, sheol (under the earth), and sea—*all* that is in them.[34] Although most interpreters comment on John's depiction of the whole creation joining in praise to God, many unfortunately fail to note the importance of this verse for determining John's understanding of salvation.[35]

That all nations will worship God is also stated in 15:4: "Lord, who will not fear and glorify your name? For you alone are holy.

---

[32]Isa 47; 63:6; 66:15-16; Jer 25:15-29; Ezek 39:1-20; Joel 3; Obad 15-18; Zech 14:1-15; Dan 7:11-12; 2 Esdras 13:37-38; Ps Sol 17:22, 24; 2 Apoc Baruch 40; 72:6; Sib Or 3:303-651; Test Simeon 6.

[33]E.g., Isa 2:2-4; 45:22-23; 49:6; 51:4-5; 55:1-5; 56:6-8; 60:1-3; 66:18-21; Jer 3:17; 16:19-21; Dan 7:14; Zeph 3:9; Zech 2:13; 8:20-23; 14:9; Tobit 13:11; 14:6; 1 Enoch 10:21; 48:4-5; Test Levi 18:9; Test Naphtali 8:3-4; Test Asher 7:3; Sil Or 3:710-23; Ps Sol 17:34.

[34]The reference to *sheol* is quite remarkable. The Old Testament understanding of the dead as completely separated from God in a shadowy existence (Psa 6:5; 30:9; 88:10-12; 115:17; Isa 38:18) is here replaced by a joyous vision of hymnic worship. Even death cannot ultimately restrain any creature from joining this cosmic doxology.

[35]Representative of the minority who do note the importance of this verse are Caird, 77; Sweet, 126, 132; and Boring, *Revelation*, 112. As Boring noted, "the hearer-reader is now prepared to appropriate the violent message of judgment presented in the opening of the seven seals and will not misunderstand the penultimate pictures of judgment as representing God's last word, the word of salvation which already resounds in this scene."

All nations will come and worship before you, for your judgments have been revealed." This verse is part of the song of Moses and the song of the Lamb sung by those who have conquered the beast.[36] But rather than rejoicing over a defeated enemy, as does the song of Moses in Exodus 15, this song focuses on God whom *all* nations will worship. The question with which 15:4 begins—"Lord, who will not fear and glorify your name?"—refers back to the eternal gospel proclaimed by an angelic messenger "to every nation and tribe and tongue and people" (14:6-7). The remainder of the song expresses the conquerors' confidence that "all nations" will come to worship God. Scholars who think that John held out no hope of repentance for the wicked are embarrassed by the song and so pass over the troublesome clauses in silence, or assert that because it is poetic it should not be pressed, or argue that in this context the terms "fear," "glorify," and "worship" indicate grudging submission to brute power rather than genuine conversion on the part of the nations.[37] But ignoring the troublesome clauses does not make them go away, asserting that because the language is poetic it should not be understood as having universal import is hardly convincing, and arguing that the terms merely mean the nations will be forced to acknowledge God as sovereign sounds quite strained. Although the seven plagues—like the plagues of Moses on which they are based—do not bring about repentance (16:9, 11, 21; cf. 9:20-21), they are introduced by a song which celebrates a new and greater exodus. Thus, the song not only interrupts[38] but interprets the seven last plagues.[39] The carnage which people bring on themselves—the

---

[36]That they have in their hands the harps of God indicates that the reader is to identify them with the 144,000 who appeared with the Lamb on Mount Zion (14:1-5), who were sealed from the twelve tribes of Israel (7:1-8), and who are in actuality an innumerable multitude from all nations, tribes, peoples, and tongues (7:9-17).

[37]E.g., Morris, 189-90; James Moffat, "The Revelation of St. John the Divine" in *The Expositor's Greek Testament* (repr.: Grand Rapids MI: Eerdmans, 1951) 444; and John P. Newport, *The Lion and the Lamb* (Nashville: Broadman Press, 1986) 257, respectively. Charles (2:37) argued that this verse refers to the conversion of the nations that survive the judgments of Revelation 16–19; their conversion occurs during the millennium (20:1-6).

[38]The "bowl" series (seven last plagues) begins in 15:1.

[39]The violent imagery of the *seven bowls* (16:1ff.) which follow must be seen in

wrath of God symbolized by the bowls[40]—does not have the final word. In the end all nations will experience the salvation of God.

One of the most striking passages portraying the inclusion of Gentiles and the universal worship of Yahweh is 21:24-26. As part of his lengthy description of the New Jerusalem, John records that the nations and the kings of the earth—the very ones destroyed in chapters 6-20[41]—are part of the new order. Indeed, the kings of the earth who once brought their glory to Babylon are pictured bring their glory, as well as the glory and honor of the nations, into the city through gates which stand forever open. And in the New Jerusalem the nations will walk by the light of God's glory whose lamp is the Lamb.[42]

The ideas expressed in 21:24-26 are, of course, literally inconsistent with the ideas expressed in passages such as 19:17-18 and 20:12-15. In an attempt to avoid the obvious difficulty this passage creates in a consistent reading of the book, interpreters have developed four alternative interpretations. (1) A few commentators have suggested that in 21:24-26 the terms nations and kings of the earth "stand for the people of the earth who are the servants of Christ . . . the redeemed nations who follow the Lamb and have resisted the beast and Babylon."[43] However, to suggest that "nations" and "kings of the earth" here refer to Gentiles converted to Christianity clearly runs counter to the consistent usage of the terms through out the book.

(2) This and other contradictions found throughout the book have led several interpreters to suggest that the Apocalypse in its present form is the result of a process of redaction involving several authors/editors. On the whole, however, this suggestion has failed to convince most scholars for the following reasons. First, in-

---

light of this introductory scene, just as the seven seals must be interpreted in light of the preceding scene of universal worship at the end of chapter five.

[40]Cf. Rom 1:18, 24, 26, 28 where the wrath of God is described as people experiencing the consequences of their decisions.

[41]See Rev 6:15; 10:11; 11:2, 9, 18; 12:5; 13:7; 14:6, 8; 16:14, 19; 17:2, 10, 12, 15, 18; 18:3, 9, 18, 19, 23; 19:15; 20:3, 8.

[42]Rev 21:23-26 is a condensed adaptation of Isaiah 60, although John's picture is more generous than Isaiah's which portrays the nations as captives or second-class citizens bowing down at Israel's feet.

[43]Newport, 320.

terpreters arguing for a process of redaction do not agree in their reconstructions or in the number of redactors involved. Second, the book as a whole generally reflects a unity of style, vocabulary, and grammar. And third, it is highly improbably that a redactor or redactors so careful to reflect the style, vocabulary, and grammar of the first author would leave such glaring contradictions.[44]

(3) In a modification of the redaction approach, R. H. Charles argued that the numerous contradictions found in 20:4-22:21 are due to a major disarrangement. According to Charles, "John died either as a martyr or by a natural death, when he had completed [1:1-20:3] of his work, and that the materials for its completion, which were for the most part ready in a series of independent documents, were put together by a faithful but unintelligent disciple in the order which he thought right."[45] When properly rearranged, the nations are those who have survived the judgments in Revelation 19 and are evangelized by the inhabitants of the New Jerusalem during the millennuim.[46] Whereas Charles' modification of the redaction approach overcomes the second and perhaps the first objections noted above, it still falls prey to the third. Such a well-intentioned disciple would have to be more than unintelligent!

(4) According to other interpreters, the discrepancy created by this passage is merely apparent. The details of vv. 24 and 26 are simply poetic and imaginative, drawn from conventional Jewish descriptions of the complete triumph of the messianic kingdom; the inclusive language should not be pressed for the Apocalypse is "entirely free from any such complacent estimate of Gentile outsiders."[47] This interpretation correctly asserts both that the passage draws on one strand of Jewish eschatological thought and that mythopoetic language should not be read literally; nevertheless, one wonders whether the argument could not be reversed. Could not one argue that those passages which picture the destruction and/or eternal torment of the wicked—details clearly

---

[44]Charles, 2:146-7; and Beckwith, 769.
[45]Charles, 2:147. See 2:148-54 for his supporting arguments as well as his rearrangement of Rev 20:4–22:21.
[46]Charles, 2:172, 177.
[47]Moffatt, 486. Cf. Beckwith, 769-70.

drawn from the other strand of Jewish eschatological thought—are simply poetic and should not be read literally? Because John used both strands of conventional eschatological thought at various points in the Apocalypse, the interpreter must discern some hermeneutical key in order to know how to understand such contradictory language. Traditionally, exegetes have approached the Book of Revelation assuming it should be read as a thorough-going apocalypse. But as was argued in the preceding chapter, this assumption may be incorrect. Recently a number of scholars have viewed the Apocalypse as using apocalyptic language within the context of prophecy. It was further argued that John provided the reader one hermeneutical key in the dialectical relationship he established between seeing and hearing; each explains the other. This key allows the reader to understand John's use of traditional imagery through the "rebirth of images" it fosters.[48] If John's purpose in the abrupt collision of contradictory pictures is to evoke a rebirth of images, then one should not be quick to dismiss the tension 21:24-26 creates with other passages as "merely apparent."

Rather than resorting to tactics designed to explain away 21:24-26, some interpreters approach the passage as another of John's attempts to evoke a radical rebirth of traditional images. Scholars such as G. B. Caird boldly assert that John "did not believe that God would be content to save a handful of martyrs and allow the rest of [humankind], along with all their achievements of culture and civilization, to perish in the abyss."[49] Several other passages in the Apocalypse point in the same direction. For example, in 7:9 the 144,000 from the 12 tribes of Israel become "a great multitude that no one could count, from every nation, from all tribes and peoples and tongues." In 21:3 the best manuscripts read "they will be his peoples" (plural) whereas John's source, Ezek 37:27, reads "they shall be my people" (singular). (Another example of John's inclusive expansion of his sources occurs in the discussion on 22:1-3a below.) And as Caird noted, "nothing from the old order which

---

[48]E.g., in 5:5-6 the audition (Lion of Judah/Root of David) explains the vision (slain Lamb) and vice versa. The death of Jesus is not weakness and defeat but power and victory; likewise, God's power and victory lie in suffering, redemptive love.

[49]Caird, 279. Cf. Sweet, 307-10; and Boring, *Revelation*, 219-22.

has value in the sight of God is debarred from entry into the new."[50] The glory and honor of the nations formerly given to adorn the worldly city, Babylon (the great whore), will be brought into the heavenly city, the New Jerusalem (the bride).

The second group of texts supportive of the notion of universal salvation in the Apocalypse are those depicting repentance of the wicked. As early as 1:7 the reader encounters such a verse. Occasionally called the "motto" of the book,[51] 1:7 is a textual conflation of Dan 7:13 and Zech 12:10. At his second advent—in contrast to his first—all people will recognize the sovereignty of the Messiah; that much is agreed upon by all. The disagreement concerns the meaning to be assigned to the verb "will wail." Although Zech 12:10 clearly pictures repentance on the part of those who "wail (or mourn) for him" (that is, for the good shepherd martyred by Israel) followed by divine pardon and cleansing, most interpreters think that John, in agreement with Matt 24:30, transformed Zechariah's image of repentance into "wailing for themselves" on account of the judgment Christ's parousia will entail.[52] Yet, John's use of the Old Testament usually demonstrates marked awareness of context, and Zechariah is one of his chief sources. Moreover, after verbs of emotion *epi* with the accusative usually denotes the object toward which the emotion is directed; hence, the wailing is *for* him, for what they had done to him rather than for what he will do to them (see Rev 18:9, 11). Thus, the verse is better understood as depicting repentance rather than fruitless remorse for the consequences of evil deeds.[53] The in-

---

[50]Caird, 279. Cf. Boring, *Revelation*, 220-21: "John envisioned transcendent salvation as a world in which all that is human is taken up and transformed, a world in which nothing human is lost. Salvation is beyond but not without this world. Concretely, this means that the 'religious' deeds of humanity are by no means all that is preserved in the eternal city. This 'secular' city-without-a-temple is in continuity with and ultimately redeems and makes worthwhile every effort in our little this-worldly lives to have a decent city: all our striving for a just and fulfilling human society. The Bride-City is clothed in the 'righteous deeds of the saints' (19:8): not only the expressions of piety but actions in behalf of justice." Cf. Rev 14:13 which states that the deeds of those who die in the Lord follow them.

[51]Barclay, 1:36; Boring, *Revelation*, 79; and Schüssler Fiorenza, *Invitation*, 42.

[52]E.g., Charles, 1:17; Moffatt, 339-40; Morris, 50; and Schüssler Fiorenza, *Invitation*, 42.

[53]E.g., Sweet, 63-64, 67; Caird, 18; Boring, *Revelation*, 79-80.

terpretation of this motto verse is important because it introduces the major themes of the book and thus functions as a hermeneutical key to assist in its interpretation.

At 11:13 the reader encounters another verse depicting the repentance of the wicked. Although 11:1-13—the second scene of the interlude between the sixth and seventh trumpets—has occasioned a variety of interpretations, there is widespread agreement that that the concluding verse describes a massive repentance among those formerly hostile to God and God's people. Although the word "fear" is capable of conflicting interpretations—either faithless terror or religious awe—the idiomatic phrase "gave glory to the God of heaven" clearly denotes repentance, "paying the honor due God by changing one's attitude and confessing, speaking, or doing the truth as the truth of God."[54] Moreover, the expression is echoed in the eternal gospel proclaimed by the angel in 14:7 and the songs of Moses and the Lamb in 15:4.

This verse helps the reader interpret the interlude as a whole. In the first scene, John eats a little bitter-sweet scroll and is commanded to "prophesy about many peoples and nations and tongues and kings." The second scene concerns two witnesses whose prophetic message results in their death at the hands of the beast. But death does not have the last word; the witnesses are raised and ascend into heaven in the sight of those celebrating their deaths. In the face of this divine vindication of the prophetic message, accompanied by an earthquake, the people repent. The point of the interlude appears to be that although acts of judgment *by themselves*—as expressed in the seals (6:15-17), the trumpets (9:20-21), and the bowls (16:9-11, 21)—fail to move the wicked to repentance, when they are accompanied by the faithful prophetic witness of the Lamb's followers (even to the point of death) repentance does occur.[55]

---

[54]Beckwith, 604. Cf. Josh 7:19; 1 Sam 6:5-6; Jer 13:16; 1 Esdras 9:8; 1 Enoch 48:4-5; John 9:24; 1 Pet 2:12; Rev 16:19.

[55]How one interprets the acts of judgment found throughout Revelation is of the utmost importance for understanding the book as a whole. If the judgments are viewed as the *direct* acts of God it is hard to understand why such a minor judgment as reflected in 11:13 (an earthquake that destroys only one-tenth of the city and kills only 7,000 people) would lead to repentance whereas judgments of

Chapter 19 contains two verses which can be interpreted as depicting the repentance of the wicked. In verses 15a and 21 Christ smites the nations with the sharp sword which issues from his mouth (cf. 1:16; 2:12, 16). That the sword is a symbol for the Word of God is acknowledged by all commentators. According to most interpreters, these verses symbolize "the death-dealing power of the words uttered by the Messiah against his foes."[56] Certainly there is no lack of parallels to this idea (cf. Isa 11 4; Wis 18:15-16; 1 Enoch 62:2; 2 Thes 2:8). Some interpreters, however, view these verses as portraying the conversion of the beast's army by the Word of God.[57] A "mouth like a sharp sword" can also symbolize God's prophet who speaks words of judgment *and* healing (cf. Isa 49:2; Hos 6:5; Heb 4:12; Eph 6:17).

If the preceding discussion has succeeded in demonstrating that Revelation contains passages in which the author hopes for the conversion of the nations in response to the witness of the Lamb's followers, then the widespread notion that the book advocates a "theology of resentment and vengeance" can be dispelled. In its place one can begin to discern a "theology of justice and hope."[58]

The third group of texts which portray salvation as universal in scope are those describing the renewal of creation. The most significant of these are 21:5 and 22:1-2. The idea of a new heaven and a new earth (Rev 21:1) was common in eschatological texts.[59] The

---

cosmic proportion found elsewhere only harden the hearts of the wicked. But if the acts of judgments are viewed as the *self-destructiveness of evil* rather than the direct acts of God (as in Rom 1:18, 24, 26, 28), then the point of this interlude is that the judgments portrayed by the seals, trumpets, and bowls will not in themselves lead to repentance. The judgments need the prophetic interpretation provided by the followers of the Lamb. Now John is quite realistic; he knows that this message may result in persecution, even martyrdom, if it is faithfully proclaimed. But such has always been the lot of God's prophets (e.g., Elijah, Jeremiah, John the Baptist, Jesus, Stephen, Antipas). If God's purpose is to be accomplished, however, John's readers must follow in the footsteps of the Lamb. Only in this manner can evil be overcome.

[56]Beckwith, 731. Cf. Charles, 2:136, 140; Morris, 231-33; Moffatt, 468-70.

[57]E.g., Caird, 245; and Sweet, 283, 286.

[58]Cf. Lawrence, *Apocalypse*, 14-15; and Schüssler Fiorenza, *Invitation*, 119.

[59]E.g., Isa 66:22; 1 Enoch 45:4; 72:1; 91:16; Jub 1:29; 2 Bar 32:6; 44:12; 57:2; 2 Esdras 7:75; Matt 19:28; 2 Pet 3:13.

new element in 21:5 is John's use of the present tense: God is *continually* making all things new, here and now not just in the future.[60] As Caird remarked:

> This is not an activity of God within the new creation, after the old has been cast as rubbish to the void; it is the process of re-creation by which the old is transformed into the new. . . . God is for ever making all things new, and on this depends the hope of the world. . . . Blind unbelief may see only the outer world, growing old in its depravity and doomed to vanish before the presence of holiness; but faith can see the hand of God in the shadows, refashioning the whole.[61]

In his vision of the transformation of all things (Rev 21-22), John mixes the traditional images of the New Jerusalem and the regained Garden of Eden. This is most clearly seen in 22:1-2.

In describing "the river of the water of life . . . flowing from the throne of God and of the Lamb" John is heir to a rich heritage. Chief among his inheritance are the notions of the river which watered the Garden of Eden making it fruitful (Gen 2:10-14; cf. 2 Enoch 8:5) and Ezekiel's river flowing from the Temple giving life to the Dead Sea and making the wilderness fruitful (Ezek 47:1-12; cf. Joel 3:18; Zech 14:8). Also significant for John's symbolism are numerous passages using the symbolism of living water (Jer 2:13; Ps 36:9; 1 Enoch 96:6; John 4:13-14; 7:37-39; Rev 7:17; 21:6; 22:17).

In picturing "the tree of life" whose leaves "were for the healing of the nations" John again draws upon a rich storehouse of images. Especially important are the tree of life in the Garden of Eden (Gen 2:9; 3:22-24; cf. 1 Enoch 24-25; 2 Esdras 8:52; T Levi 18:10-11) and Ezekiel's continuously-bearing trees growing beside the river flowing from the Temple (Ezek 47:7, 12). Noteworthy is John's inclusive expansion of Ezek 47:12; whereas Ezekiel merely says the leaves are for healing, John adds that the leaves were for the healing "of the nations" (cf. 21:4; 2 Esdras 7:123). As was the case with respect to 21:24-26, many commentators limit the reference of the term "nations" to Gentiles converted to Christiani-

---

[60]Cf. Isa 43:18-19; 2 Cor 3:18; 4:16; 5:17.
[61]Caird, 265-66.

ty; however, the imagery of the passage suggests to some interpreters the notion of universal salvation.[62]

• Statement of the Paradox •

Having examined representative passages portraying or implying both limited salvation and universal salvation, it is important to recall a statement from the introduction. Some scholars interpret one set of texts in light of the other set and in effect "explain away" the troublesome texts. For example, with reference to 20:15 John Newport remarked, "when taken seriously, this final note evaporates all theories of universalism. God's mercy is vast beyond comprehension, but . . . not limitless."[63] Consequently, he is forced to interpret "the nations" in 21:24-26 and 22:2 as a reference to Gentiles converted to Christianity; in these verses the term cannot carry the meaning it has elsewhere in the Apocalypse without contradicting 20:15. R. H. Charles approached the problem of contradictory texts in a more technical manner. Convinced that the text of the Apocalypse has suffered a number of interpolations and major dislocations at the hands of a "profoundly stupid and ignorant editor,"[64] Charles achieved a forced harmony by means of an extensive rearrangement of the text and the removal of the editor's heretical insertions.

Increasingly, however, scholars are coming to affirm that the Apocalypse contains passages portraying both notions of salvation and that it is impossible to fit them into one conceptual picture. The following remarks are typical:

> John works with pictures which are formally contradictory and does not explicitly resolve the enigma. . . . the nations who bear

---

[62]See the discussion of 21:24-26 above.

[63]Newport, 304.

[64]Charles, 1:xviii. Charles confidently asserted that "this shallow-brained fanatic and celibate, whose dogmatism varies directly with the narrowness of his understanding, has often stood between John and his readers for nearly 2,000 years. But such obscurantism cannot outlive the limits assigned to it; the reverent and patient research of the present age is steadily discovering and bringing to light the teaching of this great Christian prophet whose work fitly closes the Canon" (1:lv).

the beast's mark and are not written in the Lamb's book are destroyed, but God the Creator and Redeemer gathers all the nations . . . into his renewed creation . . . Both pictures are all embracing.[65]

Neither group of texts can be subordinated to the other. . . . John was a profound thinker, a dialectical theologian who intends to present both sets of pictures, and does so using paradoxical language. [He] intends to present pictures in which the one sovereign and gracious God is finally victorious and restores all . . . creation to its intended blessedness, redeeming all . . . creatures . . . He also intends to present pictures which portray human beings as responsible for their decisions, pictures of how inexpressibly terrible it is to reject one's creator and live one's life in allegiance to false gods . . . By offering pictures of both unconditional/universal and conditional/limited salvation and thus affirming both poles of the dialectic, John . . . guards against the dangers inherent in a superficial "consistency" obtained by affirming only one side of the issue. The interpreter's task is not to seek ways to reconcile the tension in the text; the task is to find the thrust of Revelation's message precisely in this tension.[66]

Informed by literary criticism, this new generation of scholars is taking a second look at the language of the Apocalypse. John is being viewed as an artist who gave "ancient images new life and meaning by combining them in the unity of a great work of art."[67] In the past interpreters approached John's imagery as steno-symbols which need to be decoded into univocal statements. Recent interpreters, however, who view his language primarily as tensive language do not feel the compulsion to resolve his images into consistent doctrinal statements. Eugene Boring has conveniently summarized in five points the differences between the two understandings of the language of the Apocalypse which he termed propositional language and pictorial language.[68]

---

[65]Sweet, 308-309. Likewise with reference to 6:15-17 Sweet stated: "But in his final vision the kings of the earth, who here cower in terror, bring their glory into the new Jerusalem, and the leaves of its tree are for the healing of the nations. There is no formal resolution of the paradox" (145).

[66]Boring, *Revelation*, 228.

[67]Caird, 289.

[68]The following is a summary of Boring, *Revelation*, 51-59.

(1) *Propositional language is objectifying language; pictorial language is nonobjectifying.* Propositional language claims to be descriptive of objects "out there" in the "real" world. Indeed, it assumes that language expresses "truth" only when it accurately describes this real world. Language which fails to meet this criterion is labeled "merely subjective"; subjectivity is deplored because it is assumed that truth can only be described objectively, from a nonparticipatory standpoint.[69] In sharp contrast, the pictorial language of Revelation asserts that human language cannot describe but can only point to ultimate reality. The reality with which the Apocalypse deals is incapable of being grasped by finite minds or expressed in finite language. Although pictorial language abandons any attempt to describe reality objectively, this does not mean it has abandoned the notion of referentiality. It points to, or talks about, this reality by means of expressive mythopoetic language which creates vivid pictures. These pictures are not painted from the standpoint of a detached observer. Far from being descriptive spectator language, the language of Revelation is the participatory, confessional language of the involved worshiper. Such language is not "merely subjective," however, because it points to something external.

(2) *Propositional language may use "symbols," but only in a literalizing manner, as "signs" or "steno-symbols"; pictorial language uses symbols which are tensive, evocative, and polyvalent.* A sign or steno-symbol has a one-to-one relationship to that which it represents. For example, in mathematics the Greek letter *pi* is a steno-symbol representing the relationship between the circumference and the radius of a circle. Because such symbols are "codes" for literal, objectifying meanings, they can be translated into propositional language quite easily, provided one has the interpretive key. The Apocalypse's pictorial language is not allegorical code language composed of steno-symbols whose interpretation consists of mere translation into discursive, objectifying language. On the contrary, the pictorial language of the Apocalypse uses tensive symbols which are evocative and polyvalent. In contrast with a steno-symbol, a tensive symbol evokes a whole set of meanings (with many overtones) that cannot be exhausted or adequately expressed

---

[69]See the discussion of the descriptive phase of language in chapter 2.

by any one referent. The evocative and polyvalent nature of John's language allows it to speak meaningfully in a host of different historical and cultural settings; the message is not confined to the original context. For example, the simple substitution of Rome for Babylon does not exhaust the meaning of John's vision; in fact, such a reductionistic reading may actually insulate a modern reader from the book's message today.

(3) *Propositional language is logical; pictorial language is nonlogical and noninferential.* Propositional language operates within the normal canons of logic and inference; thus, consistency is one of the criteria of truth. The pictorial language of Revelation, however, is not logically consistent, as the preceding two sections of the present chapter have demonstrated. One should not infer from this that John is irrational; rather, the ultimate realities with which he was concerned shatter the logic of propositional language. Moreover, because John's language does not presuppose a logical system, his statements are not premises from which logical inferences can be drawn that can then be used to construct doctrine.

(4) *Propositional language is diachronic; pictorial language is synchronic.* Propositional language deals with things one at a time in a chronological manner. Pictorial language does not follow linear logic but opts instead for web of simultaneous images. John typically paints more than one picture of the same reality, and often the images he uses are logically inconsistent.

(5) *Propositional language contrasts myth with truth; pictorial language uses myth as the vehicle of truth.* From the standpoint of propositional language, at best, myth is understood simply as a decorative way of saying something which could be said more clearly in propositional language; at worse, anything mythical is simply false. From the standpoint of pictorial language, however, ultimate realities can only be expressed in mythological language. The mythical pictures of Revelation are not mere illustrations of something that could be said more directly. A picture makes its own statement and cannot be reduced to discursive, objectifying language. This does not mean that one cannot comment on a picture or that discourse cannot help one "get at" a picture. The point is that discursive language about a picture cannot replace the picture; the picture always has a surplus of meaning.

In light of these five points, one can understand why scholars such as Boring feel no compulsion to resolve the paradox. The paradox is an essential part of John's message.

• Transforming the Paradox •

An interpreter working with a process hermeneutic is quite sympathetic to the concerns expressed by interpreters informed by literary criticism; in fact, the process-informed interpreter often expands and intensifies those concerns. For example, whereas the literary critic is concerned that John's mythopoetic or pictorial language be understood as evocative and polyvalent rather than as descriptive and objectifying, the process-informed interpreter understands *all* language—even that which claims to be descriptive and objective—to be analogical, indeterminate, imprecise, and value-laden. Because process thought conceives of reality as a fluid environment composed of myriads of internally related momentary events (actual entities) rather than a world of discrete substantial objects, words can never be understood in a univocal sense. The application of a name to a group of entities—such as those entities comprising this "page" at this moment—requires that *some* aspects of that actuality be lifted out of the complex and dynamic set of relationships within which it occurs (its concrete connectedness) and that *other* aspects of the actuality be ignored—such as its relationship to the tree from which it came and the hand which now holds it. Consequently, language is always abstract—an imprecise, incomplete, and indeterminate representation of concrete actuality. The plurisignificant nature of language so conceived is obvious. Due to the "elliptical" character of language, each word is potentially capable of designating a whole host of meanings; no word can indicate precisely one singular and individual meaning. Thus, what is true of John's pictorial language is true to some degree of all language; it is simply more readily apparent in the case of mythopoetic or religious language.

An important distinction exists between the tensive symbol character of poetry and religious language and the steno-symbol character of ordinary and scientific language. Languages of the steno-symbol variety have as their goal the development of terms that are univalent and precisely defined. These languages "are enormously useful for the formulation of rational explanations, and for exercising control over the world for specific purposes." But they "constitute a high abstraction from, and therefore a quite limited representation of, the concrete totality of the world." Languages of the tensive symbol variety employ "multivalent words laden with innumerable associational and valuational and emotional ligatures" and as a result convey "the essential connectedness and concrete particularity of things." These features render tensive languages incapable of serving the limited functional purposes of the special sciences, but these same features enable them "to report the world most richly and concretely." Indeed, "such language not only reports, but in some sense conveys, or re-enacts what it reports."[70]

As with all types of language, religious language can be misleading. The problem occurs when an interpreter takes any form of language to be literally descriptive rather than analogical. With respect to religious language, this occurs when an interpreter understands religious statements "as dogmas, as denoting the content of faith in a direct, precise, literal fashion"[71] to be grasped intellectually by an externally-related reader. Properly understood, religious language (like all language) is primarily a donation of "propositions" for appropriation in the self-creation of an internally-related reader. The distinctive Whiteheadian meaning of the word "proposition" will be reviewed.

In Whitehead's terminology a "proposition" is a proposal or a suggestion about the way things might be. For example, the propo-

---

[70]Janzen, "The Old Testament in 'Process' Perspective," 492-93. Janzen's statement that tensive language "in some sense conveys, or re-enacts what it reports" is similar to Amos Wilder's description of metaphor as "a bearer of the reality to which it refers. The hearer not only learns about that reality, he [or she] participates in it. . . . is invaded by it." *Early Christian Rhetoric: The Language of the Gospel* (Cambridge MA: Harvard University Press, 1971) 84.

[71]Pregeant, *Christology beyond Dogma*, 39. Cf. Caird (228): "To ask 'what does Rev. teach—eternal torment or eternal destruction?' is to use (or misuse) the book as a source of 'doctrine', or of information about the future. John uses pictures, as Jesus used parables . . . , to ram home the unimaginable disaster of rejecting God, and the unimaginable blessedness of union with God, while there is still time to do something about it"; and Boring, *Revelation* (170): "To even ask whether Revelation 'teaches' eternal torment for the damned is to misconstrue the book as a source of doctrines, to mistake its pictures for [objective discourse]."

sition "the paper is white" proposes that the eternal object "whiteness" is ingredient in those actual entities indicated by the word paper. A proposition, however, should not be equated with a sentence for the following reasons. First, a sentence can evoke an indefinite number of related propositions which fit its verbal form, and each of these propositions becomes a possible meaning for the sentence. Second, a sentence cannot express any given proposition exhaustively or precisely; language can only approximate the full meaning of a proposition because language attempts to express a proposition without reference to its system of relations, its concrete connectedness.

Now the primary function of a proposition is to serve as a "lure for feeling"; it lures a subject to feel or appropriate a datum in a particular way in that subject's process of self-creation. And according to Whitehead, it is more important that a proposition be interesting than that it be true; the importance of truth is that it adds to interest.[72]

From a process perspective, then, all texts are clusters of propositions or proposals for creative, perhaps even alternative, ways of constituting oneself. But propositions are suggestions, not demands; they may be adopted as they are, or modified, or even rejected. The preceding sections of this chapter testify to some of the ways interpreters have modified or rejected certain proposals in the Apocalypse. Unlike other hermeneutical models, a process hermeneutic does not excise propositions incompatible with its worldview; on the contrary, it encourages special attention to those dimensions of a text. In this respect it supports the literary critics' argument against explaining away one pole of the paradox in order to achieve a superficial consistency. The entertainment of lures foreign to the interpreter's sensibilities may result in the emergence of a novel pattern large enough to include both the foreign and the familiar in a harmonious "contrast." When this occurs, the interpreter experiences "creative transformation." The preceding two sentences need careful unpacking.

Occasionally an interpreter will encounter conflicting propositions. Instead of immediately choosing between the disparate

---

[72]Whitehead, *Process and Reality*, 259.

propositions, the process interpreter will seek to create a harmonious contrast of the propositions. A contrast is the unity had by the many components in a complex datum (for example, holding many colors together in a unified pattern, as in a kaleidoscope, as opposed to a single color). Contrast is the opposite of incompatibility, for incompatibility results in the exclusion of one or more elements to achieve a (more trivial) harmony. The more a subject holds the items of its experience in contrasts and contrasts of contrasts, the more it elicits depth and intensity of experience. In order to achieve the unity of a contrast, the interpreter must discern a novel, more inclusive pattern which can contain the discordant propositions in such a manner that the contrast between them contributes to the intensity of the whole. When this occurs, the interpreter experiences creative transformation.[73] A process hermeneutic does not propose that all propositions can be brought into harmonious contrasts. Nor does it presuppose that every transformation is creative; for transformation to be creative it must manifest openness toward the insights of new propositions without abandoning the insights of old propositions, thereby resulting in an enlargement of perspective. How might creative transformation occur with respect to the discordant propositions at hand: that salvation is both universal and limited in scope?

In the preceding chapter it was argued that John was probably unaware of the tension he created by means of the "undercurrent"[74]—those lures suggesting that divine power be understood as persuasive, all-influencing, and relational. However, the tension John created by proposing both universal and limited salvation can hardly be unintentional because neither lure can be described as an undercurrent. Neither is confined to a handful of text; on the contrary, both are prominent throughout the Apocalypse. Thus, John clearly wanted the reader to entertain both proposals. Now according to a process hermeneutic, for these contradictory proposals of salvation to be held in the unity of a contrast, a novel,

---

[73]The experience of creative transformation in the process of interpreting a text is similar to Gadamer's fusion of horizons.

[74]An undercurrent is a cluster of lures operating in a manner quite at odds with the dominant or surface textual lures.

more inclusive pattern must emerge in which the most important aspects of both propositions have a place. In order to appreciate what is at stake in transforming the present paradox, it will be helpful to note that each proposal of salvation lures the reader to entertain an entire cluster of component propositions. The cluster of propositions evoked by John's images of limited salvation include the following:

(1) The inescapability of human responsibility. Human decisions and conduct matter, indeed, they matter eternally. In John's pictorial language, "their deeds follow them" (14:13); "the books" will be opened and the dead will be judged by what has been written in the books, what they have done (20:12).

(2) The certainty of final judgment. There is no escape; all will be judged.

(3) Evil must be exposed in all its hideousness. John uses the most graphic and offensive language he can to describe the allies of evil (Balaamites, Jezebel, fornication, dragon, beast, whore) because "he is aware that they present themselves to the world in a much more attractive light. No [one] chooses evil because he [or she] recognizes it to be evil, but always because, for the moment at least, it appears to be good. The essence of evil is deception and counterfeit."[75]

(4) Evil has a cumulative, transpersonal effect assuming forms far beyond the control and responsibility of any individual. In the Apocalypse the social or corporate nature of evil is portrayed by the beast and the whore, John's symbols for political tyranny and economic seduction respectively.

(5) Evil will be overcome. It has absolutely no place in the new order.

The cluster of propositions evoked by John's images of universal salvation include the following:

(1) The self-destructiveness of evil. Much of the violent imagery forming so large a part of the Apocalypse—the seals, the trumpets, the bowls, the judgment of the whore, and so forth—is designed not to picture the punishment of the

---

[75]Caird, 294.

wicked but rather to portray God using the self-destroying power of evil "to batter down the defences of those who try to find security in that which is not God."[76]

(2) The importance of proclamation and mission. Although evil has within itself the germ of its own ruin, the self-destructiveness of evil *by itself* is not sufficient to bring about repentance. Also needed is the prophetic witness of the followers of the Lamb. John calls his readers to imitate Jesus, to hold fast the testimony of Jesus even unto death, to conquer as Jesus conquered. In issuing this call John reveals God's secret weapon in the overthrow of evil.

(3) The value of creaturely accomplishment. Any achievement of value in the present order, however imperfect, will find its place in the healed and transformed life of the new order.

(4) Final judgment, although certain, is neither vindictive nor unfair. God neither lusts for revenge nor punishes beyond measure (eternal torment for finite sins).

(5) God's purpose will be accomplished. For God to destroy the created order would be a confession of failure. For the purpose of God to be accomplished the whole of a transformed creation must join in worship (5:13).

From the perspective of a process hermeneutic, one can view John as having perceived two aspects of a unified pattern of religious truth: final judgment and redemption of the entire created order. But given the first-century thought world, he did not have access to an overarching framework within which these two aspects could be stated harmoniously. As he presented them in the Apocalypse they form a paradox: an affirmation of both limited and universal salvation. The modern interpreter, however, is not restricted to the first-century thought world. Given the enormous changes that have transpired with respect to worldview is it possible for the process-informed interpreter to hold the two proposals of salvation in the unity of a contrast without denying any of the preceding component lures? Can John's paradox be creatively transformed? I believe the process understanding of reality allows these questions to be answered in the affirmative.[77]

---

[76]Caird, 295.

[77]The following brief discussion of process eschatology relies heavily on the

According to the process worldview, upon attainment of satisfaction each actual occasion is appropriated or prehended by God in the consequent nature. Because God prehends actual occasions in their totality—no negative prehensions are involved—an occasion which attained consciousness is reenacted (or resurrected!) in God in its full consciousness. Although God prehends all actual occasions, the following discussion of process eschatology will be limited to human occasions of experience.[78]

Resurrection in God is not contingent upon one's death but rather occurs throughout one's life as God prehends the succession of momentary occasions comprising each human personality.[79] This resurrection in God is first experienced as judgment; in fact, the judgment is threefold. The first phase of judgment occurs as each actual occasion is compared with what it could have been had it followed God's initial aim for it precisely. Thus, people come to know themselves as God knows them: as they are and as they could have been. The second phase of judgment involves each momentary occasion experiencing itself in terms of all the preceding moments in that person's total life experience. There is a cumulative "regathering" of one's total personality in God in contrast to the "stretched out" manner in which human existence occurs in the temporal realm. The most recent moment feels the earlier moments and vice versa. The third phase of judgment is an extension of the second. Because God prehends all actual occasions, each momentary occasion experiences itself in terms of all other actual occasions of the created order. Each actual occasion experiences itself as all others experienced it. Joys that it gave to others will be experienced, and so will the evils that it inflicted. The relational nature of reality will be fully felt.

---

work of Marjorie Hewitt Suchocki. See her *God, Christ, Church: A Practical Guide to Process Theology* (esp. chap. 17) and *The End of Evil: Process Eschatology in Historical Context* (Albany: SUNY Press, 1988) for a thorough discussion.

[78]Because the process of resurrection, judgment, and transformation about to be described is not limited to human occasions of experience, one can truly speak of the process as resulting in "a new heaven and a new earth"!

[79]According to the process worldview, the human "self" or "soul" is a succession of occasions, a serially-ordered society.

This threefold judgment experienced by actual occasions is the result of God integrating the many feelings into increasing modes of unity. This movement toward a unification of feelings is a result of divine concrescence (or growing together), and this concrescence is governed exclusively by the divine aim or will. Thus, actual occasions resurrected in God have no choice but to experience judgment. To the degree that the occasion has conformed itself to the initial aim, it will experience the process of divine concrescence as wonderfully liberating, as heaven; to the degree that it has departed from the initial aim, it will experience the process as painful, as hell.

But judgment is not the final word. The breaking down of the boundaries of the finite ego which results from experiencing the full relationality of existence—that is, feeling others' feelings—also makes possible redemptive transformation. As an individual occasion moves beyond the narrow confines of self to experience the feelings of others—others in that occasion's own historical route of occasions and others outside its own historic route—that occasion's self becomes wider and wider. For hell to remain hell, the narrow boundaries of ego would have to be reinforced. But as the occasion's notion of self becomes wider and wider, it experiences redemptive transformation. That which the occasion lacks it finds in other occasions; thus, each occasion has the possibility of contributing to the redemptive transformation of others. Of course, some occasions contribute far more than do others, hence, the importance of what one does in this life. In the process of divine concrescence, that which is of value gains increased importance and is brought into the "depths" of God. As a result, actualizations of value can be experienced by those occasions which lack them as supplementations to their own actuality. In sharp contrast, that which is evil loses importance during the divine concrescence and is relegated to the "edges" of God. In this manner evil is finally overcome.

The preceding sketch of process eschatology provides an understanding of salvation inclusive enough to appropriate the most important aspects of John's contradictory notions of salvation. Although the two proposals cannot be affirmed as they stand because they involve a logical contradiction, all of the component lures evoked by the respective notions of salvation can be incorporated within this more inclusive framework. With respect to the cluster of propositions evoked by John's images of limited salvation, one can affirm:

(1) The inescapability of human responsibility. Human decisions and conduct matter, indeed, they matter eternally. *What* is relegated to the edges of God as evil and *what* is brought into the depths of God as having value (and therefore is of use in the transformation of others) is dependant upon what humans make of themselves in their process of self-creation.

(2) The certainty of final judgment. Judgment is a part of the divine concrescence.

(3) Evil must be exposed in all its hideousness. Evil is most clearly revealed for what it is when the relational nature of reality is understood.

(4) Evil has a cumulative, transpersonal effect assuming forms far beyond the control and responsibility of any individual. What it is possible for an occasion to become is in part determined by past occasions; in this respect evil precedes the becoming occasion. Also, the past which partially determines what the occasion can become is composed of innumerable occasions, no one of which is responsible for the total weight of the past; in this respect evil is cumulative and transpersonal.

(5) Evil will be overcome. In the process of divine concrescence, evil is relegated to the edges of God.

With respect to the cluster of propositions evoked by John's images of universal salvation, one can affirm:

(1) The self-destructiveness of evil. Due to the relational nature of reality, the evil one does not only destroys others, it destroys oneself as well.

(2) The importance of proclamation and mission. The prophetic witness of the Lamb's followers is used by God to shape what "hearer" occasions become. And because what occasions become matters eternally, proclamation and mission are vitally important to the purpose of God.

(3) The value of creaturely accomplishment. Any achievement of value finds its place everlastingly in the depths of God and enriches all occasions.

(4) Final judgment, although certain, is neither vindictive nor unfair. The goal is not eternal punishment but redemptive transformation.

(5) God's purpose will be accomplished. In the divine concrescence value is preserved, evil is relegated to the edges, and creation is redemptively transformed.

• Conclusion •

The purpose of this chapter has been to demonstrate that a process hermeneutic enables an interpreter to move beyond the current impasse in the study of the Apocalypse's conflicting portraits of salvation. Most interpreters today feel forced to choose between either denying one pole of John's paradox, thereby achieving a forced consistency, or simply allowing the paradox to stand. Although the process-informed interpreter will initially affirm the presence of two distinct understandings of salvation in the Apocalypse, he or she will attempt to move beyond simply affirming the presence of the paradox. By holding both propositions in the unity of a contrast, the interpreter hopes that a novel, more inclusive pattern will emerge. If a more inclusive pattern should emerge, then the paradox will be creatively transformed.

In my opinion, the understanding of salvation suggested by process eschatology is inclusive enough to transform the paradox because it is able to incorporate the component lures evoked by both poles of the paradox. And as the paradox is transformed one also observes that a more comprehensive definition of justice results than is typically associated with either limited or universal salvation. God's justice involves both judgment and redemptive transformation.

Excursus

Reimaging the Apocalyptic "End"

One recurrent aspect of biblical narrative that is rejected by most interpreters as incompatible with the modern worldview is the notion of the apocalyptic End. In many forms of religious narrative, chaos is repelled "by periodic re-presentations of the life-giving reality." Apocalyptic narrative, however, is not satisfied with this partial and never-ending approach but rather "thirsts for the total victory, the all-inclusive transformation of reality." This thirst for the "all" manifests itself in two ways: narrative movement toward inclusiveness (for example, a redemption of all of nature, not just humankind) and concentration on the End conceived of as a reversal of present reality resulting in a static perfection.[1] In some ways this longing for an all-inclusive, static perfection resembles Gnosticism, yet there is an important difference. The apocalyptic hope does not involve a loss of differentiation; on the contrary, God is viewed as taking so seriously differentiated, concrete existence that it is incorporated into the final perfection, rather than being absorbed into God and thereby loosing its differentiated existence (as is the case in Gnosticism).[2]

In an effort to render the apocalyptic End meaningful to modern readers, some interpreters have tried to interpret the language in a nonliteral fashion. One approach has been to view the notion of the End as embodying some deep symbolic meaning

---

[1]Beardslee, *Literary Criticism of the New Testament*, 53-54.
[2]William A. Beardslee, "Hope in Biblical Eschatology and in Process Theology," *Journal of the American Academy of Religion* 38 (1970): 228-29.

drawn from the past (e.g., Jung's archetypal method). Another approach has been to understand the End in terms of the ultimacy of the moment (e.g., Bultmann's existential interpretation of eschatological language). While these interpretations of the End have proven useful, there nevertheless remains something in apocalyptic narratives—a basal lure—"which deeply cries out to be told differently. . . . The core of this something is suffering. It is suffering that opens the story to the future, and it is the hope of some resolution of the terrible imbalance of suffering that keeps alive the narratives of the End."[3]

Process interpreters must agree with other interpreters that a literal understanding of the End is not meaningful today; the creative advance never comes to a static end.[4] Nevertheless, the basal lure identified in the preceding paragraph must not be ignored. The biblical scholar who has explored the relationship between apocalyptic literature and process thought most extensively is William Beardslee.[5] According to Beardslee, the process-informed interpreter can view the End as a mythological symbol embodying two meanings: "the meaning of ultimacy" and "the meaning of fulfillment or functional participation in a later reality." With respect to the first meaning—the end viewed in terms of ultimacy—the process interpretation agrees with the existentialist interpretation of eschatology. That is, "the ultimacy of the moment of decision, its unique irreversibility, is suggested by the symbol of each moment's having to bear the weight of that definitive significance which the end has." Expressed in process terminology, each actual occasion has ultimate significance; it is an eschatological moment. "But unlike existentialist theology, process theology can join this

---

[3]Beardslee, "Narrative Form in the New Testament and Process Theology," 313-15.

[4]"Neither God, nor the World, reaches static completion. Both are in the grip of the ultimate metaphysical ground, the creative advance into novelty" (Whitehead, *Process and Reality*, 349).

[5]In addition to Beardslee's works cited in the preceding footnotes, see also *A House for Hope: A Study in Process and Biblical Thought* (Philadelphia: Westminster Press, 1972) and "Openness to the New in Apocalyptic and in Process Theology," *Process Studies* 3 (1973): 169-78.

emphasis with an insight into how the moment reaches beyond itself."[6]

The ability of process thought to go beyond the existentialist interpretation of eschatology is revealed in the second meaning noted above—"the end as that to which one looks forward as a fulfillment of the process in which one is involved, or as the functional participation of the passing moments in a later reality." This understanding of the End has two dimensions. First, as a superject each actual occasion lives on in the sense of being prehended by succeeding occasions. The objective immortality of each occasion means that the future must appropriate it in some fashion. Because the occasion may not be objectified in the manner anticipated, waste or loss can occur. In fact, succeeding occasions can only prehend the objectified occasion perspectivally, or partially, so there is always some loss. But, as Beardslee noted, "the other side of this situation is that the resources which the present contributes to the future may be used in unexpectedly creative ways." Indeed, process theology expects such future creativity due to "the boundless potentiality of the primordial nature of God" whence come novel initial aims for future occasions.[7]

So far the second meaning of the End has been discussed only in terms of objective immortality in the temporal world. According to the process model, however, there is another dimension to this meaning, a dimension which involves immortality in God.[8] As was noted in chapters 3 and 9 above, God everlastingly prehends each actual occasion in its totality; there is no waste, no loss. Each element in an occasion is felt for what it truly is. In the process of the divine concrescence, that which is of value gains increased importance and is brought into the "depths" of God. That which is evil is relegated to the "edges" of God (as Whitehead so beautifully put it, "God is the great companion—the fellow sufferer

---

[6]Beardslee, "Hope in Biblical Eschatology and in Process Theology," 236-37.
[7]Beardslee, "Hope in Biblical Eschatology and in Process Theology," 237-38.
[8]For arguments in favor of "subjective immortality" in God for those actual entities which attain consciousness, see Suchocki, *The End of Evil.* The most suggestive Whiteheadian passages for the formulation of a process eschatology are found in the final two chapters of *Process and Reality,* esp. 340 and 350-51.

who understands"[9]). Therefore, "it is the confidence that in spite of the waste in the world, the occasions that pass are not finally lost, but [are] recognized everlastingly in God, that gives an ultimate ground to hope in a process perspective."[10]

Clearly, process thought offers a new way to interpret the apocalyptic notion of the End. Rather than viewing the End as a final, static perfection, the process concept of consequent nature of God suggests that the End should be thought of as an ongoing, serially enriched totality.

---

[9]Whitehead, *Process and Reality*, 351.
[10]Beardslee, "Hope in Biblical Eschatology and in Process Theology," 238.

Appendix

An Overview
of Whitehead's Cosmology

One always runs the risk of oversimplification when attempting to present an overview of a metaphysical system. The potential for oversimplification is especially great with respect to the cosmology formulated by Alfred North Whitehead due to the complexity of his thought, his many neologisms, and the nature of his writing style.[1] Yet because it is likely that for many readers the process hermeneutic developed in this book will raise questions which go beyond the scope of the brief discussion of the process worldview presented in chapter 3, a more detailed overview must be attempted. Doubtless, the following overview is deficient as an introduction to Whitehead's cosmology as a whole in that there are aspects of his thought which are not included; all that is attempted here is a presentation of those aspects which are needed to deal with questions the hermeneutic is likely to provoke.

According to Whitehead, a metaphysical system should be coherent, logical, applicable, adequate, and necessary. By coherent, he meant that "the fundamental ideas, in terms of which the

---

[1] In the preface to *Process and Reality* (xii) Whitehead wrote: "the unity of treatment is to be looked for in the gradual development of the scheme, in meaning and relevance, and not in the successive treatment of particular topics." Sherburne (*A Key to Whitehead's Process and Reality*, 2) labeled this weblike rather than linear writing style "the straw-that-breaks-the-reader's-back." Moreover, as Christian (*An Interpretation of Whitehead's Metaphysics*, 2-3) observed, Whitehead's understanding of language led him to write "imaginatively as well as logically, to suggest as well as to state his meaning. . . . This appeal to concrete imagination . . . makes an added demand on the reader. One must learn to understand both his poetry and his logic without confusing one with the other."

scheme is developed, presuppose each other so that in isolation they are meaningless"; that is, the fundamental ideas "shall not seem capable of abstraction from each other." The term logical "has its ordinary meaning, including 'logical' consistency, or lack of contradiction, the definition of constructs in logical terms, the exemplification of general logical notions in specific instances, and the principles of inference." Applicable means "that some items of experience" are interpretable by the system; that is, these items have the character of particular instances of the general scheme. Adequate means "that there are no items incapable of such interpretation." And because the system bears in itself "its own warrant of universality throughout all experience," it may be said to be necessary. One should also note that the terms coherent and logical exhibit the rational side of metaphysics, whereas the terms applicable and adequate exhibit its empirical side.[2]

The following overview introduces a number of Whiteheadian terms. Lest the reader think that Whitehead merely coined neologisms for novelty's sake, it is imperative to recall the discussion in chapter 2 about the struggle involved in expressing event thinking in Indo-European languages. In an effort to reduce to a minimum the inevitable confusion and misunderstandings which result from this struggle, Whitehead attempted to use terminology which was not already loaded with connotations evoking substance thinking. To assist the reader in mastering this terminology, the key terms are set in boldface type.

• Actual Entities/Occasions •

As the designation itself indicates, process thought affirms that process is fundamental to reality. This does not mean that everything is in process; "there are unchanging principles of process and abstract forms. But to be *actual* is to be a process."[3] Central to process thought is the concept of **actual entities** or **actual occasions**.[4] Actual occasions are the final, real "things" which compose

---

[2]Whitehead, *Process and Reality*, 3-4.
[3]Cobb and Griffin, *Process Theology: An Introductory Exposition*, 14.
[4]The word "actual" denotes concrete and real. Although the terms actual entity and actual occasion are often used interchangeably, Whitehead noted one

the universe; "there is no going behind actual entities to find anything more real."[5] Aggregates of actual entities, which Whitehead termed **nexuses** or **societies**,[6] form the objects of everyday experience (for example, rocks, trees, animals, and people).[7] One could say that the process metaphysic conceives of reality "atomistically," that is, the world is composed of a vast number of microscopic entities. This statement is somewhat misleading, however. Whereas most atomistic views of reality understand these "atoms" as inert bits of matter, actual occasions are events or "organisms" that grow, mature, and perish. Also, whereas a materialist or substantialist view of reality maintains that relations are only accidental or external to these atoms, process thought claims that relations are essential or internal to actual occasions. That is, an actual occasion is not first something "in itself" which then enters into relations with other actualities; rather, its relations are constitutive of itself. An actual occasion does not *have* relations; it *is* its relations.[8]

The patterns of relations among actual entities can only be described as an **extensive continuum**. According to human perception, this extensive continuum is four-dimensional. Two observations are necessary to avoid error on this point, however. (1) Because actual entities are the ultimate reality, space-time is an abstraction from the patterns of relations between actual entities. That is, although this pattern of relations include the temporal relations of successiveness and contemporaneity, "time" is not a

---

important exception. Because the term "occasion" implies spatial-temporal extensiveness, God—the one nontemporal actual entity—is never referred to as an actual occasion.

[5]Whitehead, *Process and Reality*, 18.

[6]Nexuses (Whitehead used nexüs as the plural) and societies will be discussed in some detail below.

[7]"In the actual world we discern four grades of actual occasions, grades which are not to be sharply distinguished from each other. First, and lowest, there are the actual occasions in so-called 'empty-space'; secondly, there are the actual occasions which are moments in the life histories of enduring nonliving objects, such as electrons or other primitive organisms; thirdly, there are the actual occasions which are moments in the life histories of enduring living objects; fourthly, there are the actual occasions which are moments in the life histories of enduring objects with conscious knowledge" (Whitehead, *Process and Reality*, 177).

[8]The process does not presuppose a subject; rather, the subject emerges from the process (see the discussion on "subject-superject" below).

single, smooth flow, infinitely divisible; rather, time comes into being as "droplets of experience" (each actual occasion "is the enjoyment of a certain quantum of time"[9]). Likewise, "space" is not to be thought of as a fixed container whose existence precedes events and in which events happen. On the contrary, space is an abstraction from the spatial relations between actual entities. (2) Although the extensive relationships of actual entities, as perceived by humans, is four-dimensional (that is, actual entities have spatial and temporal relations), this does not mean that all entities have had or will have precisely this number of dimensions. The four-dimensional universe is simply the form that the present **cosmic epoch**[10] takes; all that is *necessary* is that actual entities be in relation with other actual entities.

Each actual occasion comes into being through a process labeled **concrescence**, a "growing together" of a diverse "many" into a unified "one."[11] A becoming occasion takes into account, or appropriates as its own, or "grasps" data arising from the objectification of past actual occasions. This process of appropriating or grasping an element from a past actual occasion is termed a **prehension**. In a prehension, a datum element moves from the objectivity of a past actual occasion ("there-then") to the subjective immediacy of the becoming actual occasion ("here-now").[12] Every prehension consists of three elements: the **subject**[13] which is

---

[9]Whitehead, *Process and Reality*, 283. For discussion of Whitehead's "epochal theory of time" see *Process and Reality*, 67-69, and *Science and the Modern World* (New York: Free Press, 1967; New York: Macmillan, 1925) 113-27. Also see the brief discussion of "duration" below.

[10]The term cosmic epoch refers to "that widest society of actual entities whose immediate relevance to ourselves is traceable" (Whitehead, *Process and Reality*, 91).

[11]The phases of concrescence will be discussed in some detail below.

[12]Thus, a prehension has a "vector character" in that it transforms what is "there-then" into what is "here-now." Prehensions are the concrete or particular "facts of relatedness which give unity and continuity to the world" (Christian, *An Interpretation of Whitehead's Metaphysics*, 233). One should note that actual entities prehend entities of all eight of "The Categories of Existence": actual entities, prehensions, nexuses, subjective forms, eternal objects, propositions, multiplicities, and contrasts (Whitehead, *Process and Reality*, 22). Each of these categories will be discussed below.

[13]Although Whitehead usually used the familiar term subject, he felt that it is misleading and so coined the neologism **subject-superject** to express his thought

prehending (that is, the becoming occasion); the **datum** which is prehended (that is, the element from the past); and the **subjective form** which is "how" that subject prehends that datum (examples at the human level include consciousness, joy, anger, and dread).[14] A **positive prehension**, also termed a **feeling**, is the definite inclusion of a datum into positive contribution to a subject's internal constitution. A **negative prehension** is the definite exclusion of a datum from positive contribution. By means of its positive and negative prehensions, an actual occasion has a definite—though generally faint—bond with each entity in its past **actual world**;[15] it prehends, either immediately or mediately, the totality of the past. In the final analysis, then, an actual occasion is a concrescence or "growing together" of prehensions. This concrescence of prehensions is governed by the occasion's **subjective aim** which is a feeling of what the process may achieve together with appetition toward its realization.[16] Through a process of selection, harmonization, and supplementation[17]—which indicates creative self-determination and decision on the part of the becoming occasion[18]—the

---

more precisely.
    The philosophies of substance presuppose a subject which then encounters a datum, and then reacts to the datum. The philosophy of organism [Whitehead's designation for his system] presupposes a datum which is met with feelings, and progressively attains the unity of a subject. But with this doctrine, "superject" would be a better term than "subject." . . . The subject-superject is the purpose of the process originating the feelings. The feelings are inseparable from the end at which they aim; and this end is the feeler. The feelings aim at the feeler, as their final cause.
Process and Reality, 155, 222. Thus, an actual occasion is both the subject (the experiencer) of its feelings and the superject of (that which is produced by) its feelings. Expressed in terms of the "many" and the "one" (see the discussion on creativity below), the one is both the *subject* of the prehensions of the many (emphasis on the one) and the *superject* of the many (emphasis on the many).

[14]"Datum" (which is subdivided into "initial datum" and "objective datum") and "subjective form" will be discussed in more detail below in connection with the phases of concrescence.

[15]The "actual world" of an actual entity is the collection of past actual entities which are given as data for the concrescence of that actual entity. No two actual entities share exactly the same actual world.

[16]"The subjective aim . . . is at intensity of feeling (a) in the immediate subject, and (b) in the *relevant* future" (Whitehead, *Process and Reality*, 27). The origin of the subjective aim will be discussed below.

[17]See the discussion of the phases of concrescence below.

[18]"Creativity," "self-determination," "decision," and other such terms in

many prehensions of the past actual world are unified into one final, complex, integrated feeling known as the **satisfaction** of the actual occasion. (See fig. A-1, below, p. 242.)

Upon attaining satisfaction, the occasion ceases to be an experiencing subject and presents itself to succeeding occasions as a datum for prehension. Thus, an actual occasion "is to be conceived of both as a subject presiding over its own immediacy of becoming, and a superject which is the atomic creature exercising its function of objective immortality" (that is, the character it has as a datum for prehension by subsequent occasions).[19] The effect of an actual occasion on succeeding occasions is labeled its **objective immortality** because it "lives on"[20] in the finite world through being prehended by succeeding occasions. Because an actual occasion is a subject-superject, it can be considered both "formally" and "objectively." The formal reality of an occasion belongs to its concrescence; the objective reality of an occasion belongs to its satisfaction.

An actual occasion is exclusive of all other occasions in the sense that no two occasions—past, present, or future—have any immediacy of feeling in common. (1) The "flow of feeling" from a past occasion into the becoming occasion does not involve any sharing of immediacy; rather, it occurs through objectification of the datum occasion by the subject occasion.[21] (2) Contemporary occasions[22] are causally independent of each other; they do not

---

process thought do not imply conscious judgment, although in higher entities consciousness can be a factor (see the discussion of the phases of concrescence below). "'Decision' is used in its root sense to mean a 'cutting off' of alternatives. This is 'the very meaning of actuality' . . . for the existence of an actuality means that some 'pure' possibilities are excluded" (Christian, *An Interpretation of Whitehead's Metaphysics*, 32).

[19]Whitehead, *Process and Reality*, 45. "Thus an actual entity has a threefold character: (i) it has the character 'given' for it by the past; (ii) it has the subjective character aimed at in its process of concrescence; (iii) it has the superjective character, which is the pragmatic value of its specific satisfaction qualifying the transcendent creativity" (87).

[20]The occasion is no longer an experiencing subject, no longer an "actuality," for actuality involves immediacy of feeling; rather, the occasion is now a "potentiality" for prehension, an "object."

[21]See the discussion of the phases of concrescence below.

[22]A discussion of contemporary occasions requires that one also discuss

influence each other nor is there any *direct* perception of each other. Although a becoming occasion has **strain-feelings**[23] in which the regions composing the contemporary world are differentiated, the occasions occupying those regions are not prehended *in their concrete actuality.*[24] (3) From the standpoint of a becoming occasion, all future occasions are merely hypothetical. Future occasions are immanent in a present occasion only by means of **anticipatory feelings**. The becoming occasion "embodies a creative urge toward the future beyond itself"; that is, it anticipates future concrescences which will prehend it as a datum. Thus, "the character of future actualities is now being partly determined by the activity of the present occasion."[25]

Whitehead emphasized the importance of actual entities in the **ontological principle**:

> every condition to which the process of becoming conforms in any particular instance, has its reason *either* in the character of some actual entity in the actual world of that concrescence, *or* in the character of the subject which is in process of concrescence. . . . This ontological principle means that actual entities are the only *reasons*; so that to search for a *reason* is to search for one or more actual entities.[26]

Whitehead's understanding of a **duration**. A duration is "a cross section of the universe," a set of occasions "defined by the characteristic that any two of its members are contemporaries" (Whitehead, *Process and Reality*, 125). In general, the term duration corresponds to the common sense notion of the immediate present; yet, whereas the classical theory of time assumed that an occasion could be a member of only one duration, Whitehead (in agreement with the relativity theory of time) asserted that an occasion is a member of more than one duration. The duration which includes all of an occasions immediate present is termed the **presented duration**. (See fig. A-2, below, p. 243.)

[23]Whitehead also used the expression **regional feelings** to refer to these feelings "in which the forms [eternal object (see below)] exemplified in the datum concern geometrical, straight, and flat loci" (*Process and Reality*, 316, 310). These feelings express the geometrical relations of the extensive continuum *from the perspective of* the region or standpoint of a becoming occasion (thus, space-time is relative to the perspective or standpoint of each becoming occasion).

[24]See the discussion of "perception in the mode of presentational immediacy" in chap. 4 for an explanation of what appears to be the perception of contemporary entities.

[25]Christian, *An Interpretation of Whitehead's Metaphysics*, 123.

[26]Whitehead, *Process and Reality*, 24.

• Creativity •

Actual entities may be central to process thought, but they are not ultimate. In all metaphysical systems there is an ultimate category. In itself the ultimate is not actual; therefore, it is capable of characterization only through its accidental embodiments (that is, specific instances of actuality are instantiations of the ultimate; the ultimate does not exist apart from these actual instances). In process metaphysics this ultimate is termed **creativity**.[27] Creativity is the dynamic rhythm between the many and the one. "'Creativity,' 'many,' 'one' are the ultimate notions involved in the meaning of the synonymous terms 'thing,' 'being,' 'entity.' These three notions complete the Category of the Ultimate and are presupposed in all the more special categories."[28] (Thus, reality is pluralistic, dynamic, and internally related instead of monistic, static, and externally related.) According to this ultimate metaphysical principle, there is continual advance from the universe disjunctively (that is, the universe existing as separate entities; the "many") to the universe conjunctively (that is, the universe unified in a single entity; the "one"). The universe expands through unifications of itself in *novel* actual entities; yet each new concrescence offers itself as a member of a new multiplicity in need of unification. "The many become one, and are increased by one."[29] This is the rhythm of process. Thus, the universe is never complete; it is "a creative advance into novelty"[30] with history never repeating itself exactly.

---

[27]Whitehead, *Process and Reality*, 7. He noted that
in monistic philosophies, Spinoza's or absolute idealism, this ultimate is God, who is also equivalently termed "The Absolute." *In such monistic schemes, the ultimate is illegitimately allowed a final, "eminent" reality, beyond that ascribed to any of its accidents.* In this general position the philosophy of organism seems to approximate more to some strains of Indian, or Chinese, thought, than to western Asiatic, or European, thought. One side makes process ultimate; the other side makes fact ultimate [emphasis added].
[28]Whitehead, *Process and Reality*, 21.
[29]Whitehead, *Process and Reality*, 21.
[30]Whitehead, *Process and Reality*, 222.

Two ideas follow from the assertion that creativity is ultimate. First, no actual entity is totally derived from other actual entities; preceding entities condition but do not fully determine succeeding entities. Every actual entity is to some degree self-creative. Second, every actual entity is to some degree novel;[31] its novelty results from its self-creativity.

Whitehead distinguished two types of process: **concrescence**, the process of becoming, and **transition**, the process of influencing another's becoming. Concrescent creativity begins with efficient causation (the power of past entities to influence the becoming entity) and moves to final causation (the self-creation of the becoming entity); transcendent creativity begins with final causation and moves to efficient causation. Thus, the creative process consists of an alternating rhythm: concrescent creativity, transcendent creativity, concrescent creativity, and so on.[32]

• Eternal Objects •

According to the **principle of relativity**, "it belongs to the nature of a 'being' that it is a potential for every 'becoming.'"[33] Or to reverse the perspective, in its process of becoming, an actual entity prehends other actual entities. In fact, if allowance is made for degrees of relevance from considerable to negligible, one must say that a becoming entity prehends *all* entities in its past actual world; every item in the universe is involved in each moment of concrescence. To understand how an actual entity "is present in"

---

[31]Occasions differ in their data, subjective forms, subjective aims, and satisfactions.
[32]Whitehead, *Process and Reality*, 210-11.
[33]Whitehead, *Process and Reality*, 22.

other actual entities[34]—how it "functions"[35] in their self-creation—one must consider the role of **eternal objects**.[36]

"Particulars" and "universals" are the usual philosophical terms which roughly correspond to Whitehead's terms "actual occasions" and "eternal objects." Like Plato, Whitehead did not believe that particulars could be prehended apart from universals; on the contrary, he affirmed that "they are prehended by the mediation of universals."[37] Nevertheless, he refused to adopt Plato's terms in the development of his system because of certain misleading connotations attached to them. Two examples will illustrate the difference between Platonic and Whiteheadian terminology at this point. (1) In Platonic thought universals have "real being," that is, being exempt from becoming. Universals (for example, the idea "rock") are the standards of being to which particular things in the world of becoming (for example, a particular rock) merely approximate. Particulars are but mere shadows of changeless universals, mere illusions of reality. In process thought, however, eternal objects are not "more real" than actual entities; on the contrary, nothing is more real (that is, more actual) than temporal actual entities. Eternal objects in themselves are pure potentials; they are devoid of actuality. Thus in Whitehead's opinion, the "final Platonic problem" is that it subordinates actuality (actual entities, particulars) to possibility (eternal objects, universals), flux to permanence.[38] (2) In Platonic thought there is a sharp distinction between universals and particulars. A universal

---

[34]Whitehead, *Process and Reality*, 50:
The philosophy of organism is mainly devoted to the task of making clear the notion of "being present in another entity." This phrase is here borrowed from Aristotle: it is not a fortunate phrase, and in subsequent discussion it will be replaced by the term "objectification." The Aristotelian phrase suggests the crude notion that one actual entity is added to another *simpliciter* [simply, absolutely, without qualification]. This is not what is meant.

[35]To function means to contribute determination to an actual entity (see Whitehead, *Process and Reality*, 25).

[36]Whitehead also referred to eternal objects as "pure potentials for the specific determination of fact" and "forms of definiteness." As pure potentials, they are not actual.

[37]Whitehead, *Process and Reality*, 152.

[38]Whitehead, *Process and Reality*, 209, 346-47.

is "that which can enter into the description of many particulars" (for example, the idea "rock" can describe many particular rocks), whereas a particular "is described by universals" (for example, a particular rock can be described by the ideas "rock," "hard," and "gray"). A particular does not, however, "enter into the description of any other particular." Process thought blurs this distinction between what is universal and what is particular, for "an actual entity cannot be described, even inadequately, by universals" alone because "other actual entities do enter into the description of any one actual entity. Thus every so-called 'universal' is particular in the sense of being just what it is, diverse from everything else; and every so-called 'particular' is universal in the sense of entering into the constitutions of other actual entities."[39] Because of these and other misleading ideas associated with the terms particulars and universals, Whitehead employed the expressions actual occasions/entities and eternal objects.

Eternal objects are "potentialities of definiteness" (how something *might* be actual) capable of specifying the character of actual entities (for example, grayness, whiteness, hardness, softness, and so forth, without reference to any particular actual entity). The functioning of an eternal object in the self-creation of an actual occasion is the **ingression**[40] of the eternal object into the occasion. By its ingression, it contributes to the definiteness of that occasion. In itself, however, an eternal object does not refer to any particular actual entity of the temporal world; that is, eternal objects are "timeless in their mode of existence and indeterminate as to their physical realization."[41] "An eternal object is always a potentiality for actual entities; but in itself . . . it is neutral as to the fact of its physical ingression in any particular actual entity of the temporal world."[42]

To return to the question of how one actual entity is present in another, Whitehead explained that a becoming actual entity prehends a datum actual entity by one of the datum entity's

---

[39]Whitehead, *Process and Reality*, 48.

[40]Other equivalent expressions are realization, participation, exemplification, and illustration.

[41]Christian, *An Interpretation of Whitehead's Metaphysics*, 217.

[42]Whitehead, *Process and Reality*, 44.

component feelings. There is a "flow of feeling" from the datum entity to the becoming entity as the subject entity feels one of the feelings of the datum entity. Now ingredient in the datum entity's feelings are eternal objects. The becoming entity's prehension (or objectification) of the datum entity by one of the datum entity's feelings results in the two entities sharing the eternal object (or group of eternal objects) ingredient in the datum feeling. Or to view the matter from a different perspective, this eternal object has a two-way functioning: it is a partial determinant of the datum entity and of the subject entity. (See fig. A-3, below, p. 244.)

According to Whitehead, "the fundamental types of entities are actual entities, and eternal objects; . . . the other types of entities only express how all entities of the two fundamental types are in community with each other, in the actual world."[43] For the purpose at hand, two differences between the fundamental entities can be underscored. First, an actual entity can occur only once and only at one place, but an eternal object can occur at more than one time and at more than one place at the same time (that is, an eternal object may have multiple ingressions and, consequently, multiple locations). Second, no two actual entities have the same place and time, but two or more eternal objects may exist at the same time and place (that is, two or more eternal objects may be ingredient in the same actual entity). In noting these two differences, however, one must beware of committing what Whitehead called the **fallacy of simple location**—the idea that something is located at one point in space-time in the sense that it "does not require for its explanation any reference to other regions of space-time."[44]

---

[43]*Process and Reality*, 25. "The other types of entities" Whitehead referred to are the six that with actual entities and eternal objects make up the "Categories of Existence": prehensions, nexuses, subjective forms, propositions, multiplicities, and contrasts. Two points should be noted about Whitehead's ontology. First, he does not distinguish between "existence" and "being." All entities exist, and anything one can think of is an entity. Second, existence is not the ultimate category. "'Creativity,' 'many,' 'one' are the ultimate notions involved in the meaning of the synonymous terms 'thing,' 'being,' 'entity.' These three notions complete the Category of the Ultimate and are presupposed in all the more special categories" (*Process and Reality*, 21). See below for a more detailed discussion of these entities.

[44]Whitehead, *Science and the Modern World*, 49.

Although from the perspective of its subjective immediacy an actual occasion may be said to be located at one point in space-time, from another perspective it includes its whole past (by means of positive and negative prehensions) and it pervades its whole future (by means of objective immortality). "In a certain sense, everything is everywhere at all times."[45]

Whitehead at times referred to a "realm" of eternal objects. The term can be misleading, however, since it might suggest "some fixed and necessary order among the members of the collection, so that these entities could not exist except in this order."[46] Whitehead specifically denied that eternal objects have any systematic mutual relatedness; on the contrary, they are a **multiplicity**.[47] A multiplicity "consists of many entities, and its unity is constituted by the fact that all its constituent entities severally satisfy at least one condition which no other entity satisfies."[48] Their "unity" consists simply in the fact that eternal objects are a particular category of existence (that is, they are not actual entities, or prehensions, or nexuses, or subjective forms, or propositions, or contrasts).[49] Another way to state the ontological principle is, "All real togetherness is togetherness in the formal constitution of an actuality."[50] Thus, apart from the actual entities in which they are ingredient, eternal objects have no real togetherness. Taken by themselves eternal objects are a multiplicity, a pure disjunction of abstract possibilities. Moreover, the multiplicity of eternal objects is infinite. Because of this, "something new can always come out of past achievement. Yet no new possibilities need to come into being *as possibilities*. . . . New situations affect the relevance but not the being of eternal objects."[51]

---

[45]Whitehead, *Science and the Modern World*, 91.
[46]Christian, *An Interpretation of Whitehead's Metaphysics*, 259.
[47]Whitehead, *Process and Reality*, 31, 43, 46.
[48]Whitehead, *Process and Reality*, 24.
[49]Whitehead, *Process and Reality*, 29-30.
[50]Whitehead, *Process and Reality*, 32.
[51]Christian, *An Interpretation of Whitehead's Metaphysics*, 253. According to Category of Explanation III, "in the becoming of an actual entity, novel prehensions, nexuses, subjective forms, propositions, multiplicities, and contrasts, also become; but there are no novel eternal objects" (*Process and Reality*, 22).

The absence of a fixed order means that there are no *ultimate* exclusions or incompatibilities with respect to eternal objects. Incompatibility and exclusion of eternal objects "are not laid up in heaven" (that is, are not absolute or ultimate) but "are decided by the natures of actualities" (that is, are relative to specific actualities).[52] Whitehead explained: "Whatever is realized in any one occasion of experience necessarily excludes the unbounded welter of contrary possibilities. There are always 'others' which might have been and are not."[53] For example, if the rock is gray it cannot be white or any other color. In addition, the past actual world and the subjective aim determine what is possible for a particular occasion. But what is impossible for one occasion may be possible for another, given the creative advance of nature. Thus, a distinction should be made between **pure possibilities** and **real possibilities**.[54] On the one hand, pure possibilities are eternal objects "in themselves"; such possibilities do not refer to any particular actuality, although they do refer to actualities in general. Real possibilities, on the other hand, are eternal objects relative to some particular actuality; such possibilities are permitted by the circumstances of some actual world and the subjective aim of a becoming occasion. Thus, while there is no fixed order of eternal objects, the actual world of a particular concrescence introduces an

---

[52]Christian, *An Interpretation of Whitehead's Metaphysics*, 254-5. Christian continued:

> Exclusiveness among forms [eternal objects] must be stated by contradictory propositions, and a proposition . . . has for its logical subjects some set of actual entities . . . If a proposition p predicates some eternal object of a certain set of actual entities, then the negation of p is an assertion that *those* actual entities do not have that form of definiteness. This is another way of saying that "In the nature of things there are no ultimate exclusions, expressive in logical terms."

Exclusion or "inconsistency is relative to the abstraction involved" (Whitehead, *Modes of Thought* [New York: Free Press, 1968; New York: Macmillan, 1938] 76). See below for discussions of "propositions" and "abstractions."

[53]Whitehead, *Adventures of Ideas*, 276.

[54]There is a third type of possibility to be discussed in detail below. "Propositions" are **impure possibilities**. They describe hypothetical states of affairs; thus, they are neither "pure" possibilities nor "pure" actualities, but rather are "hybrid" or "impure" entities. Propositions refer both to particular actualities and to pure possibilities.

order among eternal objects relevant to that concrescence. This incomplete and relative order is called the **objective lure** for the concrescence arising from that actual world.

• God •

The preceding discussion of actual occasions, creativity, and eternal objects raises two questions. (1) How can unrealized eternal objects be relevant to a becoming occasion? How can a becoming occasion experience possibilities (eternal objects) that are not ingredient in past actual occasions; that is, how can novelty arise? Will not the prehension of past actual occasions merely lead to the repetition of a given number of possibilities? As stated earlier, relevance implies a real fact of togetherness in the formal constitution of an actuality. Eternal objects ingredient in the past actual world have a real togetherness, but *in themselves* eternal objects have no real togetherness; they are a multiplicity, a pure disjunction of abstract possibilities. The presence of novelty in the world indicates that unrealized eternal objects *are* relevant to becoming occasions, but how? (2) What is the origin of the subjective aim which guides the concrescence of an occasion? If the subject *emerges* from rather than is presupposed by the concrescence, what is the origin of its subjective aim?

These questions require a discussion of Whitehead's conception of God as "the principle of limitation (concretion)." In *Science and the Modern World*,[55] Whitehead began his discussion of God with the fact that particular, finite, ordered actualities exist. Clearly, then, there must be some limitation on possibility. Without "the principle of limitation" there could be no ordering of possibilities, no values introducing contraries, grades, and oppositions among eternal objects. But neither "creativity" nor "the multiplicity of eternal objects" nor both together provide the needed limitation. Thus, there must be a primordial, nontemporal actual entity[56] which limits or orders the multiplicity of eternal objects.[57]

---

[55]Whitehead, *Science and the Modern World*, 173-79.

[56]Many of Whitehead's interpreters have suggested that God is better viewed as a living person rather than a single actual entity (living person is discussed below in the section on enduring objects and the macrocosmic world).

[57]Whitehead (*Process and Reality*, 31-32) called this nontemporal actual entity

The primordial created fact is the unconditioned conceptual valuation of the entire multiplicity of eternal objects. This is the 'primordial nature' of God. By reason of this complete valuation, the objectification of God in each derivate actual entity results in a graduation of the relevance of eternal objects to the concrescent phases of that derivate occasion. There will be additional ground of relevance for select eternal objects by reason of their ingression into derivate actual entities belonging to the actual world of the concrescent occasion in question. But whether or no this be the case, there is always the definite relevance derived from God. Apart from God, eternal objects unrealized in the actual world would be relatively nonexistent for the concrescence in question. For effective relevance requires agency of comparison, and agency belongs exclusively to actual occasions.** This divine ordering is itself matter of fact, thereby conditioning creativity. Thus possibility which transcends realized temporal matter of fact has a real relevance to the creative advance.[58]

This primordial instance of creativity was an unconditioned **conceptual prehension**[59] of the entire multiplicity of eternal objects by the nontemporal actual entity, God.[60] This creative act was

---

God "because the contemplation of our natures, as enjoying real feelings derived from the timeless source of all order, acquires that 'subjective form' of refreshment and companionship at which religions aim."

[58]Whitehead, *Process and Reality*, 31. The double asterisk indicates that the editors of the corrected edition offer an alternative reading. They remark (395): "It has been suggested that 'actual occasions' should read 'actual entities,' since Whitehead has God's agency in view here and yet says elsewhere that the term 'actual occasions' excludes God . . . It is possible that, when writing the present passage, Whitehead had not yet settled upon this distinction between the two terms."

[59]A prehension whose datum is an eternal object is termed a "conceptual prehension" in distinction from a **physical prehension** whose datum is an actual entity. A physical prehension involves an eternal object, but an eternal object as immanent, as ingredient in a particular actual entity (e.g., gray ingredient in a particular actual occasion). In contrast, a conceptual prehension is the feeling of an eternal object without reference to any particular actual entity, a feeling of the eternal object "in itself" (e.g., grayness nowhere in particular).

[60]Whitehead (*Process and Reality*) noted that "by the principle of relativity there can only be one nonderivative actuality, unbounded by its prehensions of an actual world" (32). "Unfettered conceptual valuation . . . is only possible once in the universe; since that creative act is objectively immortal as an inescapable

devoid of negative prehensions since it was not limited (conditioned) by any presupposed actuality. This concrescence of conceptual prehensions, this primordial satisfaction, results in a real togetherness of all eternal objects because God is an actual entity.[61] The multiplicity of eternal objects thus obtains a graded relevance to each stage of the creative advance. All succeeding actualities presuppose this primordial creative act "while *it* merely presupposed the *general* metaphysical character of creative advance, of which it is the primordial exemplification."[62]

This ordering of the multiplicity of eternal objects in the **primordial nature** of God should not be understood to contradict what was said earlier about there being no final and necessary order of eternal objects. "If there were such an order, then this would itself be a complex eternal object, and then there would be an eternal object which included all other eternal objects."[63] Whitehead specifically denied this when he called the totality of eternal objects a multiplicity. No eternal object can escape membership in this multiplicity, but a complex eternal object which included all other eternal objects would do just that. Moreover, such an eternal object would have to be created by God, but this is impossible, for there can be no novel eternal objects (God's nature requires eternal objects in the same degree that they require God).[64] Thus, there is not one fixed and necessary order of eternal objects in the primordial nature of God. "There is not one and only one way in which all things *must* happen. There is not even a preexisting concept in the mind of God of how all things *will* happen. There is not even an ideal pattern of how all things *may* happen."[65]

How, then, should one conceive of this "order" of eternal objects within the primordial nature of God? According to William Christian, "it is truer to say that God envisages possibilities of

---

condition characterizing creative action" (247).

[61] According to the ontological principle, "All real togetherness is togetherness in the formal constitution of an actuality" (Whitehead, *Process and Reality*, 32).

[62] Whitehead, *Process and Reality*, 344.

[63] Christian, *An Interpretation of Whitehead's Metaphysics*, 272.

[64] Whitehead, *Process and Reality*, 257.

[65] Christian, *An Interpretation of Whitehead's Metaphysics*, 273.

order than that God envisages an order of possibilities."[66] In God's envisagement all eternal objects are together. God values—that is, has appetition for the realization of—each eternal object; consequently, all eternal objects are relevant to each other.

> To say that there is a general scheme of relatedness among eternal objects is only to say that all relations are possible . . . If some certain eternal object were actualized, then all other eternal objects would be relevant in *some* way or other. It does *not* mean that if some certain eternal object were actualized, then there is some *particular* way in which it would be necessary for all other eternal objects to be relevant.[67]

The result of this divine envisagement is that the entire multiplicity of eternal objects is relevant for each becoming occasion. But the past actual world determines to a large degree what is possible for a becoming occasion; it necessitates decision and exclusion (that is, real possibility limits pure possibility). Thus, although there is a general relevance of all eternal objects for each becoming occasion due to their envisagement in the primordial nature of God ("the reservoir of potentiality"[68]), the character of the actual world of each becoming occasion adds special relevance to some eternal objects resulting in the grading of the entire multiplicity. "In this way the pattern of relevance of eternal objects changes with the creative advance of nature."[69]

It is now possible to answer the first question with which this section began (How can unrealized eternal objects be relevant to a becoming occasion?). Although many eternal objects are neither physically nor conceptually realized in the past actual world of a

---

[66]Christian, *An Interpretation of Whitehead's Metaphysics*, 276.

[67]Christian, *An Interpretation of Whitehead's Metaphysics*, 274. Cf. Cobb (*A Christian Natural Theology*, 155-56):

> the eternal ordering of the eternal objects is not one simple order but an indefinite variety of orders. God's ordering of possibilities is such that every possible state of the actual world is already envisioned as possible and every possible development from that actual state of the world is already envisioned and appraised. Thus, the one primordial ordering of eternal objects is relevant to every actuality with perfect specificity.

[68]Whitehead, *Modes of Thought*, 94.

[69]Christian, *An Interpretation of Whitehead's Metaphysics*, 270.

becoming occasion, all eternal objects have their graded relevance to the occasion through the prehension of God in the initial phase of concrescence.[70] In addition, this answer points to the answer to the second question (What is the origin of the subjective aim which guides the concrescence of an occasion?).

The subjective aim cannot originate with the subject because the subject emerges from, rather than is presupposed by, concrescence. The aim cannot be derived from a past occasion because it is a novel possibility not realized in the actual world; nor can it be derived from a contemporary occasion because contemporary occasions are causally independent; nor can it be derived from a future occasion because future occasions are merely hypothetical (not actual). How, then, does this novel idea of what the becoming occasion may become originate? According to the ontological principle, to seek a reason is to seek an actual entity; the only actual entity remaining to consider is the nontemporal entity, God.

According to Whitehead, the initial stage of a subjective aim "is an endowment which the subject inherits from the inevitable ordering of things, conceptually realized in the nature of God. . . . The initial aim is the best for that *impasse.*" This **initial aim** is relevant to the actual world of the occasion in question[71]—that is, it "determines the initial gradations of relevance of eternal objects for conceptual feeling"[72]—but it does not determine the final form of the subjective aim. The initial aim, the lure of God "toward that way of becoming which is most in line with God's own aim of creating intensity of harmonious feeling in the world,"[73] may be

---

[70]See below for a discussion of the phases of concrescence.

[71]The initial aim for a particular concrescence is not predetermined from eternity because there is no fixed order of eternal objects in the primordial nature of God; nor is it totally determined by the past actual world. The initial aim is determined jointly by the past actual world and the creative self-determination of God in reaction to that past actual world.

[72]Whitehead, *Process and Reality*, 244.

[73]Sherburne, *A Key to Whitehead's Process and Reality*, 28. According to Whitehead (*Process and Reality*), "God's purpose in the creative advance is the evocation of intensities" (105); or in more poetic language, God "is the poet of the world, with tender patience leading it by his vision of truth, beauty, and goodness" (346). Cf. Cobb and Griffin (*Process Theology: An Introductory Exposition*, 26): "God is the divine Eros urging the world to new heights of enjoyment."

accepted as is or may be modified by the becoming occasion in the succeeding phases of its concrescence.

Because God supplies the initial aim, "God can be termed the creator of each temporal actual entity. But the phrase is apt to be misleading by its suggestion that the ultimate creativity of the universe is to be ascribed to God's volition."[74] According to process metaphysics, God is the primordial instance of creativity and therefore conditions each succeeding act of creativity. Moreover, because God is nontemporal, God is not merely *"before* all creation, but *with* all creation. . . . the lure for feeling, the eternal urge of desire."[75] Yet all actual entities are to some degree self-creative; therefore, God is not the sole creator. Nevertheless, God's supplying of the initial aim is quite significant. For one thing, the initial aim determines what standpoint a becoming occasion will occupy, and the standpoint determines which occasions will constitute the past actual world for the becoming occasion.[76] The initial aim also significantly influences—but does not determine—what satisfaction will be attained because it presents a graded set of related, relevant possibilities for actualization; the satisfaction actually attained will be among them although it may not be the ideal possibility.[77]

Whitehead's notion of the divine primordial nature does not exhaust his understanding of God. If God is nontemporal and thus "available" to each becoming occasion, then according to the principle of relativity not only must God affect the evolving world, but also the evolving world must, in turn, affect God. This effect on God Whitehead labelled the divine **consequent nature**, God's physical prehension of the actual occasions of the temporal world.[78] These prehensions are then integrated with the primordial vision[79] in such a way that there is no loss or obstruction; the

---

[74]Whitehead, *Process and Reality*, 225.

[75]Whitehead, *Process and Reality*, 343-44.

[76]Whitehead, *Process and Reality*, 128, 283-84.

[77]Whitehead, *Process and Reality*, 164, 207, 344.

[78]Thus, the nature of God is **dipolar**: one side is "free, complete, primordial, eternal, actually deficient, and unconscious"; the other side is "determined, incomplete, consequent, 'everlasting,' fully actual, and conscious" (Whitehead, *Process and Reality*, 345). See below for a discussion of the dipolar nature of all actual entities.

[79]Thus, this nature is "consequent" in a twofold way: it follows from the

actual occasions are prehended in their totality and preserved everlastingly in God. The resulting satisfaction (the **superjective nature** of God) is then available to the world in the form of new initial aims relevant to new becoming occasions, and the process repeats itself.[80] (See fig. A-4, below, p. 245.) Thus, temporal actualities matter, both to the experiences of succeeding temporal occasions *and* to the divine experience. In a relational universe temporal entities affect each other, God affects the world, and the world affects God.

At this point it should be clear that Whitehead does not introduce God as a *deus ex machina*. (Such an ad hoc notion of God would be uncorrelated with the fundamental principles of his metaphysical system rendering the system incoherent.) In fact, Whitehead explicitly argued that "God is not to be treated as an exception to all metaphysical principles, invoked to save their collapse." On the contrary, God "is their chief exemplification."[81] The following statements demonstrate the importance of the matter to him.

> There is no going behind actual entities to find anything more real. They differ among themselves: God is an actual entity, and so is the most trivial puff of existence in far-off empty space. But, though there are gradations of importance, and diversities of function, yet in the principles which actuality exemplifies all are on the same level.
>
> God's existence is not generically different from that of other actual entities, except that [God] is 'primordial' . . .
>
> The presumption that there is only one genus of actual entities constitutes an ideal of cosmological theory to which the philosophy of organism endeavours to conform. The description of the generic character of an actual entity should include God, as well

---

primordial nature of God and from the actual happenings in the universe.

[80]Because the rhythm of process never ends, the consequent nature of God is a serially enriched totality; the preserving of temporal value is cumulative in nature.

[81]Whitehead, *Process and Reality*, 343. See also *Science and the Modern World*, 92-93, and *Adventures of Ideas*, 169.

as the lowliest actual occasion, though there is a specific difference between the nature of God and that of any occasion.[82]

If God is the chief exemplification of, rather than the exception to, the fundamental metaphysical principles, then the minimal description of an actual entity should apply to God (with the exception that God is primordial). According to Whitehead, "an actual entity has a threefold character: (i) it has the character 'given' for it by the past; (ii) it has the subjective character aimed at in its process of concrescence; (iii) it has the superjective character, which is the pragmatic value of its specific satisfaction qualifying the transcendent creativity."[83] Because God is primordial, there is no past actual world for God; thus, the first instance of creativity would be an unconditioned envisagement of eternal objects. Nevertheless, God demonstrates the same threefold character common to actual entities. (1) The primordial nature is a concrescence of conceptual prehensions whose data include all eternal objects. The subjective aim guiding this concrescence is that the subjective forms of the prehensions will result in an ordering of the eternal objects so as to establish their graded relevance to each stage in the creative advance, because God desires the actualization of all possibilities. (2) The consequent nature is God's physical prehensions of the actual occasions of the evolving universe. The subjective aim derived from the primordial nature guides the divine concrescence, integrating these physical prehensions with the primordial conceptual prehensions. (3) The resulting satisfaction or superjective nature then qualifies the transcendent creativity.[84]

Similarities between God and other actual entities, therefore, include: conceptual and physical prehensions, concrescence, subjective aim, subjective forms of feeling, satisfaction, and superjective nature. Differences between God and other actual entities include: God is primordial as well as consequent; God's concrescence "originates" with conceptual prehensions and is "completed" with physical prehensions which is the reverse of actual occasions; God's conceptual experience is unlimited; God is everlasting[85]

---

[82]Whitehead, *Process and Reality*, 18, 75, 110.
[83]Whitehead, *Process and Reality*, 87.
[84]Whitehead, *Process and Reality*, 87-88.
[85]Although God prehends all eternal objects (the primordial nature), God as

whereas actual occasions perish; God prehends every actual entity throughout the creative advance of nature whereas actual occasions prehend only those occasions which comprise their past actual worlds; because God's conceptual experience is unlimited God's prehension of every actual occasion is complete, whereas actual occasions must eliminate data by means of negative prehensions in order to achieve a unified satisfaction. Thus, Christian's evaluation of the coherence of Whitehead's notion of God appears to be correct: "The difference between God and actual occasions does not amount to a categoreal difference."[86] Rather than being the exception to the fundamental description of actual entities, "God is the mirror image" of other actual entities, that is, "the principles governing all actual entities are in some instances exemplified in a reverse way in God."[87]

To summarize, God is both "the foundation of order" and "the goad towards novelty." "Apart from the intervention of God, there could be nothing new in the world, and no order in the world. The course of creation would be a dead level of ineffectiveness, with all balance and intensity progressively excluded by the cross currents of incompatibility."[88] Yet order and novelty are not ends in themselves; they are instruments of God's subjective aim at creating intensity of harmonious feeling in the world.

• The Phases of Concrescence •

The preceding discussion has focused on actual occasions and the three "formative elements"—from whose mutual interaction actual occasions emerge—creativity, eternal objects, and God. It is now necessary to discuss the phases of concrescence in more detail. Whitehead provided the following overview: "The process of concrescence is divisible into an initial stage of many feelings, and a succession of subsequent phases of more complex feelings integrating the earlier simpler feelings, up to the satisfaction which is

---

a whole (which includes the consequent nature) is everlasting, not eternal, because God is affected by temporal entities.

[86]Christian, *An Interpretation of Whitehead's Metaphysics*, 288.
[87]Sherburne, *A Key to Whitehead's Process and Reality*, 226.
[88]Whitehead, *Process and Reality*, 88, 247.

one complex unity of feeling."[89] Before examining the phases in detail, one must first note the relation of the process of concrescence to time. "This genetic passage from phase to phase is not in physical time: the exactly converse point of view expresses the relationship of concrescence to physical time."[90] As was noted earlier, Whitehead adopted the relativity theory of time. According to this theory, absolute time ("a sort of container within which actual entities become"[91]) does not exist; on the contrary, time is an abstraction from the succession of actual entities. According to this "epocal theory of time," the process of concrescence "takes time" but is not "in time."

If actual entities are "droplets of time," how can one speak of successive phases in the process of concrescence? Whitehead labeled as "only intellectual" the analysis of an actual entity into successive phases of concrescence: "the actual entity is divisible; but is in fact undivided."[92] Thus while the analysis of concrescence reveals a succession of phases, this succession is not temporal.

---

[89]Whitehead, *Process and Reality*, 220.

[90]Whitehead, *Process and Reality*, 283.

[91]Sherburne, *A Key to Whitehead's Process and Reality*, 38.

[92]Whitehead, *Process and Reality*, 227. He describes the analysis of an actual entity as follows (235):

The principle, according to which a prehension can be discovered, is to take any component in the objective datum of the satisfaction; in the complex pattern of the subjective form of the satisfaction there will be a component with direct relevance to this element in the datum. Then in the satisfaction, there is a prehension of this component of the objective datum with that component of the total subjective form as its subjective form. The genetic growth of this prehension can then be traced by considering the transmission of the various elements of the datum from the actual world, and—in the case of eternal objects—their origination in the conceptual prehensions. There is then growth of prehensions, with integrations, eliminations, and determination of subjective forms. But the determination of successive phases of subjective forms, whereby the integrations have the character than they do have, depends on the unity of the subject imposing a mutual sensitivity upon the prehensions. Thus a prehension, considered genetically, can never free itself from the incurable atomicity of the actual entity to which it belongs. The selection of a subordinate prehension from the satisfaction—as described above—involves a hypothetical, propositional point of view. The fact is the satisfaction as one.

Each phase, indeed, each feeling within each phase, presupposes the entire quantum.

Analysis of the process of concrescence reveals three main phases: an initial phase of "conformal feelings"; a supplemental phase (during which novelty arises) which is subdivided into three phases comprised of "conceptual feelings," "physical purposes," and "propositional feelings and intellectual feelings" respectively; and the final phase which is the satisfaction. For ease of presentation, the following discussion will divide the process into five phases. (See fig. A-5, below, p. 246, for the following discussion.)

• Phase One. Conformal Feelings •

The initial phase of concrescence is the way in which the past actual world enters into the constitution of the becoming occasion. This initial phase consists of a multiplicity of **simple physical feelings**. A simple physical feeling is a feeling whose **initial datum** is an actual entity in the past actual world and whose **objective datum** is a feeling felt by that datum entity. This feeling (the objective datum) is the **objectification**[93] of its subject (the initial datum) for the becoming occasion. Thus, a becoming entity feels (or prehends) an entity in its past actual world by means of one of the datum entity's own feelings. (See fig. A-6, below, p. 247.) Objectification relegates into irrelevance the full constitution of the initial datum; that is, objectification involves negative prehensions as well as the positive prehension in question (the simple physical feeling). Thus, prehension of past entities by a becoming occasion is always partial or "perspectival"[94]; only God prehends past entities in their fullness.

Simple physical feelings are Whitehead's explanation of "cause and effect." "The actual entity which is the initial datum is the 'cause,' the simple physical feeling is the 'effect,' and the subject

---

[93]Just as "the functioning of an eternal object in the self-creation of an actual entity is [termed] the 'ingression' of the eternal object in the actual entity" so also "the functioning of one actual entity in the self-creation of another actual entity is [termed] the 'objectification' of the former for the latter actual entity" (Whitehead, *Process and Reality*, 25).

[94]The past actual occasion (the initial datum) is reduced to the "perspective" of one of its feelings (the objective datum).

entertaining the simple physical feeling is the actual entity 'conditioned' by the effect."[95] (Occasionally Whitehead referred to the "conditioned" actual entity itself as the "effect.") Therefore, simple physical feelings are also called **causal feelings** since these feelings constitute the causal efficacy of the world. Causation, then, is "one outcome of the principle that every actual entity has to house its actual world."[96]

Simple physical feelings are also termed **conformal feelings** because they conform to or reproduce previous feelings. Yet this conformity is never complete; the reproduction of past feelings is never exact. The same datum feeling may be prehended by many subjects, but each subject will clothe the feeling with a different—sometimes a vastly different—subjective form. There are two reasons why no two feelings (prehensions) of the same datum feeling can have the same subjective form. (1) The subjective forms of the feelings constituting a becoming occasion influence one another. Now because the actual world of a becoming occasion is not shared exactly by any other occasion, that occasion will have some feelings no other occasion has. Therefore, even if two occasions share a common feeling, the subjective forms of the shared feeling will be somewhat different due to the influence of the subjective forms of feelings unique to each occasion. (2) The overall character of an occasion's subjective forms is governed by that occasion's subjective aim. The initial aim of each occasion is to some degree unique because each occasion's actual world is somewhat unique. For these two reasons, the subjective forms of two feelings of the same datum feeling may be similar but not identical.

To summarize, in the multiplicity of simple physical feelings which constitute the initial phase of concrescence there is a "flow of feeling" from the past to the present, a transformation of objective data into subjective feeling. Yet this reenaction or repetition of past feelings is never exact; there is always some degree of novelty with regard to the new subjective forms of the feelings.

---

[95] Whitehead, *Process and Reality*, 236.
[96] Whitehead, *Process and Reality*, 80.

• Phase Two. Conceptual Feelings •

In phase two a conceptual feeling is derived from each simple physical feeling in phase one. The datum of this conceptual feeling is the eternal object exemplified in the simple physical feeling. That is, in a simple physical feeling in phase one, an eternal object is felt as being immanent, as being a *realized* determinant of the datum entity (for example, "gray-there"); in the derivate conceptual feeling in phase two this same eternal object is "pried out" of its immanence and felt as transcendent, as a *capacity* for determination (for example, "gray nowhere in particular"; "grayness in and of itself").[97] The physical feelings of a becoming occasion are termed its **physical pole**; the conceptual feelings, its **mental pole**. Each actual entity is thus "dipolar," although the relative importance of each pole differs in different entities. In the actual entities which are moments in the life history of a rock the physical pole dominates, whereas in the actual occasions of the human psyche the mental pole dominates.[98]

Two points warrant special attention before preceding with a description of the second phase. (1) As presented thus far, "mental operations" arise from previous physical operations. As will be noted below, further mental operations can arise from previous mental operations. (2) Expressions such as "mental pole" and "mental operations" do not necessarily indicate a state of consciousness. As subsequent discussion will indicate, consciousness does not arise until the fourth phase of concrescence, a phase not attained by most actual entities.

If the eternal object of the derivate conceptual feeling is identical with the eternal object ingredient in the simple physical feeling, then **conceptual reproduction** is said to have occurred. If the eternal object is partially identical with but partially diverse from the eternal object ingredient in the physical feeling—that is, is a proximate eternal object—then **conceptual reversion** is said to have occurred. (Conceptual reproduction always occurs; conceptual reversion may or may not occur.) Because conceptual reversion

---

[97]Sherburne, *A Key to Whitehead's Process and Reality*, 47.
[98]Whitehead, *Process and Reality*, 239.

refers to the prehension of an eternal object not realized in the actual world of a concrescent occasion, conceptual reversion indicates that a prehension of God has occurred in the initial phase of concrescence.[99] A description of this prehension of God requires a discussion of the subcategories of simple physical feelings.

Table A-1

Types of Physical Feelings
    1. simple physical feelings
        a. pure physical feelings
        b. hybrid physical feelings
    2. transmuted physical feelings

Types of Propositional Feelings
    1. perceptive feelings
        a. authentic
            (1) direct
            (2) indirect
        b. unauthentic
    2. imaginative feelings

Types of Intellectual Feelings
    1. conscious perceptions
    2. judgments
        a. affirmative
        b. negative
        c. suspended
        d. conscious imagination

The category of simple physical feelings is subdivided into **pure physical feelings** and **hybrid physical feelings**. (See table A-1.) In a pure physical feeling, the datum actual entity is objectified by one of its own physical feelings. In a hybrid physical feeling, the datum entity is objectified by one of its own conceptual feelings. Thus, "a hybrid physical feeling originates for its subject a conceptual feeling with the same datum [eternal object] as that of

---

[99]According to the ontological principle, "everything must be somewhere; and here 'somewhere' means 'some actual entity.' . . . It is a contradiction in terms to assume that some explanatory fact can float into the actual world out of nonentity" (Whitehead, *Process and Reality*, 46). Thus, the proximate eternal object has to be "somewhere," and because it is not ingredient in the past actual world, it must have been derived from God's primordial nature.

the conceptual feeling of the antecedent subject [the datum entity]"; the subjective form of the conceptual feeling will be somewhat different, however. There are two types hybrid physical feelings: those which prehend the conceptual feelings of temporal actual entities, and those which prehend the conceptual feelings of God. The conceptual feelings of God which are positively prehended "are those with some compatibility of contrast, or of identity, with physical feelings transmitted from the temporal world"; that is, they are relevant to the becoming occasion. The conceptual feeling resulting from this hybrid physical prehension of God is the initial aim discussed above. Such novel feelings are "the foundations of progress."[100]

The subjective form of a conceptual feeling (*how* the datum eternal object is felt) is called a **valuation**: either valuation upward (adversion) or valuation downward (aversion).[101] This valuation determines the importance the eternal object will have in its ingression into subsequent feelings in the process of concrescence, that is, whether it will be enhanced or attenuated. The valuation of one conceptual feeling is influenced by the subjective forms of all other feelings in the phase, and their overall character is determined by the subjective aim guiding the concrescence. This mutual influencing introduces the notion of a **contrast**.[102] A contrast is the unity had by the many components in a complex datum (for example, holding many colors together in a unified pattern, as in a kaleidoscope, as opposed to a single color); it is the opposite of incompatibility (which results in exclusion by means of a negative prehension). The more an actual entity holds the items of its experience in contrasts and contrasts of contrasts, the more it elicits depth and intensity for its satisfaction. Thus, the valuation of a conceptual feeling is dependent upon whether or not the datum eternal object can be integrated into a harmonious contrast with other feelings.

---

[100]Whitehead, *Process and Reality*, 245-47.

[101]Subjective forms occur in a variety of types, e.g., emotions, valuations, purposes, and consciousness.

[102]As Sherburne noted (*A Key to Whitehead's Process and Reality*, 216), "The name is somewhat misleading, for *to set in contrast with* means *to put in a unity with.*"

• Phase Three. Physical Purposes •

In phase three simple comparative feelings, termed **physical purposes**, arise. A comparative feeling may be defined as the comparison of actuality with possibility. In the case of a comparative feeling of the type termed physical purpose, a feeling arises that compares a simple physical feeling from phase one and a conceptual feeling from phase two. There are two species of physical purposes.

In the first species the comparison involves the integration of a simple physical feeling and the conceptual feeling resulting from conceptual *reproduction*. In effect, a physical purpose of this species is "a reiteration of the physical feeling felt in phase [one], except that the subjective form of the conceptual feeling in phase [two] may be either adversion or aversion." If the subjective form is adversion, then the subject occasion "tends to preserve that physical feeling and transmit it to future occasions"; if the subjective form is aversion, then the physical feeling will to some degree "lose importance in the future beyond the subject."[103] Thus, "adversions promote stability; and aversions promote change."[104] Assuming a subjective form of adversion, the first species of physical purposes, therefore, accounts for the persistence of the order of nature and the transference of energy in the physical world.

In the second, more complex, species of physical purposes the comparison involves the integration of a simple physical feeling and the conceptual feeling resulting from conceptual *reversion*. If the subjective form of the reverted conceptual feeling is adversion, then the reverted eternal object ("b′″" in fig. A-5, below, p. 246) is transmitted to the next generation of occasions as ingredient in the physical feeling, and the eternal object that was actually ingredient in the original physical feeling ("b" in fig. A-5) becomes the datum for a reverted conceptual feeling in the next generation of occasions (that is,"b′″" and "b" exchange places for the next generation of occasions). An enduring object[105] composed of a succession of

---

[103]Sherburne, *A Key to Whitehead's Process and Reality*, 234.
[104]Whitehead, *Process and Reality*, 277.
[105]See below for a discussion of enduring objects.

occasions in which this more complex physical purpose occurs "gains the added intensity of feeling arising from a contrast between inheritance and novel effect, and also gains the enhanced intensity arising from the combined inheritance of its stable rhythmic character throughout its life history."[106] The second species of physical purposes, therefore, accounts for vibration and rhythm in the physical world as well as the persistence of the order of nature and the transference of energy.

Physical purposes are terminal, that is, they inhibit further integrations so that the process of concrescence comes to an end in phase three. Because consciousness does not arise until phase four, physical purposes are devoid of consciousness as well. Although all actual entities include physical purposes, this type of activity characterizes the primitive actual occasions which compose inanimate objects.

• Phase Four. Propositional Feelings and Intellectual Feelings •

In phase four more sophisticated comparative feelings, termed **intellectual feelings**, arise. A discussion of intellectual feelings requires an understanding of what Whitehead called **propositional feelings**.

In some respects a propositional feeling resembles a physical purpose. Like a physical purpose, a propositional feeling is the integration of a physical feeling in phase one with a conceptual feeling in phase two, but whereas a physical purpose compares a possibility with an actuality, a propositional feeling predicates a possibility of an *abstracted* actuality. A **proposition** makes an incomplete abstraction from the actual entity which is the initial datum of the physical feeling in phase one, reducing the actual entity to a bare "it"; that is, the eternal objects actually ingredient in the physical prehension of the actual entity are eliminated. This abstracted actual entity, the bare "it," is termed the **logical subject** of the proposition. The eternal object of the conceptual feeling in phase two is then "predicated" of the abstracted actual entity (the bare "it"); this eternal object is termed the **predicate** of the proposition.[107] Whereas eternal objects in themselves "tell no tales

---

[106]Whitehead, *Process and Reality*, 279.

[107]Thus, propositions are "impure potentials"; they describe hypothetical states

as to their ingressions," propositions are "tales that perhaps might be told about particular actualities."[108] For example, one can compare the role of the eternal object "gray" (1) in a pure conceptual prehension (gray nowhere in particular), (2) in a physical purpose (gray physically realized in *that* actual entity), and (3) in a proposition (*that* actual entity *might* be gray). A proposition, then, is the *possibility* of a particular predicate applying to a particular logical subject.[109]

There are two types of propositional feelings: **perceptive feelings** and **imaginative feelings**. (See table A-1, above, p. 226.) An explanation of these two types of feelings requires a more detailed analysis of the emergence of propositions and propositional prehensions. (See fig. A-7, below, p. 248.) A proposition requires a physical feeling in phase one whose datum (an actual entity) is the logical subject of the proposition. In becoming the logical subject of a proposition, the physical feeling of this actual entity undergoes incomplete abstraction—that is, is reduced to a bare "it"—and is termed an **indicative feeling**. Yet the physical feeling in phase one actually involves an eternal object. A physical feeling which does not undergo this process of abstraction is termed a **physical recognition**. A conceptual feeling in phase two supplies the predicate for a proposition. This eternal object may arise from either conceptual reproduction or conceptual reversion; that is, the eternal object felt by the conceptual feeling may be derived from the physical recognition, or it may be a proximate eternal object derived from a hybrid physical prehension of God in phase one. In either case, a conceptual feeling whose datum (an eternal object) is the predicate of a proposition is termed a **predicative feeling**. A propositional feeling arises in phase three with the integration of an indicative feeling and a predicative feeling.

---

of affairs. They are neither "pure possibilities" nor "pure actualities" but rather are "hybrid entities" because the statement of a proposition involves reference both to particular actualities and to pure possibilities. (Likewise, a propositional feeling is not a "pure conceptual feeling" but an "impure conceptual feeling.")

[108]Whitehead, *Process and Reality*, 256.

[109]This is a simplified description of a proposition, for the logical subject of a proposition may be a nexus of actual entities, and the predicate, a set of eternal objects summarized as a complex eternal object.

The distinction between the two types of propositional feelings is based on whether the indicative feeling (from which is derived the logical subject) and the physical recognition (from which is derived the predicate) are the same physical feeling. (Compare figs. A-7 and A-8.) If they are identical, the propositional feeling is a **perceptive feeling**. There are two types of perceptive propositional feelings. (See table A-1.) If the eternal object forming the predicate arises from conceptual reproduction, the propositional feeling is termed an **authentic perceptive feeling**; the predicate is actually realized in actual entity from which the logical subject is abstracted.[110] If the eternal object forming the predicate arises from conceptual reversion, the propositional feeling is termed an **unauthentic perceptive feeling**; conceptual reversion produces a proximate eternal object which in some respects is similar to but in other respects is different from the eternal object actually ingredient in the actual entity.[111] There are two types of authentic perceptive feelings. If a proposition predicates of its logical subject the *physical* enjoyment of the eternal object (that is, that the logical subject felt the eternal object as ingredient in a physical prehension) when the logical subject actually enjoyed the eternal object *mentally* (that is, the eternal object was the datum of a conceptual prehension), then the authentic perceptive feeling is termed **indirect**. But if a proposition predicates of its logical subject the *physical* enjoyment of the eternal object and the logical subject actually enjoyed the eternal object *physically*, then the authentic perceptive feeling is termed **direct**.[112]

If the indicative feeling and the physical recognition are not the same physical feeling, the propositional feeling is an **imaginative feeling**. (See fig. A-8, below, p. 249.) The two physical feelings may differ greatly or may be quite similar; nevertheless, the difference in the two feelings allows for some degree of free imagination because the predicate is derived from an actual occasion different from the actual occasion which provides the logical subject.[113]

---

[110]Whitehead, *Process and Reality*, 262.
[111]Whitehead, *Process and Reality*, 263.
[112]Whitehead, *Process and Reality*, 262.
[113]An unauthentic perceptive propositional feeling is similar to an imaginative propositional feeling; but because the indicative feeling and physical recognition

Because the logical subject of a proposition is an actual entity, a proposition must be either true or false; either the eternal object predicated of the logical subject has ingression in that actual entity or it does not. But the truth or falsehood of a proposition is not its most important aspect. According to Whitehead:

> The interest in logic, dominating overintellectualized philosophers, has obscured the main function of propositions in the nature of things. They are not primarily for belief, but for feeling at the physical level of unconsciousness. They constitute a source for the origination of feeling which is not tied down to mere datum.
>
> Unfortunately ... [propositions] have been handed over to logicians, who have countenanced the doctrine that their one function is to be judged as to their truth or falsehood. ... The doctrine here laid down is that, in the realization of propositions, 'judgment' is a very rare component, and so is 'consciousness.'
>
> The result [of the logicians' treatment of propositions] is that false propositions have fared badly, thrown into the dustheap, neglected. But in the real world it is more important that a proposition be interesting than that it be true. The importance of truth is, that it adds to interest.
>
> In that purely logical aspect, nonconformal propositions are merely wrong, and therefore worse than useless. But in their primary rôle, they pave the way along which the world advances into novelty. Error is the price which we pay for progress.[114]

The primary purpose of a proposition is to serve as a lure for feeling. When a conformal proposition—one that conforms to the actual world—is admitted into feeling, "the reaction to the datum has simply resulted in the conformation of feeling to fact, ... prehension of the proposition has abruptly emphasized one form of definiteness [an eternal object] illustrated in fact [an actual entity]." When a nonconformal proposition—one that does not conform to the actual world—is admitted into feeling, "the reaction

---

are derived from the same physical feeling, the unauthentic perceptive feeling will have some of the vivid relevance to the actual occasion as does an authentic perceptive feeling.

[114]Whitehead, *Process and Reality*, 186, 184, 259, 187.

to the datum has resulted in the synthesis of fact with the alternative potentiality of the complex predicate. A novelty has emerged into creation. The novelty may promote or destroy order; it may be good or bad. But it is new, . . . or at least, an old form in a new function."[115] Propositions, then, are lures "to creative emergence in the transcendent future"[116] because they provide for the origination of feeling which is not tied down to mere datum in the actual world. Moreover, "new propositions come into being with the creative advance of the world."[117]

According to the ontological principle, a proposition must be somewhere; the "locus" of a proposition consists of those actual occasions whose actual worlds include the actual occasions which are the logical subject of the proposition. As a datum or "lure for feeling," a proposition awaits a prehending subject to feel it. The positive prehension of a proposition by an actual occasion belonging to the proposition's locus is termed a **propositional feeling**. As will be seen, propositional feelings are lures for more sophisticated integrations that may result in consciousness.

The preceding analysis of propositional feelings makes it possible to discuss intellectual feelings. As was noted earlier, comparative feelings compare actuality with possibility. The datum for an intellectual feeling is the comparison of the physical prehension of a nexus[118] (or aggregate) of actual entities and a proposition whose logical subjects are members of that nexus, that is, the comparison a group of simple physical feelings and a propositional feeling. Thus, an intellectual feeling has as its datum a comparison of a "fact" in the actual world (the nexus) and a "theory" about that fact (the proposition).

One element in the subjective form of an intellectual feeling is **consciousness**, the degree of which varies according to the intensity of effort on the part of the subject. According to Whitehead, this account of consciousness arising by means of intellectual feelings

---

[115]Whitehead, *Process and Reality*, 186-87.
[116]Whitehead, *Process and Reality*, 263.
[117]Whitehead, *Process and Reality*, 259.
[118]Nexus will be discussed in some detail below.

agrees with the plain facts of our conscious experience. Consciousness flickers; and even at its brightest, there is a small focal region of clear illumination, and a large penumbral region of experience which tells of intense experience in dim apprehension. . . . this character of our experience suggests that consciousness is the crown of experience, only occasionally attained, not its necessary base.[119]

Thus, "consciousness presupposes experience, and not experience consciousness."[120]

There are two types of intellectual feelings: **conscious perceptions** and **judgments**. (See table A-1, above, p. 226.) A conscious perception is the comparative feeling of the integration of a perceptive propositional feeling and the physical feeling from which the perceptive propositional feeling is derived. (See fig. A-9, below, p. 250.) If the perceptive feeling is authentic and direct, then the conscious perception is correct, that is, the proposition conforms to "fact." If the perceptive feeling is authentic but indirect, then the conscious perception results in some degree of error (and hence novelty, for good or for ill). If the perceptive feeling is unauthentic, then the conscious perception results in the awareness that the proposition is to some degree erroneous; the eternal objects predicated of the logical subject are proximate to those actually ingredient in the logical subject.

A **judgment** is the comparative feeling of the integration of an imaginative propositional feeling and the physical feeling from which the logical subject of the proposition is derived.[121] (See fig. A-10, below, p. 251, and table A-1, above, p. 226.) If the difference

---

[119]Whitehead, *Process and Reality*, 267. Thus, "Whitehead's philosophy agrees with the depth psychologists in emphasizing the priority and greater massiveness of what is unconscious" (Cobb, *A Christian Natural Theology*, 80).

[120]Whitehead, *Process and Reality*, 53. Whitehead used this idea to refute Hume and Kant, as discussed in chap. 4.

[121]Whitehead (*Process and Reality* 192) divided judgments into two types: **intuitive** and **derivative**. In an intuitive judgment there is a comparison of the full and complex detail of both the proposition and the physically prehended datum. In a derivative judgment there is a comparison of the complete detail of the proposition with only partial detail of the physical datum. Most judgments belong to the derivative category.

between the indicative feeling and the physical recognition is trivial, then the predicate derived from physical recognition may be identical with that exemplified by the physical feeling from which is derived the indicative feeling. When this is the case, the proposition is judged to be true and the subjective form of the judgment will include definite belief. Such a judgment (termed **affirmative**) is similar to a conscious perception. If the difference between the indicative feeling and the physical recognition is significant, then the predicate derived from physical recognition may be incompatible with the eternal objects exemplified by the physical feeling from which is derived the indicative feeling. When this is the case, the proposition is judged to be false and the subjective form of the judgment will include definite disbelief. Such a judgment is termed **negative**. More frequently, however, the predicate is not identical with the eternal objects ingredient in the logical subject, but it is not incompatible with them either. As a result, it may be possible to hold the predicate and the ingredient eternal objects in some form of compatible contrast. When this is the case, the subjective form need not be either belief or disbelief; rather, **suspended** judgment (analogous to a hypothesis) may result. Whitehead cautioned against equating suspended judgments with negative judgments.

> Our whole progress in scientific theory, and even in subtility of direct observation, depends on the use of suspended judgments. It is to be noted that a suspended judgment is not a judgment of probability. It is a judgment of compatibility. The judgment tells us what *may* be additional information respecting the formal constitutions of the logical subjects, information which is neither included nor excluded by our direct perception.[122]

In each of the preceding judgments, the emotional pattern is dominated by attention to truth. It is possible, however, for the emotional pattern to be dominated by an indifference to truth and falsehood (this indifference arising from the subjective aim guiding the concrescence and from the "mutual sensitivity" of the totality of feelings comprising the prehending subject). In such a case (for

---

[122]Whitehead, *Process and Reality*, 274-75.

example, daydreaming) the judgment is labeled **conscious imagination**.

Determining whether a proposition expresses truth, error, or whether judgment should be suspended is not the major function of intellectual feelings, however. "By the sharp-cut way in which they limit abstract valuation to express possibilities relevant to definite logical subjects" intellectual feelings are a "concentration of attention involving increase of importance." A proposition is "a lure for the conditioning of creative action"; thus, the entertainment of a proposition "effects a modification of the subjective aim" of the prehending subject.[123]

• The Final Phase. Satisfaction •

The preceding discussion of the phases of concrescence reveals that the process begins with a multiplicity of feelings in the initial phase which, through succeeding phases, are integrated and reintegrated—that is, feelings of an earlier phase become component feelings of more complex feelings in a later phase—until they are finally integrated into one complex, unified feeling termed the satisfaction. This progressive integration of feelings is controlled by the subjective aim and the subjective forms of the various feelings which arise in the process. Upon attaining satisfaction, an actual entity looses subjectivity and becomes objectively immortal thereby conditioning the creative advance of the world: "the many become one, and are increased by one."[124]

• **Enduring Objects and the Macrocosmic World** •

So far this overview of process metaphysics has focused on the microcosmic world of actual entities which become and then perish; the data of ordinary human experience, however, are macrocosmic entities such as rocks, trees, animals, and people which endure through a period of time. "Our lives are dominated by enduring things," acknowledged Whitehead.[125] Movement from

---

[123]Whitehead, *Process and Reality*, 273.
[124]Whitehead, *Process and Reality*, 21.
[125]Whitehead, *Adventures of Ideas*, 280.

the microcosmic world of actual entities to the macrocosmic world of objects which endure is made possible by **transmutation**.

Transmutation occurs in the following manner. (See fig. A-11, below, p. 252.) In phase two of its concrescence, a prehending subject derives the same conceptual feeling from a number of simple physical feelings in phase one. The simple comparative feeling in phase three then contrasts the conceptual feeling in phase two with *all* of the aforementioned simple physical feelings in phase one. The simple comparative feeling, in effect, prehends this particular group of datum occasions as one entity qualified by the datum eternal object of the conceptual feeling (differences among the datum occasions are eliminated). This simple comparative feeling is called a **transmuted physical feeling** whose datum is a *group* of actual occasions—a macrocosmic entity—in contrast to a simple physical feeling whose datum is a *single* actual occasion—a microcosmic entity.[126] (See table A-1, above, p. 226.)

Conscious human experience normally involves prehending the world by means of transmuted physical feelings, though transmuted feelings themselves occur at a preconscious level of experience (consciousness arises in phase four of concrescence). That the process of transmutation is a prerequisite for the rise of consciousness reveals that conscious experience involves **abstraction** from reality.[127]

> The irrelevant multiplicity of detail is eliminated, and emphasis is laid on the elements of systematic order in the actual world. . . . [In contrast, a] low-grade organism is merely the summation of the forms of energy which flow in upon it in all their multiplicity of detail. It receives, and it transmits; but it fails to simplify into intelligible system.

---

[126]Sherburne (*A Key to Whitehead's Process and Reality*, 73) offered the following concise definition: "Transmutation is the operation whereby an aggregate of many actual occasions, forming a nexus, is prehended not as an aggregate, not as a many, but as a unity, as one macrocosmic entity."

[127]"An abstraction . . . is a disjoining of entities which are in fact joined. . . . an entity considered apart from some of the roles or functions it has in the actual world. Since it is not possible, in a finite and conditioned act of experience, to prehend *all* of the functions of any entity in nature, thought essentially involves abstraction." Christian, *An Interpretation of Whitehead's Metaphysics*, 207.

Apart from transmutation our feeble intellectual operations would fail to penetrate into the dominant characteristics of things [that is, would fail to discern "elements of systematic order" in the world]. We can only understand by discarding.[128]

Two points relative to transmutation warrant additional attention. First, the conceptual feeling involved in a transmuted feeling may arise from conceptual reproduction or conceptual reversion. If conceptual reversion occurs, the transmuted feeling introduces novelty; "and in unfortunate cases this novelty may be termed 'error.'"[129] Second, transmutation presupposes "order." A group of actual occasions manifesting elements of systematic order—for example, the group of datum occasions of a transmuted feeling—is termed a **nexus**. "A nexus is a set of actual entities in the unity of the relatedness constituted by their prehensions of each other, or—what is the same thing conversely expressed—constituted by their objectifications in each other."[130] A nexus, then, is a group of actual entities interrelated to one another in any way. (See fig. A-12, below, p. 253.)

A nexus enjoys what Whitehead termed **social order** when "(i) there is a common element of form [an eternal object] illustrated in the definiteness of each of its included actual entities, and (ii) this common element of form arises in each member of the nexus by reason of the conditions imposed upon it by its prehensions of some other members of the nexus, and (iii) these prehensions impose that condition of reproduction by reason of their inclusion of positive feelings of that common form." A nexus which meets these criteria is called a **society**, and the common eternal object (or complex eternal object) is called the **defining characteristic** of the society.[131]

---

[128]Whitehead, *Process and Reality*, 254, 251.

[129]Whitehead, *Process and Reality*, 253. The notion of "error" received additional attention in the discussion of perception in chap. 4.

[130]Whitehead, *Process and Reality*, 24.

[131]Whitehead, *Process and Reality*, 34. Whitehead discussed a variety of societies and nexuses—e.g., enduring objects, corpuscular, noncorpuscular, structured, subordinate, stabilized, unstable, specialized, unspecialized, living, inorganic, subservient, and regnant. Only those most relevant to the development of a process hermeneutic will be discussed here.

A society of occasions, only one of which exists at a time, and each of which inherits its data primarily (not exclusively of course) from the immediately preceding occasion in the series, is termed an **enduring object**. An enduring object, then, is a society whose social order has taken the special form of **serial** or **personal order**.[132] The vast majority of enduring objects are characterized by repetition of the past rather than novelty since repetition is required for endurance. Each occasion in the series tends to repeat or reenact the feelings of its immediate predecessor (the influence of other past occasions is weak and the novelty of the becoming occasion is trivial). As a result, there is considerable stability in the universe.

The objects which comprise the macrocosmic world of ordinary human experience are composed of collections or strands of enduring objects. Such a macrocosmic object is termed a **corpuscular society**. (See fig. A-13, below, p. 253.) Whitehead stressed the significance of viewing macrocosmic objects as societies rather than actual occasions: "It is the mistake that has thwarted European metaphysics from the time of the Greeks, namely, to confuse societies with the completely real things which are the actual occasions."[133] Thus, the world is a plurality of real individual things (actual entities) organically interrelated; but the world of ordinary human experience—rocks, trees, animals, and people—is composed of societies of these real individual things.

Whitehead noted that "a society may be more or less corpuscular, according to the relative importance of the defining characteristics of the various enduring objects compared to that of the defining characteristic of the whole corpuscular nexus."[134] That is, a society may be composed of actual occasions, some of which are and some of which are not members of enduring objects. For example, a living cell is composed of many strands of enduring objects (for example, molecules) as well as much "empty space." This space is not really empty but rather is "occupied" by actual occasions which are characterized by novelty rather than repetition.

---

[132]Whitehead, *Process and Reality*, 34.
[133]Whitehead, *Adventures of Ideas*, 204.
[134]Whitehead, *Process and Reality*, 35.

Because of this predominance of novelty, the successive occasions occupying this space do not constitute an enduring object (there is no defining characteristic). Now where there is no enduring object, humans can detect nothing, hence the term "empty space."

Although the succession of actual occasions occupying the empty space of a living cell does not form an enduring object, this does not mean that these occasions are insignificant; on the contrary, these occasions constitute the life of the cell.[135] A **living society** "is one which includes some 'living occasions.'" And as with corpuscular societies, "a society may be more or less living, according to the prevalence in it of living occasions." And "an occasion may be more or less living according to the relative importance of the novel factors in its final satisfaction." Thus, "there is no absolute gap between 'living' and 'nonliving' societies."[136]

Because the succession of occasions in the empty space of the cell does not exhibit social order, this group of occasions must be termed a **subordinate nexus**—rather than a **subordinate society**, which would be the designation proper for a molecule—within the **structured society** of the living cell.[137] As the terms subordinate and structured societies indicates, the world of human experience is composed of societies of societies. For example, electrons are organized into subordinate societies within atoms; atoms are organized into subordinate societies within molecules; molecules are organized into subordinate societies within cells; and cells are

---

[135]Whitehead, *Process and Reality*, 104-105:

Life is a bid for freedom . . . "life" means novelty . . . a single occasion is alive when the subjective aim which determines its process of concrescence has introduced a novelty of definiteness not to be found in the inherited data of its primary phase. The novelty is introduced conceptually and disturbs the inherited "responsive" adjustment of subjective forms. . . . The mere response to stimulus is characteristic of all societies whether inorganic or alive. Action and reaction are bound together. The characteristic of life is reaction adapted to the capture of intensity, under a large variety of circumstances. But the reaction is dictated by the present and not by the past. It is the clutch at vivid immediacy.

[136]Whitehead, *Process and Reality*, 102.

[137]A society may be labeled structured when it "provides a favorable environment for the subordinate societies which it harbors within it" (Whitehead, *Process and Reality*, 99).

organized into subordinate societies within plant and animal bodies. And just as there is no absolute gap between living and nonliving societies, there is no absolute gap between plants and animals. Rather what one observes is a gradual movement from low-grade living entities (for example, plants and very simple animals) which manifest "democracy" among their component societies, to high-grade entities (for example, higher animals and humans) which manifest considerable centralized control by a **dominant** or **reigning nexus.** This dominant nexus is composed of a series of high-grade living occasions capable of supporting a "thread of personal order along some historic route of its members." This special type of enduring object—which combines life with endurance—is termed a **living person**[138] and with respect to humans is typically referred to as the self or soul.[139]

---

[138]Whitehead, *Process and Reality*, 107-109.
The defining characteristic of a living person is some definite type of hybrid prehensions transmitted from occasion to occasion of its existence. . . . a "hybrid" prehension is the prehension by one subject of a conceptual prehension, or of an "impure" prehension [i.e., a prehension which integrates conceptual and physical prehensions], belonging to the mentality of another subject. By this transmission the mental originality of the living occasions receives a character and a depth. In this way originality is both "canalized" . . . and intensified. . . . Apart from canalization, depth of originality would spell disaster for the animal body. With it, personal mentality can be evolved, so as to combine its individual originality with the safety of the material organism on which it depends. Thus life turns back to society: it binds originality within bounds, and gains the massiveness due to reiterated character. (107)
[139]The human self or soul was briefly discussed in chaps. 3 and 4.

Figure A-1[140]

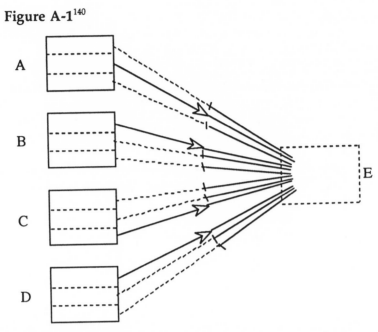

A, B, C, and D are four datum occasions in the past actual world of becoming occasion E (subject). Unbroken vector lines are the becoming occasion's positive prehensions (feelings); broken vector lines are its negative prehensions. Thus, the concrescing subject E has objectified past actual occasion A by one of A's component feelings; that is, E has positively prehended A by one of A's feeling. The other component feelings of A are negatively prehended by E.

---

[140]Process thinkers cringe when they are asked to illustrate process thought, responding that diagrams are inherently misleading. For example, diagrams inevitably place datum occasions *outside* the becoming occasion whereas one of the basis tenets of process thought is that relations are internal not external. Similarly, spatializing time is quite misleading. These and other misleading aspects of diagrams notwithstanding, I have opted to "resort" to diagrams for I feel that they can be helpful heuristic devices in an initial attempt to understand Whitehead's thought.

Figure A-2[141]

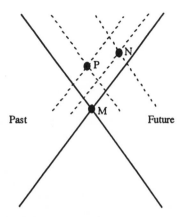

This diagram illustrates the notion of "multiple time systems." Actual occasions P and N are contemporary with M, yet P and N are not contemporary with each other. P lies in the past of N whereas N lies in the future of P.

This diagram can also illustrate the notion of "durations." A line drawn through M and P would represent one duration (one set of *mutually* contemporary occasions) to which M, P, and many other occasions belong; N does not belong to that set of mutually contemporary occasions, however. A line drawn through M and N would represent another duration to which M, N, and many other occasions belong; P does not belong to that set of mutually contemporary occasions, however. Thus, M is a member of more than one duration.

The diagram as a whole illustrates the "presented duration" of M, that duration which includes all M's immediate present (the common sense notion of the immediate present).

---

[141]Figure A-2 is adapted from Sherburne, *A Key to Whitehead's Process and Reality*, 111.

Figure A-3

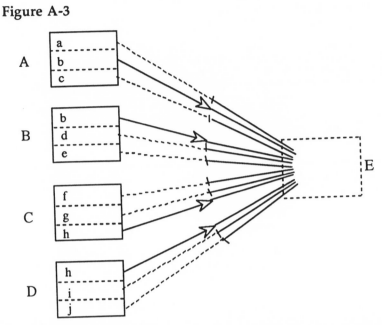

A, B, C, and D are four datum occasions in the past actual world of becoming occasion E (subject). Eternal objects ingredient in the component feelings of the datum occasions are represented by a, b, c, d, e, f, g, h, i, and j. Unbroken vector lines are the becoming occasion's positive prehensions (feelings); broken vector lines are its negative prehensions. Thus, the concrescing subject E has prehended (or objectified) past actual occasion A by one of A's component feelings, the feeling in which eternal object b is ingredient. Eternal object b thus has a two-way functioning in A and E (A and E share eternal object b). Other feelings of A and their ingredient eternal objects are negatively prehended by E; that is, E rejected A's feelings in which eternal objects a and c are ingredient.

Figure A-4[142]

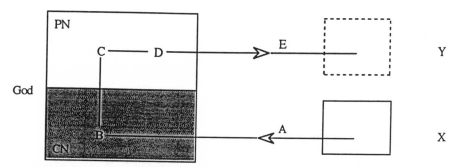

God physically prehends (A) the satisfaction of actual occasion X so that the totality of X is felt (B) in the consequent nature (CN). God then (C) integrates X with all other occasions in the past world within the primordial nature (PN). The satisfaction resulting from this integration suggests a new ordering of eternal objects (D) which is relevant to the becoming world. Arrow E represents both God's superjective nature and the world's prehension of God, represented in this figure as the initial aim for becoming occasion Y.

---

[142]Figure A-4 is adapted from Suchocki, *God, Christ, Church,* 42-43.

Figure A-5[143]

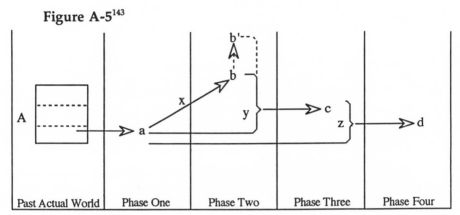

| Past Actual World | Phase One | Phase Two | Phase Three | Phase Four |

In phase one, becoming occasion B objectifies datum occasion A by one of its component feelings; this simple physical feeling is represented by (a). In phase two, the eternal object ingredient in physical feeling (a) is "pried out" of its immanence and felt as transcendent (arrow x); this conceptual feeling is represented by (b) in the case of conceptual reproduction and (b´) in the case of conceptual reversion. In phase three, the simple physical feeling in phase one (a) and the conceptual feeling in phase two (b) are held in the unity of a contrast (bracket y); this simple comparative feeling, termed a physical purpose, is represented by (c). In phase four, a nexus (a group of actual occasions prehended as a unity; a complex physical feeling; see figure A-12) in phase one and a propositional feeling (also represented in this diagram by c because propositional feelings resemble physical purposes in some reapects) are contrasted (bracket z); this complex comparative feeling, termed an intellectual feeling, is represented by (d).

---

[143]Figure A-5 is adapted from Sherburne, *A Key to Whitehead's Process and Reality*, 40.

Figure A-6

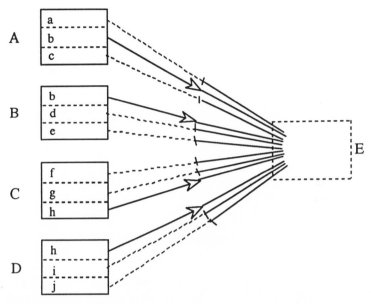

The initial phase of concrescence consists of a multiplicity of simple physical feelings. In this diagram this multiplicity is represented by the positive prehensions (the unbroken vector lines) of A, B, C, and D which are actual occasions in the past actual world of becoming occasion E. A simple physical feeling is a feeling (positive prehension) whose initial datum is an actual entity in the past actual world (such as A) and whose objective datum is a feeling felt by that datum entity (such as A's component feeling in which eternal object b is ingredient). This feeling (the objective datum, in this case A's feeling in which b is ingredient) is the objectification of its subject (the initial datum, in this case A) for the becoming occasion (in this case E). This objectification of A relegates into irrelevance the full constitution of A; that is, objectification involves negative prehensions (in this case A's feelings in which eternal objects a and c are ingredient) as well as the positive prehension in question.

Figure A-7

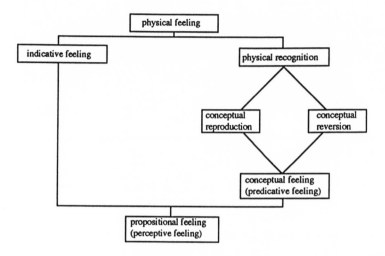

In the case of a perceptive propositional feeling the same physical feeling gives rise to both the indicative feeling (the bare "it," the logical subject of the proposition) and the physical recognition (from which is derived the predicate of the proposition, either through conceptual reproduction or conceptual reversion).

Figure A-8

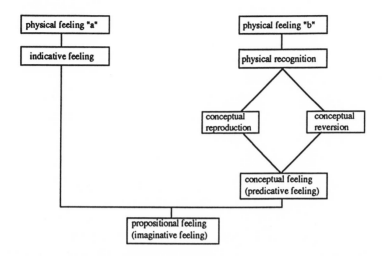

In the case of an imaginative propositional feeling different physical feelings give rise to the indicative feeling (the bare "it," the logical subject of the proposition) and the physical recognition (from which is derived the predicate of the proposition, either through conceptual reproduction or conceptual reversion).

Figure A-9

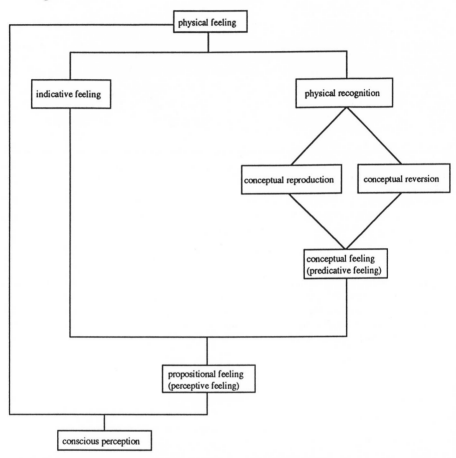

A conscious perception is the comparative feeling of the integration of a perceptive propositional feeling and the physical feeling from which the perceptive propositional feeling is derived.

Figure A-10

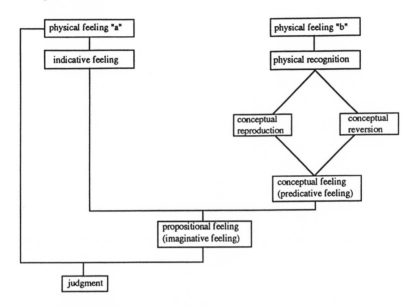

A judgment is the comparative feeling of the integration of an imaginative propositional feeling and the physical feeling from which the logical subject of the proposition is derived.

Figure A-11[144]

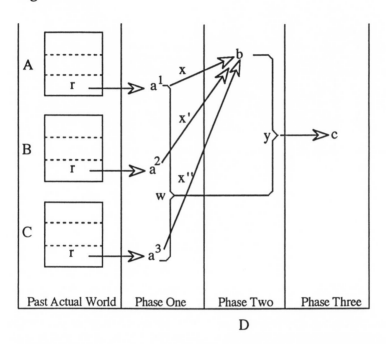

In phase one of its concrescence, becoming occasion D objectifies datum occasions A, B, and C by one of their component feelings; these simple physical feelings are represented by a1, a2, and a3. In phase two, the same eternal object "red" (r), which is ingredient in each of the physical feelings, is "pried out" of immanence and felt as transcendent (arrows x, x´, and x´´); this conceptual feeling is represented by (b). In phase three, the conceptual feeling of the eternal object "red" (b) is held in the unity of a contrast (bracket y) with all of the simple physical feelings (bracket w); this simple comparative feeling is represented by (c). This comparative feeling is termed a transmuted physical feeling because it prehends the nexus of many microcosmic datum occasions as one macrocosmic entity qualified by the eternal object "red."

---

[144]Figure A-11 is adapted from Sherburne, *A Key to Whitehead's Process and Reality*, 74.

Figure A-12

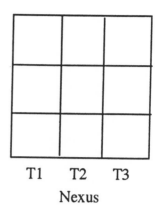

T^1, T^2, and T^3 represent three successive moments.

T1   T2   T3

Nexus

Figure A-13

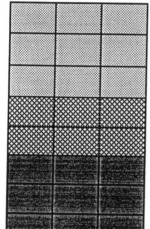

Strand One

Strand Two

Strand Three

This diagram represents an enduring object composed of strands of enduring objects. Most enduring objects in the macrocosmic world are of this type.

Bibliography

Altizer, Thomas J. J. *Total Presence: The Language of Jesus and the Language of Today.* New York: Seabury Press, 1980.

Altizer, Thomas J. J., Max A. Meyer, Carl A. Raschke, Robert P. Scharlemann, Mark C. Taylor, and Charles E. Winquist. *Deconstruction and Theology.* New York: Crossroad, 1982.

Atkins, G. Douglas. *Reading Deconstruction/Deconstructive Reading.* Lexington: University Press of Kentucky, 1983.

Barclay, William. *The Revelation of John.* Revised edition. Two volumes. Philadelphia: Westminster Press, 1976.

Barr, David. "The Apocalypse as a Symbolic Transformation of the World: A Literary Analysis." *Interpretation* 38 (1984): 39-50.

_____. "The Apocalypse of John as Oral Enactment." *Interpretation* 40 (1986): 243-56.

Barr, James. *Old and New in Interpretation: A Study of the Two Testaments.* New York: Harper & Row, 1966.

_____. *The Semantics of Biblical Language.* London: Oxford University Press, 1961.

Barth, Karl. "Rudolf Bultmann—An Attempt to Understand Him." In *Kerygma and Myth II.* Edited by Hans Werner Bartsch. London: S.P.C.K., 1962.

Beardslee, William A. *A House for Hope: A Study in Process and Biblical Thought.* Philadelphia: Westminster Press, 1972.

_____. *Literary Criticism of the New Testament.* Philadelphia: Fortress Press, 1969.

_____. "Christ in the Postmodern Age: Reflections Inspired by Jean-Francois Lyotard." In *Varieties of Postmodern Theology.* By David R. Griffin, William A. Beardslee, and Joe Holland. Albany: SUNY, 1989.

_____. "Christology in Scripture and Experience: The Case of Process Theology." In *Scripture in History and Theology. Essays in Honor of J. Coert Rylaarsdam.* Edited by Arthur L. Merrill and Thomas W. Overholt. Pittsburgh: Pickwick Press, 1977.

_____. "Hope in Biblical Eschatology and in Process Theology." *Journal of the American Academy of Religion* 38 (1970): 227-39.

_____. "Narrative Form in the New Testament and Process Theology." *Encounter* 36 (1975): 301-15.

_____. "Openness to the New in Apocalyptic and in Process Theology." *Process Studies* 3 (1973): 169-78.

_____. "Recent Hermeneutics and Process Thought." *Process Studies* 12 (1982): 65-76.

_____. "Saving One's Life by Losing It." *Journal of the American Academy of Religion* 47 (1979): 57-72.

_____. "Stories in the Postmodern World: Orienting and Disorienting." In *Sacred Interconnections: Postmodern Spirituality, Political Economy, and Art.* Edited by David R. Griffin. Albany: SUNY, 1990.

_____. "The Motif of Fulfillment in the Eschatology of the Synoptic Gospels." In *Transitions in Biblical Scholarship* Edited by J. Coert Rylaarsdam. Chicago: University of Chicago Press, 1968.

_____. "Whitehead and Hermeneutic." *Journal of the American Academy of Religion* 47 (1979): 31-37.

Beardslee, William A., and David J. Lull. "Introduction." *Semeia* 24 (1982): 1-6.

Beardslee, William A., John B. Cobb, Jr., David Lull, Russell Pregeant, Theodore J. Weeden, Sr., and Barry A. Woodbridge. *Biblical Preaching on the Death of Jesus.* Nashville: Abingdon Press, 1989.

Beckwith, I. T. *The Apocalypse of John.* New York: Macmillan, 1920.

Bible and Culture Collective, The. *The Postmodern Bible.* New Haven: Yale University Press, 1995.

Birch, Charles, and John B. Cobb, Jr. *The Liberation of Life: From the Cell to the Community.* Cambridge: Cambridge University Press, 1981.

Boozer, Jack, and William A. Beardslee. *Faith to Act: An Essay on the Meaning of Christian Existence.* New York/Nashville: Abingdon Press, 1967.

Boring, M. Eugene. *Revelation.* Interpretation. Louisville: John Knox Press, 1989.

_____. "The Theology of Revelation: 'The Lord Our God the Almighty Reigns.'" *Interpretation* 40 (1986): 257-69.

Bornkamm, Günther. *Jesus of Nazareth.* New York: Harper & Row, 1960.

Brock, Rita Nakashima. *Journeys by Heart: A Christology of Erotic Power.* New York: Crossroad, 1988.

Bultmann, Rudolf. "Bultmann Replies to His Critics." In *Kerygma and Myth I.* Edited by Hans Werner Bartsch. New York: Harper & Row, 1961; London: S.P.C.K., 1953.

_____. "New Testament and Mythology." In *Kerygma and Myth I.* Edited by Hans Werner Bartsch. New York: Harper & Row, 1961; London: S.P.C.K., 1953.

Buri, Fritz. "Entmythologisierung oder Entkerygmatisierung der Theologie." In *Kerygma and Myth II.* Edited by Hans Werner Bartsch. London: S.P.C.K., 1962.

Caird, G. B. "A Commentary on the Revelation of St. John the Divine." In *Harper's New Testament Commentaries.* Edited by Henry Chadwick. New York: Harper & Row, 1966.

Charles, R. H. *A Critical and Exegetical Commentary on the Revelation of St. John.* Two volumes. International Critical Commentary. Edinburgh: T.&T. Clark, 1920.

Childs, Brevard S. *Biblical Theology in Crisis.* Philadelphia: Westminster Press, 1970.

Christian, William A. *An Interpretation of Whitehead's Metaphysics.* New Haven: Yale University Press, 1959; repr.: Westport CT: Greenwood Press, 1977.

Clark, Kevin C. "An Analysis of Isaiah 40-44:23, Utilizing the Creation-Redemption Model of the Creator-King and Process Theology." D.Min. project, School of Theology at Claremont, 1977.

Coats, George W. "The King's Loyal Opposition: Obedience and Authority in Exodus 32-34." In *Canon and Authority: Essays in Old Testament Religion and Theology.* Edited by G. W. Coats and B. O. Long. Philadelphia: Fortress Press, 1977.

_____. "The Way of Obedience: Traditio-Historical and Hermeneutical Reflections on the Balaam Story." *Semeia* 24 (1982): 53-79.

Cobb, John B., Jr. *A Christian Natural Theology: Based on the Thought of Alfred North Whitehead.* Philadelphia: Westminster Press, 1965.

_____. "The Authority of the Bible." In *Hermeneutics and the Worldliness of Faith: A Festschrift in Memory of Carl Michalson. The Drew Gateway* 45 (1974–1975): 188-202.

_____. *God and the World.* Philadelphia: Westminster Press, 1969.

_____. *The Structure of Christian Existence.* Philadelphia: Westminster Press, 1967.

_____. "A Theology of Story: Crossan and Beardslee." In *Orientation by Disorientation.* Edited by Richard A. Spencer. Pittsburg: Pickwick Press, 1980.

_____. "Faith and Culture." In *The New Hermeneutic.* Edited by James M. Robinson and John B. Cobb, Jr. New Frontiers in Theology 2. New York: Harper & Row, 1964.

_____. "Feminism and Process Thought: A Two-Way Relationship (The Harvard University Dudelian Lecture)." In *Feminism and Process Thought.* Edited by Shelia Greeve Davaney. New York: Edwin Mellen Press, 1981.

_____. "Trajectories and Historic Routes." *Semeia* 24 (1982): 89-98.

Cobb, John B., Jr., and David Ray Griffin. *Process Theology: An Introductory Exposition.* Philadelphia: Westminster Press, 1976.

Cobb, John B., Jr., with David J. Lull and Barry A. Woodbridge. "Introduction: Process Thought and New Testament Exegesis." *Journal of the American Academy of Religion* 47 (1979): 21-30.

Collins, Adela Yarbro. *The Apocalypse.* Wilmington DE: Michael Glazier, 1979.

_____. *Crisis & Catharsis: The Power of the Apocalypse.* Philadelphia: Westminster Press, 1984.

_____, editor. *Early Christian Apocalypticism: Genre and Social Setting*. *Semeia* 36. Decatur GA: Scholars Press, 1986.

Collins, John J. "Process Hermeneutic: Promise and Problems." *Semeia* 24 (1982): 107-16.

_____, editor. *Apocalypse: The Morphology of a Genre*. *Semeia* 14. Missoula MT: Scholars Press, 1979.

Crossan, John Dominic. *The Dark Interval: Towards a Theology of Story*. Niles IL: Argus Press, 1975.

_____. *In Parables: The Challenge of the Historical Jesus*. New York: Harper & Row, 1973.

_____. *Raid on the Articulate: Comic Eschatology in Jesus and Borges*. New York: Harper & Row, 1976.

Davis, Robert Con, and Ronald Schleifer. *Contemporary Literary Criticism: Literary and Cultural Studies*. Second edition. New York: Longman, 1989.

de Saussure, Ferdinand. *Course in General Linguistics*. Translated by Wade Baskin. New York: McGraw-Hill, 1959; 1915.

Derrida, Jacques. *Of Grammatology*. Translated by Gayatri Chakravorty Spivak. Baltimore: Johns Hopkins University Press, 1976.

_____. *Positions*. Translated by Alan Bass. Chicago: University of Chicago Press, 1981.

_____. "Structure, Sign, and Play in the Discourse of the Human Sciences." In *The Structuralist Controversy: The Languages of Criticism and the Sciences of Man*. Edited by Richard Macksey and Eugenio Donato. Baltimore: Johns Hopkins University Press, 1972.

Dillenberger, John. "On Broadening the New Hermeneutic." In *The New Hermeneutic*. Edited by James M. Robinson and John B. Cobb, Jr. New Frontiers in Theology 2. New York: Harper & Row, 1964.

Ebeling, Gerhard. *Word and Faith*. Translated by James W. Leitch. Philadelphia: Fortress Press, 1963.

Farmer, Ron. "Divine Power in the Apocalypse to John: Revelation 4–5 in Process Hermeneutic." In *Society of Biblical Literature 1993 Seminar Papers*. Edited by Eugene H. Lovering, Jr. Atlanta: Scholars Press, 1993.

_____. "Process Hermeneutic and Biblical Exegesis: Description and Assessment." *Parish and Process* 3/3 (1989): 3-20.

_____. "The Role of the 'Transmission of Tradition' in the 'Academic Freedom-Ecclesiastical Control' Debate: Three Models." *Perspectives in Religious Studies* 17 (1990): 129-39.

Fiorenza, Elisabeth Schüssler. "Apokalypsis and Propheteia: The Book of Revelation in the Context of Early Christian Prophecy." In *L'Apocalypse johannique et l'Apocalyptique dans le Nouveau Testament*. Edited by J. Lambrecht. Leuven: Leuven University Press, 1980.

_____. *Invitation to the Book of Revelation. A Commentary on the Apocalypse with Complete Text from the Jerusalem Bible*. Garden City NY: Image Books, 1981.

_____. "The Phenomenon of Early Christian Apocalyptic." In *Apocalypticism in the Mediterranean World and the Near East.* Edited by David Hellholm. Tübingen: J. C. B. Mohr, 1983.

Ford, Lewis S. *The Lure of God: A Biblical Background for Process Theism.* Philadelphia: Fortress Press, 1978.

_____. "Biblical Recital and Process Philosophy. Some Whiteheadian Suggestions for Old Testament Hermeneutics." *Interpretation* 26 (1972): 198-209.

_____. "God as King: Benevolent Despot or Constitutional Monarch?" *Christian Scholar's Review* 1 (1971): 318-22.

_____. "The Divine Curse Understood in Terms of Persuasion." *Semeia* 24 (1982): 81-87.

Fretheim, Terrence E. "The Repentance of God: A Key to Evaluating Old Testament God-Talk." *Horizons in Biblical Theology* 10 (1988): 47-70.

_____. "The Repentance of God: A Study of Jeremiah 18:7-10." *Hebrew Annual Review* 11 (1987): 81-92.

_____. *The Suffering of God: An Old Testament Perspective.* Philadelphia: Fortress Press, 1984.

Frye, Northrop. *The Great Code: The Bible and Literature.* New York: Harcourt Brace Jovanovich, 1982.

Fuchs, Ernst. *Studies of the Historical Jesus.* Translated by A. Scobie. London: SCM Press, 1964.

Funk, Robert W. "The Hermeneutical Problem and Historical Criticism." In *The New Hermeneutic.* Ed. James M. Robinson and John B. Cobb, Jr. New Frontiers in Theology 2. New York: Harper & Row, 1964.

_____. *Language, Hermeneutic, and Word of God: The Problem of Language in the New Testament and Contemporary Theology.* New York: Harper & Row, 1966.

Gadamer, Hans Georg. *Truth and Method.* Translated by Garrett Barden and John Comming. New York: Seabury Press, 1975.

Griffin, David Ray. "Faith and Spiritual Discipline: A Comparison of Augustinian and Process Theologies." *Faith and Philosophy* 3 (1986): 54-67.

_____. *God & Religion in the Postmodern World.* Albany: SUNY Press, 1989.

_____. "Relativism, Divine Causation, and Biblical Theology." *Encounter* 36 (1975): 342-60.

Harrington, Michael L. "Whitehead's Theory of Propositions." Ph.D. dissertation, Emory University, 1972.

Hartshorne, Charles. *Omnipotence and other Theological Mistakes.* Albany: SUNY Press, 1984.

Hellholm, David, editor. *Apocalypticism in the Mediterranean World and the Near East.* Tübingen: J. C. B. Mohr, 1983.

Holt, D. Lynn. "Metaphors as Imaginative Propositions." *Process Studies* 12 (1982): 252-56.

Janzen, J. Gerald. *Job*. Atlanta: John Knox Press, 1985.
_____. "Metaphor and Reality in Hosea 11." *Semeia* 24 (1982): 7-44.
_____. "Modes of Power and the Divine Relativity." *Encounter* 36 (1975): 379-406.
_____. "The Old Testament in 'Process' Perspective: Proposal for a Way Forward in Biblical Theology." In *MAGNALIA DEI: The Mighty Acts of God. Essays on the Bible and Archaeology in Memory of G. Ernest Wright*. Edited by Frank Moore Cross, Werner E. Lemke, and Patrick D. Miller, Jr. Garden City NY: Doubleday, 1976.
_____. "What's in a Name? 'Yahweh' in Exodus 3 and the Wider Biblical Context." *Interpretation* 33 (1979): 227-39.
Jeremias, Joachim. ἀρνίον. In *Theological Dictionary of the New Testament*, 1:340-41. Edited by Gerhard Kittel. Translated and edited by Geoffrey W. Bromiley. Grand Rapids MI: Eerdmans, 1964; orig., 1933.
Käsemann, Ernst. "The Problem of the Historical Jesus." In *Essays on New Testament Themes*. London: SCM Press, 1964.
Kelsey, David H. "The Theological Use of Scripture in Process Hermeneutics." *Process Studies* 13 (1983): 181-88.
Korsmeyer, Jerry D. "A Resonance Model for Revelation." *Process Studies* 6 (1976): 195-96.
Künneth, Walter. "Bultmann's Philosophy and the Reality of Salvation." *Kerygma and History: A Symposium of the Theology of Rudolf Bultmann*. Translated and edited by Carl E. Braaten and Roy A. Harrisville. Nashville: Abingdon Press, 1962.
Lambrecht, J., ed. *L'Apocalypse johannique et l'Apocalyptique dans le Nouveau Testament*. Leuven: Leuven University Press, 1980.
Lawrence, D. H. *Apocalypse*. Introduction by Richard Aldington. Longon: Heinemann, 1972; Harmondsworth UK: Penguin Books, 1974; original, 1931.
Leclerc, Ivor. *Whitehead's Metaphysics: An Introductory Exposition*. New York: Macmillan, 1958.
Loomer, Bernard. "Two Conceptions of Power." *Process Studies* 6 (1976): 5-32.
Lowe, Victor. *Understanding Whitehead*. Baltimore: Johns Hopkins University Press, 1962.
Lull, David J. "PNEUMA in Paul's Letter to the Churches of Galatia: An Interpretation of the Spirit in Light of Early Christian Experiences in Galatia, Paul's Message to the Galatians, and Theology Today." Ph.D dissertation. Claremont Graduate School, 1978.
_____. "The Spirit and the Creative Transformation of Human Existence." *Journal of the American Academy of Religion* 47 (1979): 39-55.
_____. *The Spirit in Galatia: Paul's Interpretation of PNEUMA as Divine Power*. Chico CA: Scholars Press, 1980.
_____. "What Is 'Process Hermeneutics'?" *Process Studies* 13 (1983): 189-201.

Lundeen, Lyman T. "The Authority of the Word in a Process Perspective." *Encounter* 36 (1975): 281-300.

_____. *Risk and Rhetoric in Religion: Whitehead's Theory of Language and the Discourse of Faith.* Philadelphia: Fortress Press, 1972.

Mays, James Luther. "Response to Janzen: 'Metaphor and Reality in Hosea 11.'" *Semeia* 24 (1982): 45-51.

McKnight, Edgar V. *Postmodern Use of the Bible: The Emergence of Reader-Oriented Criticism.* Nashville: Abingdon Press, 1988.

Meland, Bernard E. "Response to Paper by Professor Beardslee." *Encounter* 36 (1975): 331-41.

Michel, Otto. σφάζω, σφαγή. In *Theological Dictionary of the New Testament,* 7:925-38. Edited by Gerhard Friedrich. Translated and edited by Geoffrey W. Bromiley. Grand Rapids MI: Eerdmans, 1971; orig., 1964.

Miller, J. Hillis. "The Critic as Host." In *Deconstruction and Criticism.* New York: Seabury Press, 1979.

_____. "Tradition and Difference." *Diacritics* 2 (1972): 6-12.

Moffatt, James. "The Revelation of St. John the Divine." In *The Expositor's Greek Testament.* Repr.: Grand Rapids: Eerdmans, 1951.

Moore, Stephen D. *Mark and Luke in Poststructuralist Perspectives: Jesus Begins to Write.* New Haven: Yale University Press, 1992.

Morris, Leon. *The Revelation of St. John.* Tyndale New Testament Commentaries. Grand Rapids: Eerdmans, 1969.

Nelson, Herbert J. "The Resting Place of Process Theology." *Harvard Theological Review* 72 (1979): 1-21.

Newport, John P. *The Lion and the Lamb.* Nashville: Broadman Press, 1986.

Ogden, Schubert M. *Christ without Myth: A Study Based on the Theology of Rudolf Bultmann.* New York: Harper & Brothers, 1961.

Perrin, Norman. *Jesus and the Language of the Kingdom: Symbol and Metaphor in New Testament Interpretation.* Philadelphia: Fortress Press, 1976.

Petersen, Norman R. *Literary Criticism for New Testament Critics.* Philadelphia: Fortress Press, 1978.

Pittenger, Norman. *The Christian Church as Social Process.* Philadelphia: Westminster Press, 1971.

Pixley, George V. "Justice and Class Struggle: A Challenge for Process Theology." *Process Studies* 4 (1974): 159-75.

Pregeant, Russell. *Christology Beyond Dogma: Matthew's Christ in Process Hermeneutic.* Philadelphia: Fortress Press, 1978.

_____. "Grace and Recompense: Reflections on a Pauline Paradox." *Journal of the American Academy of Religion* 47 (1979): 73-96.

_____. "Matthew's 'Undercurrent' and Ogden's Christology." *Process Studies* 6 (1976): 181-94.

_____. "The Matthean Undercurrent: Process Hermeneutic and the 'Parable of the Last Judgment.'" In *Society of Biblical Literature 1975 Seminar Papers*. Missoula MT: Scholars Press, 1975.

_____. "Where Is the Meaning? Metaphysical Criticism and the Problem of Indeterminacy." *The Journal of Religion* 63 (1983): 107-24.

Prigent, Pierre. *Apocalypse et Liturgie*. Cahier Theologiques 52. Paris: Delachaux et Niestlé, 1964.

Reitz, Helga. "Biblical and Cosmological Theology: A Process View of Their Relations." *Encounter* 36 (1975): 407-32.

Richards, Kent Harold. "Beyond Bruxism." In *Society of Biblical Literature 1976 Seminar Papers*. Missoula: Scholars Press, 1976.

_____. "Cobb's Living Historic Routes: A Response." *Semeia* 24 (1982): 99-106.

_____. "Collaboration and Conceptualization: Biblical Studies and Process Philosophy." Paper read at the Center for Process Studies, January 1976.

Robinson, James M. "The German Discussion of the Later Heidegger." *The Later Heidegger and Theology*. Edited by James M. Robinson and John B. Cobb, Jr. New York: Harper & Row, 1963.

_____. "Hermeneutics Since Barth." In *The New Hermeneutic*. Edited by James M. Robinson and John B. Cobb, Jr. New Frontiers in Theology 2. New York: Harper & Row, 1964.

_____. "Introduction: The Dismantling and Reassembling of the Categories of New Testament Scholarship." In *Trajectories through Early Christianity*. With Helmut Koester. Philadelphia: Fortress Press, 1971.

_____. *A New Quest of the Historical Jesus*. Studies in Biblical Theology 25. London: SCM Press, 1959.

Schniewind, Julius. "A Reply to Bultmann." In *Kerygma and Myth I*. Edited by Hans Werner Bartsch. New York: Harper & Row, 1961; London: S.P.C.K., 1953.

Schweitzer, Albert. *The Quest of the Historical Jesus*. London: A. C. Black, 1910; New York: Macmillan, 1961.

Sherburne, Donald, ed. *A Key to Whitehead's Process and Reality*. Chicago: University of Chicago Press, 1966.

Spivak, Gayatri Chakravorty. "Translator's Preface." In Jacques Derrida. *Of Grammatology*. Baltimore: Johns Hopkins University Press, 1976.

Stendahl, Krister. "Biblical Theology, Contemporary." *Interpreter's Dictionary of the Bible*, A-D:418-32. New York/Nashville: Abingdon Press, 1962.

Suchocki, Marjorie Hewitt. "Constructing Theology in a Deconstructive Age." In *Religion and the Postmodern Vision*. Edited by Ron Farmer. Columbia MO: University Press of Missouri, 1992.

_____. "Deconstructing Deconstruction: Language, Process, and a Theology of Nature." *American Journal of Theology and Philosophy* 11 (1990): 133-42.

_____. *The End of Evil: Process Eschatology in Historical Context.* Albany: SUNY Press, 1988.

_____. *God, Christ, Church: A Practical Guide to Process Theology.* Revised edition. New York: Crossroads, 1989.

Sweet, J. P. M. *Revelation.* Westminster Pelican Commentaries. Philadelphia: Westminster Press, 1979.

Taylor, Mark C. *Deconstructing Theology.* New York: Crossroad, 1982.

_____. *Erring: A Post Modern A/Theology.* Chicago: University of Chicago Press, 1984.

Thielicke, Helmut. "The Restatement of New Testament Mythology." In *Kerygma and Myth I.* Edited by Hans Werner Bartsch. New York: Harper & Row, 1961; London: S.P.C.K., 1953.

Thompson, Leonard. "A Sociological Analysis of Tribulation in the Apocalypse of John." *Semeia* 36 (1986): 147-74.

van Unnik, W. C. "'Worthy is the Lamb': The Background of Apoc 5." In *Melanges Bibliques.* Gembloux: J. Duculot, 1970.

Via, Dan O., Jr. "Editor's Forward." In Norman R. Peterson. *Literary Criticism for New Testament Critics.* Philadelphia: Fortress Press, 1978.

Weeden, Theodore J. "Recovering the Parabolic Intent in the Parable of the Sower." *Journal of the American Academy of Religion* 47 (1979): 97-120.

_____. "The Potential and Promise of a Process Hermeneutic: A Response to William Beardslee's Paper, 'Narrative Form in the New Testament and Process Theology.'" *Encounter* 36 (1975): 316-30.

Wheelwright, Philip. *The Burning Fountain: A Study in the Language of Symbolism.* Revised edition. Bloomington: Indiana University Press, 1968.

_____. *Metaphor and Reality.* Bloomington: Indiana University Press, 1962.

Whitehead, Alfred North. *Adventures of Ideas.* New York: Free Press, 1967; New York: Macmillan, 1933.

_____. *Modes of Thought.* New York: Free Press, 1968; New York: Macmillan, 1938.

_____. *Process and Reality: An Essay in Cosmology.* Corrected edition. Edited by David Ray Griffin and Donald W. Sherburne. New York: Free Press, 1978; New York: Macmillan, 1929.

_____. *Religion in the Making.* New York: Macmillan, 1926.

_____. *Science in the Modern World.* New York: Free Press, 1967; New York: Macmillan, 1925.

_____. *Symbolism: Its Meaning and Effect.* New York: Fordham University Press, 1985; New York: Macmillan, 1927.

Wilder, Amos N. *Early Christian Rhetoric: The Language of the Gospel.* Cambridge: Harvard University Press, 1971.

_____. "The Word as Address and the Word as Meaning." In *The New Hermeneutic.* Edited by James M. Robinson and John B. Cobb, Jr. New Frontiers in Theology 2. New York: Harper & Row, 1964.

Williamson, Clark M. "Process Hermeneutics and Christianity's Post-Holocaust Reinterpretation of Itself." *Process Studies* 12 (1982): 77-93.
_____. "Whitehead as Counterrevolutionary? Toward Christian-Marxist Dialogue." *Process Studies* 4 (1974): 176-86.
Williamson, Clark M., and Ronald J. Allen. *A Credible and Timely Word: Process Theology and Preaching.* St. Louis: Chalice Press, 1991.
Woodbridge, Barry A. "An Assessment and Prospectus for a Process Hermeneutic." *Journal of the American Academy of Religion* 47 (1979): 121-28.
_____. "Process Hermeneutic: An Approach to Biblical Texts." In *Society of Biblical Literature 1977 Seminar Papers.* Missoula MT: Scholars Press, 1977.
_____. "The Role of Text and Emergent Possibilities in the Interpretation of Christian Tradition: A Process Hermeneutic in Response to the German Hermeneutical Discussion." Ph.D. dissertation, Claremont Graduate School, 1976.
Young, R. Garland. "The Role of the Spirit in Texts: James Sanders, Paul Achtemeier, and Process Theology." *Perspectives in Religious Studies* 13 (1986): 229-40.

Indexes

• Author Index •

Allen, Ronald J., 127n.9
Altizer, Thomas J. J., 33, 41n.90
Atkins, G. Douglas, 33n.67, 35n.74, 36, 37-38nn.78-81, 40n.85, 40n.87, 40-42, 44n.98
Augustine, 55n.11, 116n.17

Barclay, William, 165n.8, 176n.51
Barr, David, 144n.19, 147-48, 154n.52, 155n.56
Barr, James, 10nn.13-14
Barth, Karl, 7n.8, 14n.21
Beardslee, William A., ix-x, xiv, 24n.48, 28n.56, 83n.1, 89n.14, 91n.19, 92n.22, 92n.26, 93n.30, 123, 125n.5, 126n.9, 127n.10, 129-30nn.13-15, 155n.57, 195-98
Beckwith, I. T., 166n.11, 174n.44, 174n.47, 177n.54, 178n.56
Bible and Culture Collective, 39n.83, 42n.94
Birch, Charles, 63n.27, 65-67nn.29-30, 67n.32, 67
Bloom, Harold, 33
Boring, M. Eugene, 142n.15, 144n.19, 155n.56, 168n.23, 170, 171n.35, 175n.49, 176nn.50-51, 176n.53, 181n.66, 181-84, 185n.71
Bornkamm, Günther, 15n.25
Brock, Rita Nakashima, 138
Bultmann, Rudolf, 7n.7, 11-17, 21-22, 27, 45, 196
Buri, Fritz, 14n.23

Caird, G. B., 151n.38, 151n.41, 152n.46, 155, 164nn.2-3, 165n.4, 166-67, 168, 171n.35, 175-76, 176n.53, 178n.57, 179, 181n.67, 185n.71, 188n.75, 189n.76
Charles, R. H., 149, 151n.39, 152n.43, 159, 165nn.4-5, 168n.18, 172n.37, 174nn.44-46, 176n.52, 178n.56, 180
Childs, Brevard S., 7-9nn.9-11, 10n.15
Christian, William A., 71n.1, 86n.10, 199n.1, 202n.12, 203n.18, 205n.25, 211n.46, 211n.51, 212n.52, 215n.62, 215n.65, 215-16, 221n.86, 237n.127
Crossan, John Dominic, 33, 41nn.90-91
Cobb, Jr., John B., xiv, 24n.49, 47n.100, 63n.27, 65-67nn.29-30, 67n.32, 67n.34, 67, 71n.1, 82n.21, 85n.5, 111-14, 117n.18, 126n.9, 138, 155n.57, 200n.3, 216n.67, 217n.73, 234n.119
Collins, Adela Yarbro, 141n.13, 142n.17, 143n.18, 146n.24, 165n.6
Collins, John J., 130, 141n.13
Cox, Harvey, 41n.90

Darwin, Charles, 5
Davis, Robert Con, 32n.66, 36n.75, 36n.77
Democritus, 59
Dillenberger, John, 25n.50
de Man, Paul, 33
de Saussure, Ferdinand, 33-34
Derrida, Jacques, 30n.59, 32, 34-40, 42, 45
Descartes, René, 56, 60-62, 91
Dewart, Leslie, 41n.90

Ebeling, Gerhard, 16n.27, 17n.29, 22n.42, 22n.44

Farmer, Ronald L., 3n.1, 4n.2

Fiorenza, Elisabeth Schüssler, 142n.15, 144-45, 165n.4, 165n.8, 170, 176nn.51-52, 178n.58
Ford, Lewis S., 124n.4, 142n.16
Frye, Northrop, 52-58
Fuchs, Ernst, 16n.27, 17n.29, 22n.42, 22n.44
Funk, Robert W., 22n.43, 25-26nn.50-51

Gadamer, Hans Georg, 110-11, 116n.14, 187n.73
Griffin, David Ray, 58n.20, 61n.25, 71n.1, 115n.12, 128n.12, 136n.3, 138, 200n.3, 217n.73

Harrington, Michael L., 89n.16, 94n.33, 96n.39
Hartman, Geoffrey, 33
Hartshorne, Charles, 135-36nn.2-3
Hegel, Georg Wilhelm Friedrich, 5
Heidegger, Martin, 17-21, 30
Hellholm, David, 141n.13
Holt, D. Lynn, 97n.43
Hume, David, 61-62, 84n.4, 87, 91, 234n.120

Janzen, J. Gerald, 43, 47, 52n.1, 94, 96-97, 97nn.43-44, 185n.70
Jeremias, Joachim, 153n.48
Jung, Carl Gustav, 196

Kant, Immanuel, 43, 62-63, 84n.4, 91, 123, 234n.120
Käsemann, Ernst, 15n.25
Kelsey, David H., 47n.101, 109n.1
Kierkegaard, Sören, 17
Koester, Helmut, 131
Korsmeyer, Jerry D., 132n.21
Künneth, Walter, 14nn.21-22

Lambrecht, J., 141n.13
Lawrence, D. H., 140, 159, 178n.58
Leclerc, Ivor, 71n.1
Lévi-Strauss, Claude, 129
Loomer, Bernard, 137n.5, 138-39nn.9-10
Lowe, Victor, 71n.1
Lull, David J., 47n.100, 83n.1, 92n.23, 93n.29, 109-10, 116n.15, 117n.19, 117, 126n.9

Lundeen, Lyman T., 46, 115n.13, 118n.23, 127n.11

Mabee, Charles, xi-xii, xiv
McKnight, Edgar V., 5n.3, 28-32, 44
Meland, Bernard E., 94n.35
Michel, Otto, 153n.50
Miller, J. Hillis, 33, 39n.82, 39n.84
Moffat, James, 172n.37, 174n.47, 176n.52, 178n.56
Moore, Stephen D., 33
Morris, Leon, 150, 165n.6, 165n.10, 172n.37, 176n.52, 178n.56

Newport, John P., 172n.37, 173n.43, 180

Ogden, Schubert M., 12n.19, 14nn.22-23, 15n.24
O'Leary, Joseph S., 33

Petersen, Norman R., 26n.52, 27
Perrin, Norman, 26n.51
Pittenger, Norman, 117n.21
Plato, 62, 208
Pregeant, Russell, xiv, 47n.100, 48, 89n.17, 91n.19, 95n.38, 98nn.45-46, 101n.48, 105-106, 121-22nn.1-2, 126n.9, 185n.71
Prigent, Pierre, 150

Raschke, Carl, 33
Richards, Kent Harold, 83n.1, 131
Ricoeur, Paul, 128
Robinson, James M., 15n.25, 17-20nn.30-37, 21-22nn.39-41, 111-13, 119-20, 131
Robinson, John A. T., 41n.90

Schleifer, Ronald, 32n.66, 36n.75, 36n.77, 44n.98
Schniewind, Julius, 14n.21
Schweitzer, Albert, 6
Sherburne, Donald, 71n.1, 86n.7, 199n.1, 217n.73, 221n.87, 222n.91, 225n.97, 227n.102, 228n.103, 237n.126, 243n.141, 246n.143, 252n.144
Spinoza, Baruch, 206n.27
Stendahl, Krister, 11n.16

Suchocki, Marjorie Hewitt, 43n.97, 71n.1, 189n.77, 197n.8, 245n.142
Sweet, J. P. M., 143n.18, 148n.29, 157n.62, 158, 166n.12, 167n.17, 168n.18, 168n.23, 171n.35, 175n.49, 176n.53, 178n.57, 181n.65

Taylor, Mark C., 33
Thielicke, Helmut, 14n.21
Thompson, Leonard, 142n.17, 143n.18, 145-47
Tillich, Paul, 41n.90

van Unnik, W. C., 152
Via, Dan O., 26

Weeden, Sr., Theodore J., 126n.9
Wheelwright, Philip, 96
Whitehead, Alfred North, ix, xiii, 46, 57, 64n.28, 68, 71-82, 84-99, 104n.4, 106, 110-20, 123, 127n.10, 130, 132n.21, 140, 159n.66, 196n.4, 197n.8, 197-98, 199-253
Wilder, Amos N., 24, 185n.70
Williamson, Clark M., 111n.4, 116n.14, 127n.9
Winquist, Charles, 33
Woodbridge, Barry A., 47n.100, 103nn.1-3, 104n.5, 111n.4, 116, 118n.23, 124, 125-26nn.7-9, 130n.17

• Subject Index •

actual entities/occasions, 72, 86, 91, 94, 200-205, 207
actual world, 203
Augustinian-Pelagian debate, 136n.3
author intent vs indeterminate meaning, 27, 121-22
authority, 115n.13, 117, 126-27

biblical theology movement, 7-11, 45

categories of existence, 202n.12, 210n.43
category of the ultimate, 206, 210n.43
causal efficacy, 84-91, 128, 224
classical liberalism, 5-7, 9, 11, 12, 25, 45
classical theism, 58, 135-36
community of interpretation, 118, 130
conceptual reproduction, 225
conceptual reversion, 225
concrescence, 72, 75, 137, 191, 202
  phases of concrescence, 84-85, 87, 92, 131, 221-36
confessionalism vs public discussion, 130
contrast, 115-16, 124-25, 146n.26, 159-61, 186-87, 227
consciousness, 229, 233-36
consequent nature of God, 80, 137, 190, 218-19
constructive postmodernism, ix
cosmic epoch, 202
creative transformation, 114-17, 125, 126, 186-87
creativity, 206-207
  concrescent creativity, 207
  transcendent creativity, 207

datum
  initial datum, 203, 223
  objective datum, 203, 223
deconstruction, 30, 32-45, 58n.20, 62
descriptive vs. hermeneutical, 131
dipolar (physical/mental poles), 218n.78, 225
dualism, 60, 67n.30, 74n.9

empiricism, 62
enduring objects, 76n.11, 77, 81, 87, 236-41
error of Western epistemology, 84-85, 87
essentialist vs evolutionary approach, 5, 104-105, 107, 117, 125-26

eternal objects, 76-79, 86-88, 91, 94, 207-213
events, ix, 67, 72
  in Heidegger, 18, 21, 22n.44, 23, 46
  event thinking vs. substance thinking, 58-68
everlasting vs eternal, 220n.85
evolutionary spirituality, 4, 6, 125-26
existentialist interpretation, 11-17, 45
extensive continuum, 201-202

fallacy of misplaced concreteness, 57, 94, 96
fallacy of simple location, 210-11
fundamentalism, fundamentalist, 3-4, 7, 9

God, 78-80, 190-91, 213-21

historical-critical method, 4-5, 6, 8, 11, 22n.46, 27, 45
historic routes of living occasions, 110-14, 130, 131
history and divine activity, 128

idealism, 63-64, 67n.33, 74n.9, 76
identity through time, 113
imagination, 229-36
impasse, ix, xiii, 45-46, 51, 56, 58
ingression, 77, 209
initial aim, 79, 80-81, 115, 128, 129, 131, 157, 190, 197, 217-19, 227
intellectual feelings, 92
inspiration, 131-32

language
  descriptive phase of language, 21n.38, 55-56, 98-99, 182
  fourth phase of language, 56-58, 99
  metaphorical phase of language, 52-53
  metonymic phase of language, 53-55, 98-99
  performative language, 22n.43
  religious language, 97-99, 122-23, 184-85
  Whitehead's theory of language, 93-99, 184-86
literary criticism, 25, 26-32, 46

materialism, 60-61, 67n.33, 74n.9
multiplicity, 211

narrative and myth, 129-30

nexus of actual entities, 72n.4, 85, 91, 104, 201, 238
normative, 5
novelty, 74n.10, 77, 82, 92, 110, 113-14, 126, 128, 197, 206, 211n.51, 213, 224, 227, 232-33

objective immortality, 74, 75, 197, 204
objective lure, 213
ontological principle, 78n.15, 205, 211, 215n.61, 226n.99
order, 221, 228-29, 238

pantheism, 58
panentheism, 58
persuasive power, 79, 127, 128, 137-40, 155, 177
phenomenalism, 62, 123
pluralism, 115n.13
positivist, 6, 122-23
prehensions/feelings, 73, 75, 76-77, 202-203
    anticipatory feelings, 205
    conceptual prehensions, 93n.31, 94, 214, 224-27
    conformal feelings, 223-24
    hybrid physical prehensions, 82n.23
    intellectual feeling, 233-36
        conscious perceptions, 234
        judgments, 234-36
    physical prehensions, 93n.31, 93-94, 214n.59
    physical purposes, 228-29
    propositional prehensions, 94, 229-33
        perceptive feelings, 230-33
        imaginative feelings, 230-33
    simple physical feelings/causal feelings, 223-24
        pure physical feelings, 226
        hybrid physical feelings, 226, 241n.138
    strain-feelings/regional feelings, 205
    transmuted physical feelings, 237
presentational immediacy, 84-91, 128, 205n.24
presented duration/immediate present, 86, 87-88, 204n.22
primordial nature of God, 79-80, 137, 197, 215
principle of limitation, 79, 213
principle of relativity, 207

process eschatology, 190-91, 195-98
progressive revelation, 5-7
propositions, 91-93, 103-106, 109-10, 115-16, 185-89, 192-93, 212n.52, 212n.54
possibilities
    pure possibilities vs real possibilities, 77-78, 203n.18, 212
    impure possibilities, 212n.54, 229n.107

redemptive suffering, 140, 147-48, 153-55, 158, 177
relational power, 137-40, 155-58
revelation, 131-32

satisfaction, 73, 190, 204
societies of actual entities, 72, 81-82, 201, 238-41
    corpuscular society, 76n.11, 239
    living society, 240
space and time, 201-202, 205n.23
static spirituality, 4
steno-language vs. tensive language, 96-97, 181-83, 184-85
subject-superject, 197, 202n.13, 204
subjective aim, 73, 75, 79, 132, 203, 213, 217
subjective form, 73, 75, 77, 82, 90, 104, 110, 203, 224, 233
subjective immortality, 190-91, 197
symbolic reference, 84-91
symbolism, 89, 128-29

texts
    nature of texts, 103-107, 186
    bifocal approach to texts, 105-106
    excision of problematic elements, 123-25
the new hermeneutic, 17-26, 46, 122, 125n.5
"tool box raiding," xiii, 32, 46
transmutation, 237

undercurrent, x, 106, 158-61

validity in interpretation and theological norms, 109-120
valuation, 90, 227

Beyond the Impasse.
The Promise of a Process Hermeneutic.
   by Ronald L. Farmer
Studies in American Biblical Hermeneutics 13 (StABH 13).

Mercer University Press, Macon, Georgia 31210-3960.
Isbn 0-86554-558-8. Catalog and warehouse pick number: MUP/P126.
Text designs, composition, and layout by Edmon L. Rowell, Jr.
Camera-ready pages composed on a Gateway 2000
   via WordPerfect 5.1/5.2 and printed on a LaserMaster 1000.
Text font: (Adobe) Palatino 11/13 and 10/12.
Display font: (Adobe) Palatino 24-, 12-, and 11-point bf.
Printed and bound by McNaughton & Gunn Inc., Saline MI 48176.
   Printed via offset lithography on 50# Writers Natural (500ppi).
   Perfectbound in 10-pt. c1s stock,
      printed one color, and lay-flat laminated.

[October 1997]